WORLD OF LOGOTYPES

WORLD OF Logotypes

Volume 2

AL COOPER

ART DIRECTION **BOOK** COMPANY

19 West 44th St.
New York, N.Y. 10036

Contributors to

WORLD OF LOGOTYPES

Trademarks/Wordmarks/Symbol, entries may be submitted for reproduction consideration in World of Logotypes.

Volume 3, now in preparation, will include appropriate credit indexing of category, designer and client.

The service, which is free, includes wordmarks, logotypes, symbols, book titles, etc. These should be submitted as black-and-white stat prints approximately 1¼ inches in height or width, and wordmarks approximately 2½ inches in length, together with full particulars of the designer's and client's name, category, address and country of origin. Mail to:

World of Logotypes,
c/o 113 Dolomite Drive,
Downsview, Ontario,
Canada M3J 2N1

World of Logotypes maintains a search and find reference library service for filing or obtaining reproductions of trademarks/word-marks/symbols. Subscribers to the service may request a search for graphic designs similar to theirs that might conflict with their rights, image, services, etc. Filing each image or notification of each single item report is payable in U.S. funds. Fee schedule available on request, submit copy(s) of image and full details on company letterhead.

Write to Reference Library
        World of Logotypes
        c/o 113 Dolomite Drive
        Downsview, Ontario
        Canada M3J 2N1

ACKNOWLEDGEMENTS

Appreciation for her encouragement in compiling Volume 2 goes first to my wife, Gertrude. As with Volume 1, her understanding of the thousands of hours spent over these past two years was a constant inspiration.

Secondly, to the hundreds of graphic designers around the world for their entries and constructive suggestions.

My thanks to my associate staff design artists for the mechanical assembly, and to my office staff for their library research and help with producing this volume.

I would be remiss if I failed to mention the following reference acknowledgements:

TRADEMARKS & SYMBOLS, Yasaburo Kuwayama,
Van Nostrand Reinhold Company, Japan

THE BOOK OF AMERICAN TRADEMARKS, David E. Carter,
Art Direction Book Company, U.S.A.

TOP SYMBOLS AND TRADEMARKS OF THE WORLD,
Ricci & Ferrari, Deco Press, Italy

THE CREATIVITY ANNUALS,
Art Direction Book Company, U.S.A.

And last but not the least, gratitude to Don Barron, my publisher, for his enthusiasm, and consistent, unremitting contact and support.

The mark arrangement grid, concept and final assortment are, of course, entirely my own. Errors and omissions with regrets.

A.C.

PROLOGUE

The presentation of a trademark and symbol source reference can hardly be made without a great deal of pleasure, gratitude, relief, and a certain pinch of pride. In a sense, WORLD OF LOGOTYPES, Volume 2 has been a world-wide activity, and I'm pleased that it joins the ever growing list of books compacting this planet into one community, hospitable, we hope, to us all.

Volume 2 of WORLD OF LOGOTYPES took two years to compile, and reflects the combined help of many. Specifically, this volume marks the inclusion of almost 20,000 additional marks to our growing archive collection. This volume is a showcase collection of symbolic images and shapes, and a mixture of symbols, trademarks, wordmarks and anagram graphic words.

While compiling this book, a number of corporate design factors became highly visible. Of first importance, is the high esteem corporate designers now have. They are, to many commerce and industry decision people, professional communicators, and their services are equal in value to those of other professions involved in the manufacturing, distribution and merchandising of products and services.

As a matter of fact, many firms now feel their corporate identity is a major consideration. Millions of dollars each year are being spent for recognition, and to secure unqualified customer acceptance for product lines and services that often number in the hundreds. The aim is to present an identity the ultimate consumer trusts.

To that end, corporate graphic design is being called upon to provide the means for instant and favorable recognition from audiences of millions and even hundreds of millions, and across dozens of nation-state boundaries. The state of the art in this area is under great pressure for simplified symbols and marks that can be reproduced in country after country, exactly alike. To quote Don Barron in ART DIRECTION, The Magazine of Visual Communication, March 1977, commenting on design trends,

"Logos, trade marks, letterheads are sane and sober. Design in these categories is crystal clear—to provide clients with graphics usable for their intended purpose. Letterhead design, itself, is excellent and in one of its golden periods. Logos, incidentally, still favor the sans serifs."

The progress, however, should not imply that little remains to be done. For instance, many businesses engaged in communications do not have supporting identifying symbols or other updated corporate signatures to reflect their roles. The list includes advertising agencies, radio, television, print media and lithographers. By merely citing those above, it becomes obvious that the design requirements in corporate identity are enormous.

The recent contribution to the corporate image scene by innovative letterhead styles merits further notice. What is really happening is more of an updating. So much has been eliminated over the years from corporate business stationery that it has reached the point where they seem more appropriate for a small family business. The trend has reversed, and today's designers convey a more accurate presentation of a firm's size. The new letterheads styles are extremely well designed and contain innovations now possible due to the expanding capabilities of the graphic arts.

The new format of WORLD OF LOGOTYPES, Volume 2 retains its "at-a-glance," A to Z alphabetized sectional display. The design selections are numbered in sequence continuing with the 3,168 marks reproduced in Volume I. A numbered reference booklet cataloging Volume I is scheduled for publication.

Al Cooper

3170 AD) Andre Emmerich Gallery, Inc., USA
DES/A) Harry Zelenko

3171 AD) American-Exporter, New York, NY, USA

3172 AD) American Astrionics, Div. of Techni-colour Inc., 291 Kalmus Drive, Costa Mesa, CA, USA

3173 AD) Autosafe Training Systems Ltd., 359 Kerr St., Oakville, Ont., CANADA

3174 AD) Asazawa, JAPAN
DES/A) Kyuyo Kajino

3175 AD) Engineers of Tokyo, JAPAN

3176 AD) Allen Personnel, 362 Dundas St., London, Ont., CANADA

3177 DES/A) Stefankantschev, BULGARIA

3178 DES/A) Shigeo Katsooka, JAPAN

3179 AD) Japan Tourist Bureau, JAPAN
DES/A) Gan Hosoya
Yanagiya

3180 AD) Yanagiya
SM) Cosmetics

3181 AD) The Aluminum Assoc., New York, NY, USA

3181 AD) The Aluminum Assoc., NY, USA

3182 AD) Aids Supply Mart, 400 N. Main St., High Point, NC, USA

3183 AD) Alexander-Roberts Co., 1851 Langley Ave., Irvine, CA, USA

3184 AD) Alinve, ITALY
via muzio clementi, 68-00196 Roma

3185 AD) Howard A. Anderson Co., 5451 Marathon St., Hollywood, CA, USA

3186 AD) Aerotecnica Italiana S.p.A., 20094 Corsico (Milano) Via Volta 6, ITALY

3187 AD) The Ansul Company, Marinette, WI, USA
DES/A) Raymond Loewy & William Snaith, Inc.

3188 (AD) Appleford, Packaging Div. of Eddy Forest Products Ltd., Box 487, Hamilton, Ont., CANADA

3189 AD) Ajinomoto, JAPAN
DES/A) Takashi Kono

3190 AD) Amarillo National Bank, Amarillo, TX, USA
DES/A) Crawford Dunn

3191 AD) Aerospace Corporation, Los Angeles, CA, USA

3192 AD) Aerotron Inc., Raleigh, NC, USA

3193 AD) American Broadcasting Co., USA
DES/A) Paul Rand

3194 AD) ACF Industries, Inc., W-K-M Valve Div., Houston, TX, USA

3195 AD) Aralux, AUSTRALIA
DES/A) Neish Tutt, Grundwald Pty., Ltd.

3196 AD) Amasco Asphalt Co.
DES/A) Kenneth Holick

3197 AD) Anthony Hyde Jr., USA
DES/A) Herb Lubalin

3198 AD) Acme Hamilton Manufacturing Corp., P.O. Box 361, Trenton, NJ, USA

3199 AD) Artearredo, via C. Colombo, 171, 20036 Meda/Italia-via trento 90

3200 AD) American Business Products, Inc., Suite 330 Emerson Centre, 2814 New Spring Rd., Atlanta, GA, USA

3201

3202

3203

3204

3205

3206

3207

3208

3209

3210

3211

3212

3213

3214

3201 AD) Allen Carter, USA
      DES/A) Dean Harahara
3202 AD) Acu-Tech Corporation
      DES/A) Bill Wood; Design Shop, 68 Winsor
              Pl., Glen Ridge, NJ, USA
3203 AD) Alan Somers Associates
      DES/A) Bryan Honkawa, 1332 Crescent
              Heights, Los Angeles, CA, USA
3204 AD) Anne Hanger
      DES/A) Anne Hanger, Baltimore, MD,
              USA
3205 AD) Applewhite Mortgage Co.
      DES/A) Skin Morrow, S. Pasaden, CA,
              USA
3206 AD) Adapta, Montreal, Que., CANADA
      DES/A) Fritz Gottschalk
3207 AD) Architetti Associati, Roma
      DES/A) Michele Spera, ITALY 1973
3208 AD) Arca-Centro Commercial
      DES/A) Jesus Emilio Franco,
              VENEZUELA
3209 AD) Arthur J. Taft Co.
      DES/A) Don Primi, Great Neck, NY, USA
3210 AD) Ambience Travel, 10 Campbell St.,
              W., AUSTRALIA
      DES/A) Craig Chappelle
3211 AD) Acmos, 28 Bremen
3212 AD) The Art Group
3213 AD) Arley Properties Co.
      DES/A) Don Primi, Great Neck, NY, USA
3214 AD) Association for Non-Smokers Rights
      DES/A) Gale William, Ikola & Associates

A-15

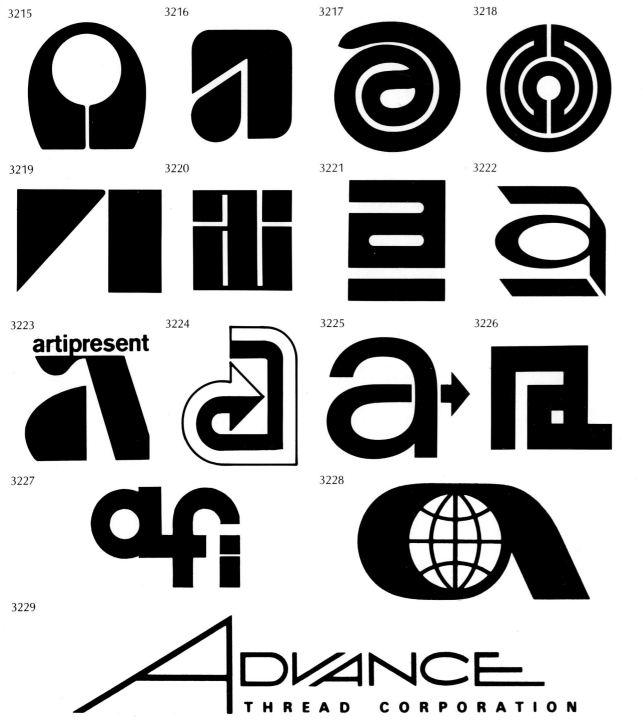

3215 AD) Acushnet Co., New Bedford, MA, USA
3216 AD) Acheson Colloids Co., Port Huron, MI, USA
3217 AD) Laboratories Ausonia, SPAIN
DES/A) Jose Baques Tomas
3218 AD) Arbeitgemeinschaft der Lukal-und, Regionalpresse, SWITZERLAND
DES/A) Erich Hanzi
3219 AD) American Motors Corp., Detroit, MI, USA
DES/A) Walter P. Margulies
ST) Arkwright-Interlaken, Inc., USA
DES/A) J. Malcolm Grear
ST) Lippincott & Margulies, Inc.
3220 AD) AD) Artwright-Interlaken, Inc., USA
DES/A) J. Malcolm Grear
3221 AD) Alliend Casting Corp., Philadelphia, PA, USA
DES/A) Kramer, Miller, Lomden & Glassman, Inc.
3222 AD) Armour-Dial Inc., Chicago, IL, USA
DES/A) Dickens Design Group
3223 AD) Artipresent, Fritz Pfizenmaier & Co., 7022 Leinfelden
3224 AD) Argus Refrigeration & Air Conditioning, 4 Blair Dr., Bramalea, CANADA
3225 AD) Amasco Amalgamated Asphalt Co., Ltd., London, ENGLAND
DES/A) Kenneth Hollick
3226 AD) Aiko Sangyo Co., JAPAN
DES/A) Masayoshi Matsushima
3227 AD) Arredamenti E. Forme Interne Via S. Teodoro 90, Rome, ITALY
3228 AD) Atlas Chemical Industries, Inc., Mentztown, PA, USA
DES/A) Raymond Lowewy & William Snaith, Inc.
3229 AD) Advance Thread Corp., Hackensack, NJ, USA

A-16

3230

3231

3232

3233

3234

3235

3236

3237

3238

3239

3240

3241

3242

alberti

3243

ARINOX

3244

ALLENAIR

3230 AD) American Protection Agencies, Los Angeles, CA, USA

3231 AD) Aquaria Inc., Los Angeles, CA, USA

3232 AD) Air Bus Industries

3233 AD) Adventure Inn, Box SM-27, Hilton Head Island, SC, USA

3234 AD) Airport Marina Hotels, (Operated by Fred Harvey Inc.)

DES/A) Primo Angeli, San Francisco, CA, USA

3235 AD) AMX Sound Corp., Ltd., 788 Alderbridge Way, Richmond, B.C., CANADA

3236 AD) Adtool Corp., 1262 Don Mills Rd., Suite 97, Don Mills, Ont., CANADA

3237 AD) Aircraft Radio Corporation, Boonton, NJ, USA

3238 AD) Canadian Arctic Gas Study Ltd., CANADA

DES/A) Chris Yaneff Ltd.

3239 AD) American Bankers Insurance Co., 234 Eglin Ave., East, Toronto, Ont., M4P 1K5, CANADA

3240 AD) All-tube Products Ltd., 380 Alliance Ave., Toronto, Ont., CANADA

3241 AD) American-Standard Power & Controls Group, 1 Blair Dr., Bramalea, Ont., CANADA

3242 AD) Alberti Arredamenti Cucine SNC, 20030 Bovisio Masciago (MI) Via Repubblica 3, ITALY

3243 AD) Arinox (Collection Design) Paris 16e: 48 Rue Vital Lyon: 125 Avenue De Saxe, FRANCE

3244 AD) Aeroquip (Canada) Ltd., 287 Bridgeland Ave., Toronto, Ont., CANADA Subsidiary of Libbey-Owens-Ford Co.

A-17

3245

3246

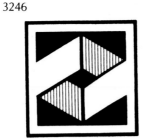

3247

3248

3249

3250

3251

3252

3253

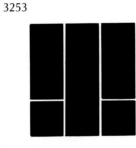

3254

3256

3257

3258

3245	AD)	Asgen-Mrk - Via N. Lorenzi 8, Genova-Cornigliano, ITALY
3246	AD)	American Institute of Interior Designers 42nd National Conference Fairmont Roosevelt Hotel, New Orleans, LA, USA
3247	AD)	Maillet, FRANCE
	C)	Exhibition Construction
	DES/A)	Jacques Nathan - Garamond
3248	AD)	Action Hardware Ltd., 115 West Dr., Bramalea, Ont., L6T 2J6, CANADA
3249	AD)	Art Director's Workshop, Inc., 219 E. 44th St., New York, NY 10017, USA
3250	AD)	Air France, P.O. Box 747, New York, NY 10011 USA
3251	AD)	American Paper Institute
	C)	Paper Stock Conservation Committee, 260 Madison Ave., New York, NY 10016 USA
3252	AD)	American Air Filter, Box 1100, Louisville, KY 40201 USA
3253	AD)	Agnew Peckham and Associates Ltd., 200 St. Clair Avenue West, Toronto, Ont., M4V 1R1 CANADA
3254	AD)	Australia and New Zealand Banking Group Ltd., North American Offices, 63 Wall St., New York, NY, USA
3256	AD)	ACI Industries Inc., 38-60 Review Ave., Long Island City, NY 11101 USA
3257	AD)	Amtrak Travel Center, P.O. Box 4733, Chicago, IL 60680 USA
3258	AD)	Associated Industrial Consultants, London, ENGLAND
	DES/A)	Henrion Design Associates

A-18

3259 AD) Ayres, Lewis, Norris & May, Consulting Engineers, 500 Wolvering Building, Ann Arbor, MI, USA

3260 AD) Allied Chemical Corporation
   C) Fibers Division, Contract Furnishings, One Times Sq., New York, NY 10036 USA

3261 AD) Arpex, Divisione Arredamenti, ITALY

3262 AD) Araya Industrial Co., Ltd., 1, 1-Chome, Takejima, Nishiyodogawa-Ku, Osaka, JAPAN

3263 AD) All-O-Matic Industries, Inc., 2099 Jericho Turnpike, New Hyde Park, NY, USA

3264 AD) Adams et Cie, 3 Quai Jean-Moulin, Lyon ler, Rhone, FRANCE

3265 AD) Air Products and Chemicals, Inc., Houdry Division, 5 Executive Mall, Swedesford Rd., Wayne, PA 19087 USA

3266 AD) American Continental Homes Inc., 1 E. Fourth St., Cincinnati, OH 45202 USA

3267 AD) Assurance vie. Rente ou capital retraite

3268 AD) Anonima Castelli, Roma, Bologna, Milano, Torino, Firenze, ITALY

3269 AD) Aquapak Respiratory Care Inc., 2420 E. Oakton St., Arlington Heights, IL 60005 USA

3270 AD) Argus Research Corporation, 140 Broadway, New York, NY 10005 USA

3271 AD) R.P. Anderson Co., Dallas, TX, USA
   DES/A) Hayward R. Blake

3272 AD) Audio-Visual Corp. of America, Richmond Hill, NY, USA
   DES/A) Appelbaum & Curtis Inc.

3273 AD) Artafax Systems Ltd., 1439 Erie Blvd. East, Syracuse, NY 13210 USA

3274

3275

3276

3277

3278

3279

3280

3281

3282

3283

3285

3286

3284

3287

3274 AD) Abstainers' Insurance Co., Div. of Maplex Management & Holdings Ltd.

3275 AD) "Automatic" Sprinkler Corp. of America, Div. of American La France Inc., Subsidiary of A-T-O Inc., USA

3276 AD) Avery Label Systems, Div. of Avery Products Corp. (CAN) Ltd., 35 McLachlan Dr., Rexdale, Ont., CANADA

3277 AD) American Demolition, Denver, CO USA

3278 AD) Architectural Design Association Providence, RI, USA

3279 AD) Anglo-Gibraltar Group, Anglo Canada General Insurance Co. and Gibraltar General Insurance Co., CANADA

3280 AD) AKM Associates Inc., 41 E. 42nd St., New York, NY, USA

3281 AD) Avicenum, CZECHOSLOVAKIA
DES/A) Josef Tyfa

3282 AD) All-Terrain Amphibian Ltd., 56 Burns Ave., R.R. 3, Belleville, Ont., CANADA

3283 AD) (Product Symbol)
via leonardo da vinci, 53-20094 corsico, Milano, ITALY

3284 AD) (Product Symbol) V. Martiri Liberta, 96 - Lissone - ITALY

3285 AD) All-Steel Inc., Aurora, IL 60507 USA

3286 AD) Allgemeine Maschinenbau Gesellschaft mbH P.O.B. 518 A 4021 Linz, AUSTRIA

3287 AD) Applied Computing Technology Inc., 17961 Sky Park Circle, Irvine, CA 92707 USA

A-20

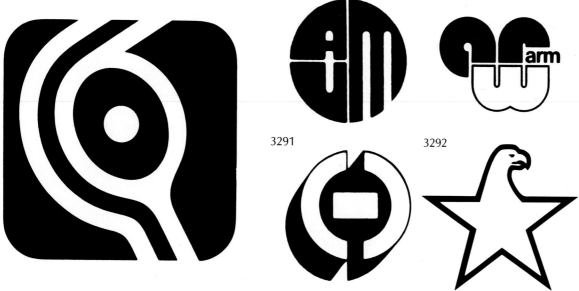

3288

3289

3290

3291

3292

3293

3294

alfa **alfa arredamenti**

Aspen Land Company

3295

3296

3297

American Trauma Society

3288 AD) American Airlines Tennis Games,
          Tucson, AZ, USA
      DES/A) Niels Diffrient & Rick Hibberd
      ST) Henry Dreyfuss Associates
          Graphics for American Airlines Tennis
          Games designed by Niels Diffrient &
          Rick Hibberd of Henry Dreyfuss As-
          sociates, New York, NY. Directional
          kiosk, scoreboard and program in-
          corporate red and blue American Air-
          lines logo. The logo and directional
          symbols were designed previously by
          the Dreyfuss office, while a new tennis
          symbol was designed expressly for this
          Tucson, AZ, tournament. The co-
          ordinated graphics provide an or-
          ganized and attractive visual identifi-
          cation of the sports event.

3289 AD) A.V. Mazzega, Murano Venezia
          Via Vivarini 3, ITALY
3290 AD) AD) Arm di Radice-Industria
          Arredamenti viale Lombardia 85-20036
          Meda/Milano, ITALY
3291 AD) American Stock Exchange Inc., USA
3292 AD) American Pioneer Centre, USA
      DES/A) Alan Leitstein
3293 AD) Alfa Arredamenti, via San Giovanni,
          33044 Manzano/Udine, ITALY
3294 AD) Aspen Land Company, USA
      DES/A) Wyatt L. Phillips
3295 AD) (Product Symbol)
          Arredamento E Decorazione Degli
          Interni, 90 Via Di S. Teodoro/Roma,
          ITALY
3296 AD) American Trauma Society, P.O. Box
          6190, Toledo, OH 43614 USA
3297 AD) Arnold Jones Insurance Agency, USA
      DES/A) Anita Soos

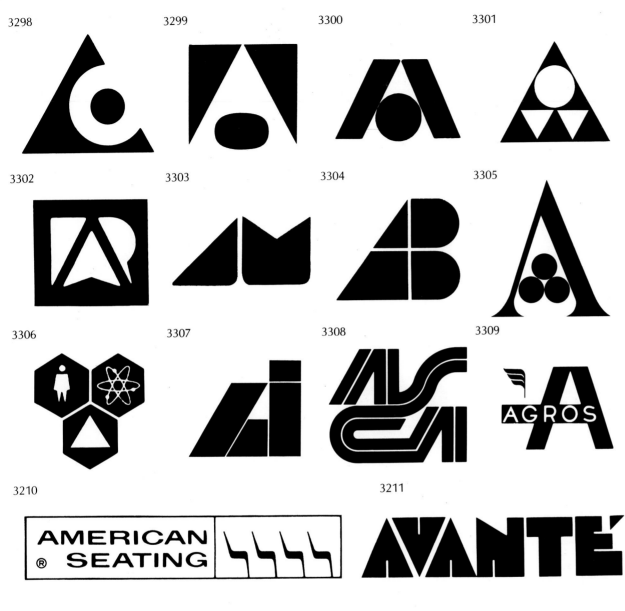

3298 AD) Allied Control Company Inc., 100 Relay Rd., Plantsville, CT 06479 USA

3299 AD) Lee Parker (1974) Ltd., 1435 Bleury St., Montreal, Que., H3A 2H8 CANADA

3300 AD) Archforma, Art and Style snc 80125 Aynamo (NA)-via Augusto Righi 32/36, Showroom-20144 Milano-via Monferrato 7, ITALY

3301 AD) Algonquin Wildlands League, Box 114, Postal Station Q, Toronto, Ont., CANADA

3302 AD) R. Angus Alberta Ltd., General Office: P.O. Box 2405, Edmonton, Alta. T5J 2S1 CANADA

3303 AD) Agua Meter, Instrument Corporation, 465 Eagle Rock Ave., Roseland, NJ 07068 USA

3304 AD) Andover Savings Bank, USA
DES/A) Selame Design Associates

3305 AD) Amigen, (Symbol Design) Baxter Laboratories, USA
ST) Ed & Jane Bedno

3306 AD) McKonnon, Allen & Associates Ltd., 631-42nd Ave., S.E., Calgary, Alta. T2G 1Y7 CANADA

3307 AD) Atlific Inns Inc., 6550 Cote de Liesse, Montreal, Que., H4T 1S7 CANADA

3308 AD) Arkansas Society of Communication Arts, Ar, USA
DES/A) Tom Henton

3309 AD) Agros National Foreign Trade Enterprise, Exporters-Importers Warszawa, Zurawia 32/34, POLAND

3210 AD) American Seating Company, Contract Division, Dept. 1-760, Grand Rapids, MI 49504 USA

3211 AD) Avante, 5900 S. Dixie Highway, South Miami, FL, USA

3312 AD) Angolo s.r.1. esposizione via emilia, 72, ITALY

A-22

3313 AD) Aichinger Ladenhau-Metallbau
85 Nurnberg, Scheurlstr. 21,
GERMANY
3314 AD) Alec Litho, USA
DES/A) Frank A. Gutierrez
3315 AD) Alfa. Paris, FRANCE
Jewelry Store
DES/A) Felix Betran
3316 AD) Amprobe Instrument
Div. of SOS Consolidated Inc.,
Lynbrook, NY 11563 USA
3317 AD) American Middle East Consultants,
USA
DES/A) Jim Lake
3318 AD) Acromag Inc., 30765 Wixom
Road, Wixom, MI 48096 USA
3319 AD) Amano Time Systems, Inc., 57 Galaxy
Blvd., Rexdale, Ont. CANADA
3320 AD) Alchem Limited,
C) Chemical & Consulting Service
Burlington, Ont., CANADA
3321 AD) Aran Line, via della Vigna Nuova 29-R,
Firenze, ITALY
3322 AD) Auma, Koln
C) German Council of Trade Fairs &
Exhibitions
DES/A) Grete Troost
ST) Troost KG.
3323 AD) Amcom
DES/A) Michael Vanderbyl
3324 AD) Graphic Design for Publication:
Nato's Magazine (Artillery Meteoro-
logical Systems—Amets)
3325 AD) M.P. Goodkin Company
(ASTRO/T.M. for Verticle Camera)
140-146 Coit St., Irvington, NJ 07111
USA
3326 AD) Arrowhead Associates, P.O. Box 3069,
Waterbury, CT, USA

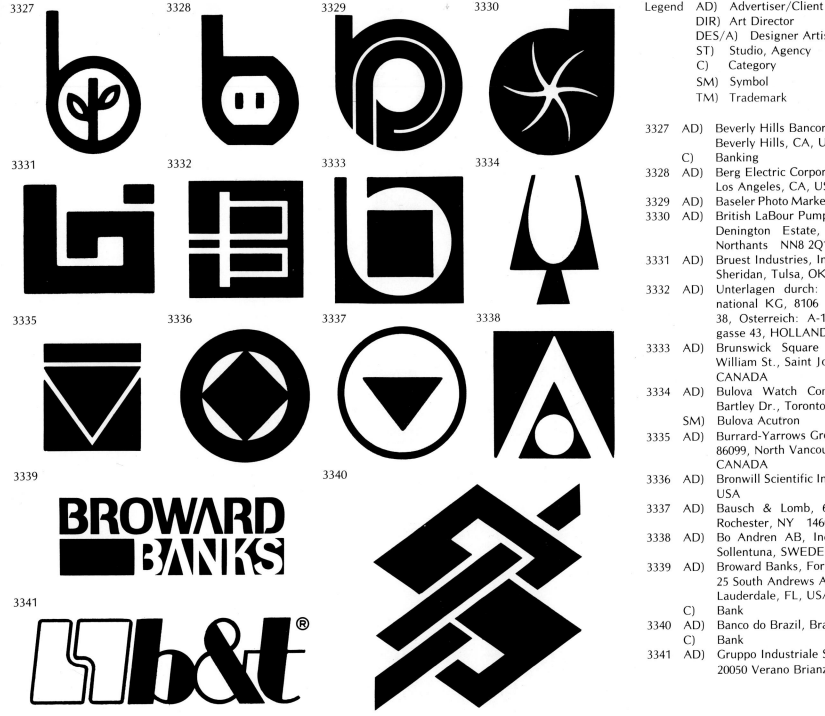

3327 AD) Beverly Hills Bancorp
Beverly Hills, CA, USA
C) Banking
3328 AD) Berg Electric Corporation
Los Angeles, CA, USA
3329 AD) Baseler Photo Marketing Co., Inc. USA
3330 AD) British LaBour Pump Co. Ltd.,
Denington Estate, Wellingborough,
Northants NN8 2Q1 ENGLAND
3331 AD) Bruest Industries, Inc., 4823 S.
Sheridan, Tulsa, OK 74145 USA
3332 AD) Unterlagen durch: Banz-Bord International KG, 8106 Oberau, Postfach
38, Osterreich: A-1060 Wien, Web-
gasse 43, HOLLAND
3333 AD) Brunswick Square Ltd., 93 Prince
William St., Saint John, N.B.,
CANADA
3334 AD) Bulova Watch Company Ltd., 105
Bartley Dr., Toronto, Ont., CANADA
SM) Bulova Acutron
3335 AD) Burrard-Yarrows Group, P.O. Box
86099, North Vancouver, B.C.,
CANADA
3336 AD) Bronwill Scientific Inc., Rochester, NY
USA
3337 AD) Bausch & Lomb, 635 St. Paul St.,
Rochester, NY 14602 USA
3338 AD) Bo Andren AB, Industriv 16, 19120
Sollentuna, SWEDEN
3339 AD) Broward Banks, Fort Lauderdale,
25 South Andrews Ave., Fort
Lauderdale, FL, USA
C) Bank
3340 AD) Banco do Brazil, Brazil, SA
C) Bank
3341 AD) Gruppo Industriale Salotti B & T
20050 Verano Brianza, Milano, ITALY

3342

3343

3344

3345

BRUKSBO

3346

3347

3348

3349

3350

3351

3352

3353

3354

3355

3356

3357

3358

3359

3360

3361

3362

3363

3364

3365

3366

3367 AD) Buhler-Miag (Canada) Ltd., 1925 Leslie St., Don Mills, Ont. M3B 2M3 CANADA

3368 AD) Bell Office Products Ltd., 141 Adelaide St. West, Suite 1507, Toronto, Ont. M5H 3L9 CANADA

3369 AD) Ciba-Geigy Corp, Ardsley, NY 10502 USA

DES/A) Stan Baker, Ciba-Geigy

SM) Blood Bank for Ciba-Geigy

3370 AD) The Belmont (A Doral Hotel) Lexington Ave., 49th to 59th St., New York, NY 10022 USA

3371 AD) John Burn & Associates, 289 Allan St., Oakville, Ont. L6J 3P3 CANADA

3372 AD) Bardmoor Reality, Cincinnati, OH, USA

DES/A) Joseph Bottoni

3373 AD) Bell Telephone

3374 AD) Bank of Tokyo, Head Office: Tokyo, JAPAN
(Affiliate in New York, USA
The Bank of Tokyo Trust Company)

3375 AD) Place Bonaventure Inc., P.O. Box 1000, Place Bonaventure, Montreal, Que. H5A 1G1 CANADA

3376 AD) Burkett & Wong, San Diego, CA, USA

3377 AD) Bank of Contra Costa, Walnut Creek, CA, USA

DES/A) Nancy Kraft

ST) Primo Angeli Graphics

3378 AD) Block China Corp., 25 East 26th St., New York, NY 10010 USA

3392

3393

3394

3395

3396

3397

3398

3399

3400

3401

3402

3403

3404

BRA
BOHAG

3405

3406

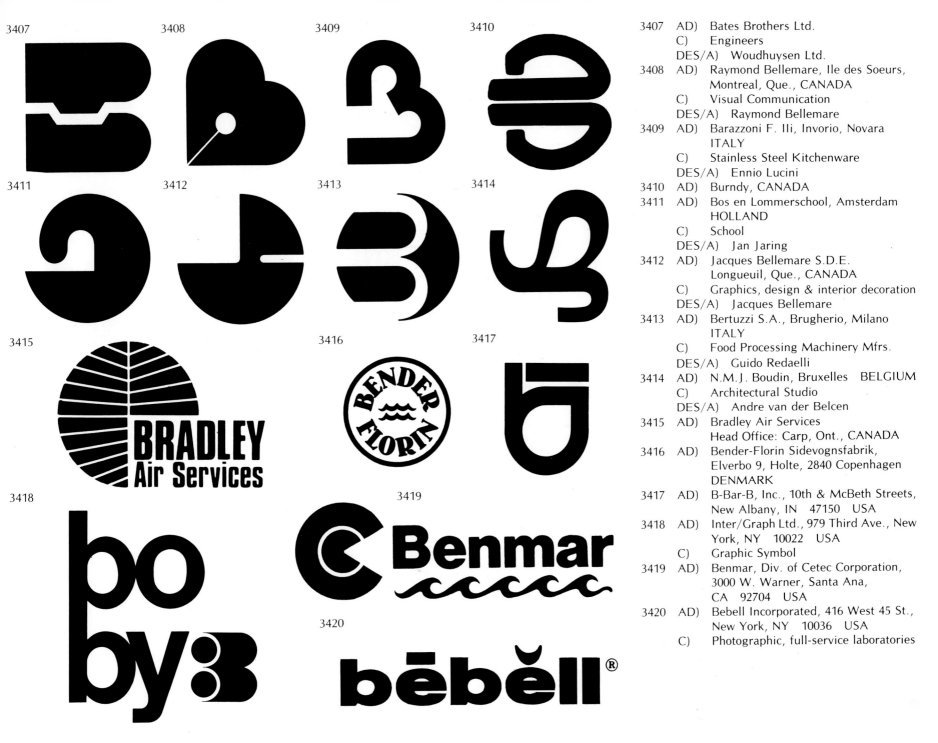

3407 AD) Bates Brothers Ltd.
C) Engineers
DES/A) Woudhuysen Ltd.

3408 AD) Raymond Bellemare, Ile des Soeurs,
Montreal, Que., CANADA
C) Visual Communication
DES/A) Raymond Bellemare

3409 AD) Barazzoni F. lli, Invorio, Novara
ITALY
C) Stainless Steel Kitchenware
DES/A) Ennio Lucini

3410 AD) Burndy, CANADA

3411 AD) Bos en Lommerschool, Amsterdam
HOLLAND
C) School
DES/A) Jan Jaring

3412 AD) Jacques Bellemare S.D.E.
Longueuil, Que., CANADA
C) Graphics, design & interior decoration
DES/A) Jacques Bellemare

3413 AD) Bertuzzi S.A., Brugherio, Milano
ITALY
C) Food Processing Machinery Mfrs.
DES/A) Guido Redaelli

3414 AD) N.M.J. Boudin, Bruxelles BELGIUM
C) Architectural Studio
DES/A) Andre van der Belcen

3415 AD) Bradley Air Services
Head Office: Carp, Ont., CANADA

3416 AD) Bender-Florin Sidevognsfabrik,
Elverbo 9, Holte, 2840 Copenhagen
DENMARK

3417 AD) B-Bar-B, Inc., 10th & McBeth Streets,
New Albany, IN 47150 USA

3418 AD) Inter/Graph Ltd., 979 Third Ave., New
York, NY 10022 USA
C) Graphic Symbol

3419 AD) Benmar, Div. of Cetec Corporation,
3000 W. Warner, Santa Ana,
CA 92704 USA

3420 AD) Bebell Incorporated, 416 West 45 St.,
New York, NY 10036 USA
C) Photographic, full-service laboratories

B-18

3421

3422

3423

3424

3425

3426

3427

3428

3429

3430

3431

3432

3433

3434

3421 AD) Bionda, Rizzi & Co., S.A., Minusio
C) Builders
DES/A) Till Neuburg
3422 AD) Bernische Lokalbanken, Bern
SWITZERLAND
C) Banking
DES/A) Hans Hartmann
3423 AD) Bestobell Canada Ltd., 235 Norseman
St., Toronto, Ont. M8Z 2R5
CANADA
3424 AD) Basic/Four Corporation,
18552 MacArthur Boulevard,
Irvine, CA 92714 USA
3425 AD) Gustl Bohler, Hard
C) Plastics Manufacturers
DES/A) Othmar Motter
ST) Voratlberger Graphik
3426 AD) Beth Tikvah Synagogue,
3080 Bayview Ave., Willowdale, Ont.,
CANADA
3427 AD) Richard T. Byrnes Co. Inc.,
West Chester, PA 19380 USA
3428 AD) Beauchemin-Beaton-Lapointe Inc.
C) Engineering, Planning and Multi-
disciplinary Services, 1134 St.
Catherine St., W, Montreal, Que.,
H3B 1H4 CANADA
3429 AD) Bergen Wire Rope Co., USA
Subsidiary of RSC Industries Inc.,
Gregg St., Lodi, NJ 07644 USA
3430 AD) Barger Packaging Corporation,
15th at Lusher Ave., Elkhart,
IN 46514 USA
3431 AD) The William J. Burns Int. Detective
Agency, New York, NY USA
C) Detective & Security Agents
DES/A) Philip Gips
ST) Gips & Danne
3432 AD) Bilbao, French/Basque Restaurant &
Cocktail Lounge, 5910 S.W. 8th St.,
Miami, Fl, USA
3433 AD) Broward Industrial Board, Fl, USA
3434 AD) Banamex-Banco Nacional de Mexico,
S.A. (International Division) Isabel la
Catolica, 44-50. Piso, MEXICO 1
C) Banking
SM) Symbol C.I. & Wordmark

B-19

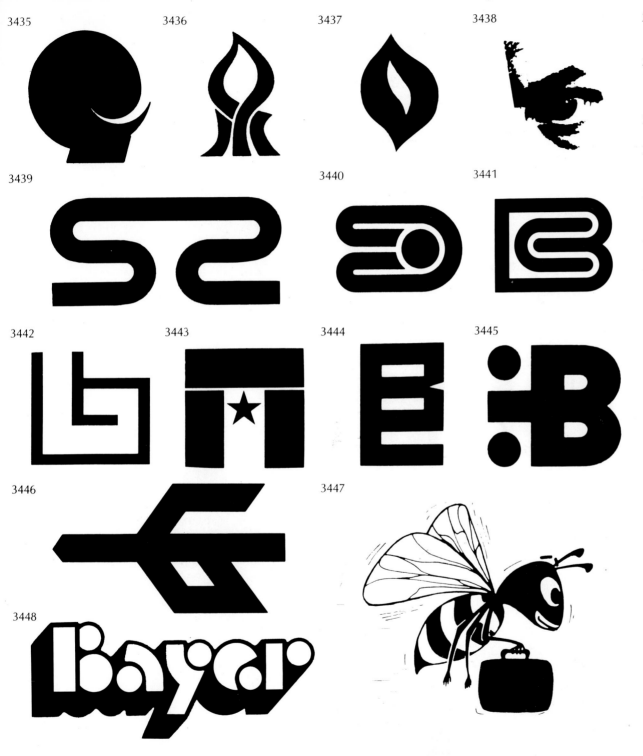

3435

3436

3437

3438

3439

3440

3441

3442

3443

3444

3445

3446

3447

3448

3435	AD)	Base Interiors, Milano-V. Montenapoleone 27, Roma-V. Condotti 24, Cannes-44 La Croisette, ITALY
3436	AD)	Canadian Associates of the Ben Gurion University of Negev, Israel c/o 5800 Cavendish Blvd., Suite 403, Montreal, Que., CANADA
3437	AD)	Brooklyn Union Gas, 195 Montague St., Brooklyn, NY 11201 USA
3438	AD)	Curt Cole Burkhart, Chicago, IL USA
	C)	Photographer & Filmmaker
	DES/A)	David L. Burkee
3439	AD)	British Transport Docks Board Melbury House, Melbury Terrace, London NW1 6JY ENGLAND
3440	AD)	Blazon-Flexible Flyer, Inc., Akron, OH, USA
3441	AD)	Bunge Corporation, New York, NY USA
	C)	Wholesale Exporters of Agricultural Products
	DES/A)	Paul Buhlmann
3442	AD)	Bank Vom Linthgebiet, Uznach, SWITZERLAND
	C)	Banking
	DES/A)	Peter Hablutzel
3443	AD)	Bank of Texas, Houston, TX, USA
	C)	Banking
	DES/A)	George K. Buckow Jr.
3444	AD)	Broderna Larsson Dressmaker, SWEDEN
	DES/A)	Ove Engstrom
3445	AD)	Autobatterier AB, SWEDEN
	DES/A)	Tom Huttgren
3446	AD)	Bulgarian Airtransport, Sofia BULGARIA
	C)	Air Transport
	DES/A)	Anton Metschkuev
3447	AD)	Brian D. Butler, 70 Alicewood Ct., Rexdale, Ont., CANADA
	SM)	Trademark
3448	AD)	A.J. Bayer Co., Box 276, Shepherdsville, Ky. 40165 USA

B-20

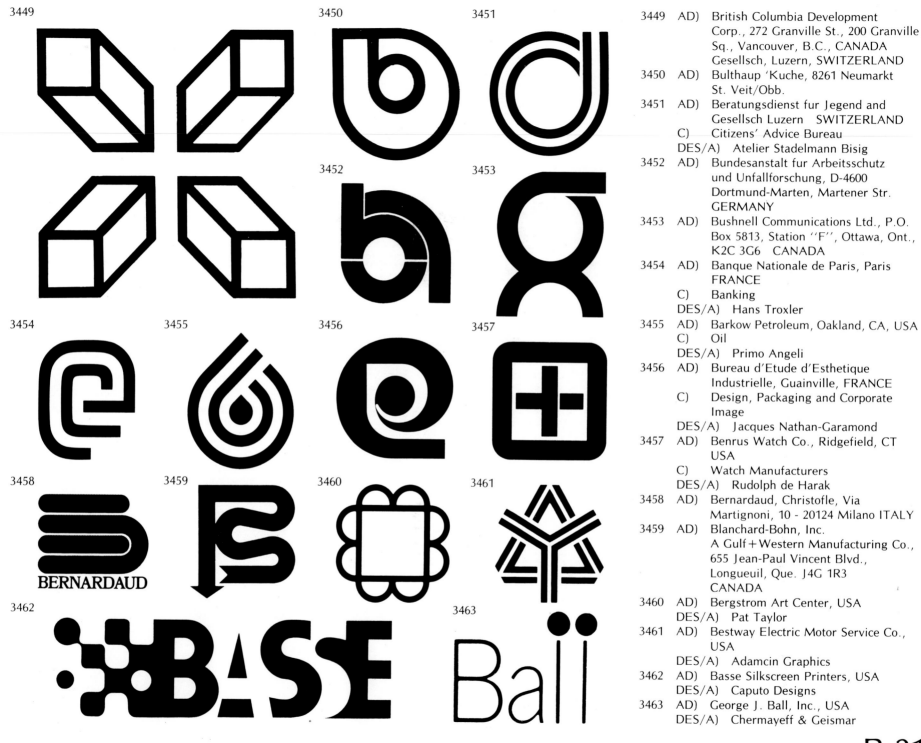

3449 AD) British Columbia Development
Corp., 272 Granville St., 200 Granville
Sq., Vancouver, B.C., CANADA
Gesellsch, Luzern, SWITZERLAND

3450 AD) Bulthaup 'Kuche, 8261 Neumarkt
St. Veit/Obb.

3451 AD) Beratungsdienst fur Jegend and
Gesellsch Luzern SWITZERLAND
C) Citizens' Advice Bureau
DES/A) Atelier Stadelmann Bisig

3452 AD) Bundesanstalt fur Arbeitsschutz
und Unfallforschung, D-4600
Dortmund-Marten, Martener Str.
GERMANY

3453 AD) Bushnell Communications Ltd., P.O.
Box 5813, Station ''F'', Ottawa, Ont.,
K2C 3G6 CANADA

3454 AD) Banque Nationale de Paris, Paris
FRANCE
C) Banking
DES/A) Hans Troxler

3455 AD) Barkow Petroleum, Oakland, CA, USA
C) Oil
DES/A) Primo Angeli

3456 AD) Bureau d'Etude d'Esthetique
Industrielle, Guainville, FRANCE
C) Design, Packaging and Corporate
Image
DES/A) Jacques Nathan-Garamond

3457 AD) Benrus Watch Co., Ridgefield, CT
USA
C) Watch Manufacturers
DES/A) Rudolph de Harak

3458 AD) Bernardaud, Christofle, Via
Martignoni, 10 - 20124 Milano ITALY

3459 AD) Blanchard-Bohn, Inc.
A Gulf + Western Manufacturing Co.,
655 Jean-Paul Vincent Blvd.,
Longueuil, Que. J4G 1R3
CANADA

3460 AD) Bergstrom Art Center, USA
DES/A) Pat Taylor

3461 AD) Bestway Electric Motor Service Co.,
USA
DES/A) Adamcin Graphics

3462 AD) Basse Silkscreen Printers, USA
DES/A) Caputo Designs

3463 AD) George J. Ball, Inc., USA
DES/A) Chermayeff & Geismar

3464
3465
3466
3467
3468
3469
3470
3471
3472
3473
3474
3475 (E)
3476 (H)
3475 (H)
3476 (E)

Designer Artist Profile / Joseph M. Bass
(Ref. World of Logotype File No. 105)
ST) P.B.S. Advertising & Public Relations Ltd.
  Tel-Aviv, 37 Shlomo Hamelech St., ISRAEL

3464	AD)	Supergas Limited, ISRAEL
	C)	The Gas Company
3465	AD)	ALCID, ISRAEL
	C)	Treatment of water and sewage
3466	AD)	Bass
	C)	Artist's trademark
3467	AD)	Mefalsim, Kibuts Mefalsim, ISRAEL
	C)	Wood Industry
3468	AD)	B.L.L.—Bank Leumi Lisrael, ISRAEL
	C)	Bank
3469	AD)	Herouth's Ltd., Lift Division, Tel-Aviv, ISRAEL
3470	AD)	Liranplast Ltd., Agencies & Marketing Ltd., ISRAEL
3471	AD)	The Country-Club Restaurant, Herzlia, ISRAEL
3472	AD)	Azmauth, ISRAEL
	C)	Conditory & Cafeteria
3473	AD)	The Assoc. of Israel Pharmaceutical, ISRAEL
3474	AD)	The First International Music Contest Jerusalem, ISRAEL
3475	AD)	Move Mills Jerusalem Limited, ISRAEL
		(H) Hebrew (E) English
3476	AD)	Herouth Limited, ISRAEL
		(H) Hebrew (E) English

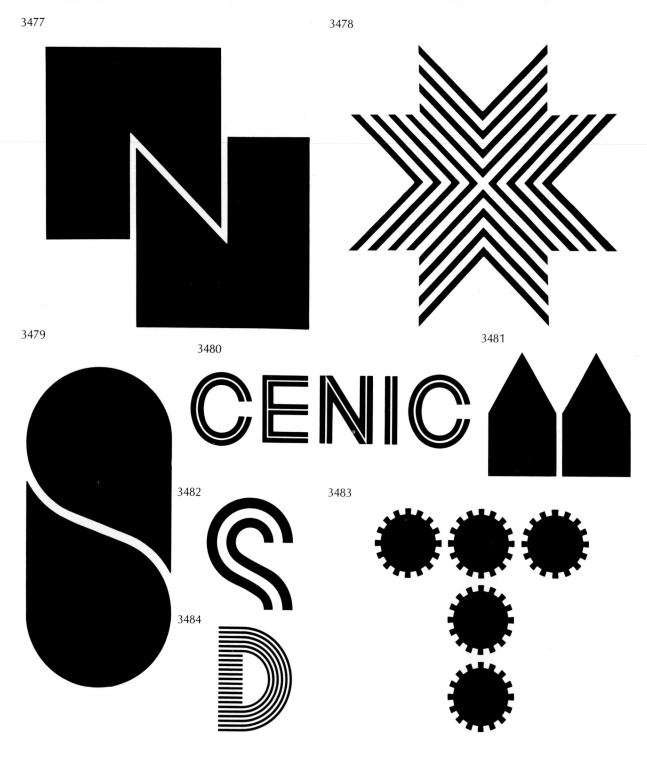

3477

3478

3479

3480

CENIC

3481

3482

3483

3484

Designer Artist Profile / Felix Beltran
(Ref. World of Logotypes File No. 186)
Professor Felix Beltran, AGI
Apartado 4109, Zona 4, Habana 4, CUBA
(Note - see profile attached)

3477 AD) Norberto - Havana   CUBA
C) Logo for a metal sculptor
3478 AD) Felix Beltran, Designer/Artist
C) Symbol for personal identification
3479 AD) Seldon - Madrid   SPAIN
C) Logotype for a medical laboratory
3480 AD) Cenic - Havana   CUBA
C) Wordmark for a research centre
3481 AD) Matecons - Havana   CUBA
C) Logotype for house construction in the
country
3482 AD) Selida - Havana   CUBA
C) Logotype for a dancer
3483 AD) Ministerio del Trabajo - Havana
CUBA
C) Logotype for a meeting on the work
3484 AD) Desarrollo Industrial - Havana   CUBA
C) Logotype for Industrial Development

Felix Beltran was born in Havana in 1938. In 1956 he went to New York to further his technical skill. He obtained an advertising design and layout diploma at the School of Visual Arts, and an easel painter diploma at American Art School. From 1965 to 1966 he attended the Circle of Fine Arts, Madrid. He has received 63 national and international awards and has held 47 one-man exhibitions in Havana, Praha Leipzig, Sofia, Darmstadt, Barcelona, Stockholm, Wroclav, Nairobi, Kent, Lancashire, Riga, Richmons, Caracas, Mexico, and Milan. He has participated in over 200 national and International collective exhibitions.

His works are included in the permanent collections of many museums. He is a professor at the School of Architecture of the University of Havana. At present he is National Chairman of the Alliance Graphic Internation, Paris; member of the International Committee for Public Symbols Standards of the National Standards Institute, Wien; a correspondent member of the International Council of Graphic Design Associations, London, and many other institutions. Recently he was awarded a National Order for 25 years of activities in the field of design.

B-23

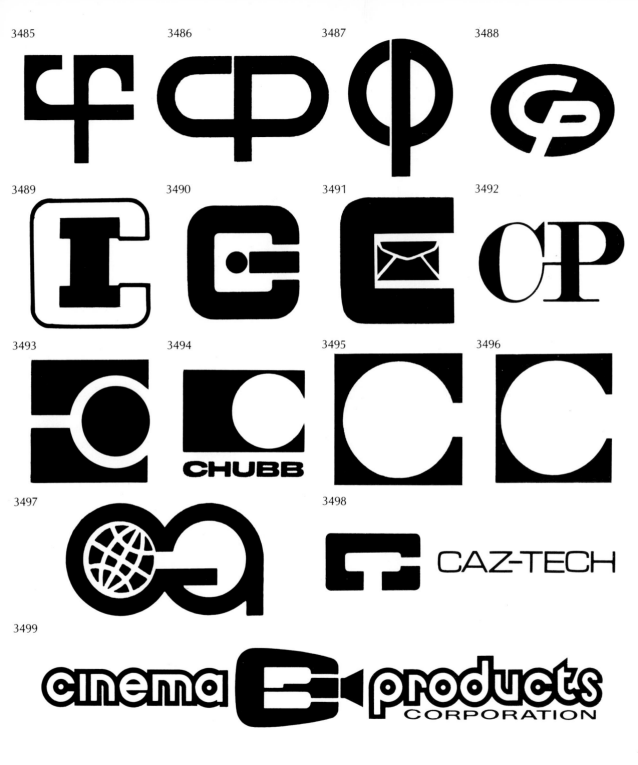

Legend
AD) Advertiser/Client
DIR) Art Director
DES/A) Designer, Artist
ST) Studio, Agency   SM) Symbol
C)   Category   TM) Trademark

3485 AD) Churchill Falls (Labrador) Corp., Ltd.,
Churchill Falls, Labrador, Newfoundland, CANADA

3486 AD) Carlo Parolini Industria Mobili Im-
bottiti, via Leonardo da Vinci 56
20036 Meda Milano, ITALY

3487 AD) Central Penn National Bank
Philadelphia, PA, USA
C)   Bank

3488 AD) Chili Plastics Inc., 2278 Westside Dr.,
Rochester, NY 14624   USA

3489 AD) Colonial Management Assoc. Inc.,
75 Federal St., Boston, MA 02110
USA

3490 AD) Cramer Industries Inc., 625 Adams St.,
Kansas City, KS 66105   USA

3491 AD) Canada Envelope Co., Toronto, Ottawa, Vancouver, Edmonton, Calgary,
Halifax   CANADA

3492 AD) Control Process Inc., 201 Atwater St.,
Plantsville, CT 06479   USA

3493 AD) Command Yachts (International) Ltd.,
a De Leuw Cather Canada Ltd., Co.,
London, Ont. CANADA

3494 AD) Chubb & Son Inc. Underwriters
Subsidiary of The Chubb Corp., 800
Dorchester Blvd, W., Montreal, Que.
CANADA
C)   Underwriters

3495 AD) Cegelec Canada Ltd., 2000 Ellesmere
Rd., Scarborough, Ont.   CANADA
Subsidiaries of Compagnie Général
D'Electricité. Paris, FRANCE

3496 AD) Chittom Equipment Ltd., 6224 2nd St.,
S.E., Calgary, Alta.   CANADA

3497 AD) Canadian Atlas Furniture Mfg. Ltd.,
2400 Finch Ave., Weston, Ont.
M9M 2L8   CANADA
C)   Slimline Steel Equipment

3498 AD) Caz-Tech, 282 Belfield Rd., Rexdale,
Ont.   CANADA

3499 AD) Cinema Products Corporation
2044 Cotner Ave., Los Angeles, CA
90025   USA

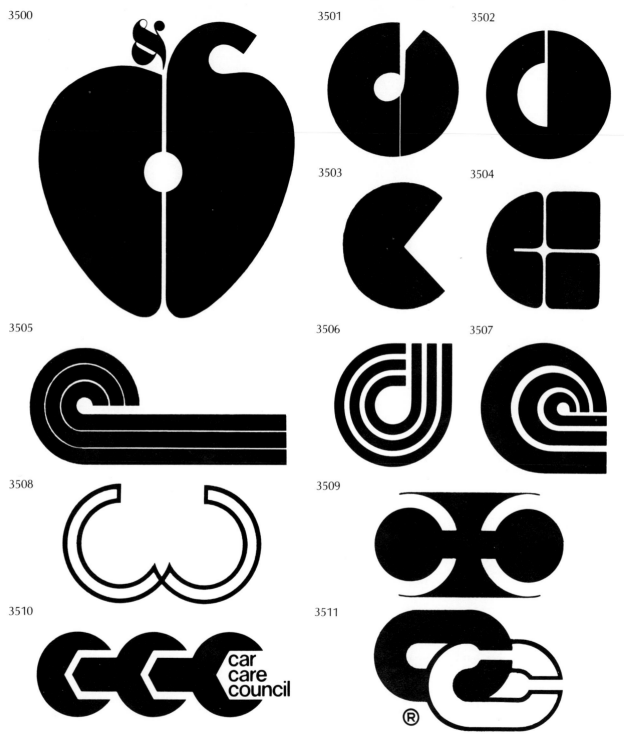

3500 AD) Caring & Sharing Productions,
73 Richmond St. West, Suite 400,
Toronto   M5H 2A1   CANADA

3501 AD) Creative Sound & Video,
Division of Perfect Television, Inc.
9541 Harding Ave., Surfside,
Hollywood, Hallandale, FL, USA

3502 AD) Consolidated Credits & Discounts,
London, ENGLAND

DES/A)   Romek Marber

3503 AD) Cranfield Sails Ltd., The Quay,
Burnham-On-Crouch, Essex,
ENGLAND

3504 AD) Carleton Towers Hotel, 150 Albert St.,
Ottawa, Ont., CANADA

3505 AD) Carpet Cushion Council

3506 AD) Chemware, (Division of Champion
International) 600 East Evergreen
Ave., Monrovia, CA   91016   USA

3507 AD) Columbia School of Broadcasting,
San Francisco, CA, USA

DES/A)   Jerry Berman

3508 AD) Charles R. Casson Ltd., 111 Miranda
Ave., Toronto, Ont.   M6B 3W8
CANADA

3509 AD) Carlo Costa, Negozio esposizione a
Milano, Piazza De Angeli, 9 ITALY

3510 AD) Car Care Council, Dearborn, MI, USA

3511 AD) Campbell Chain Co., Union City, CA
USA

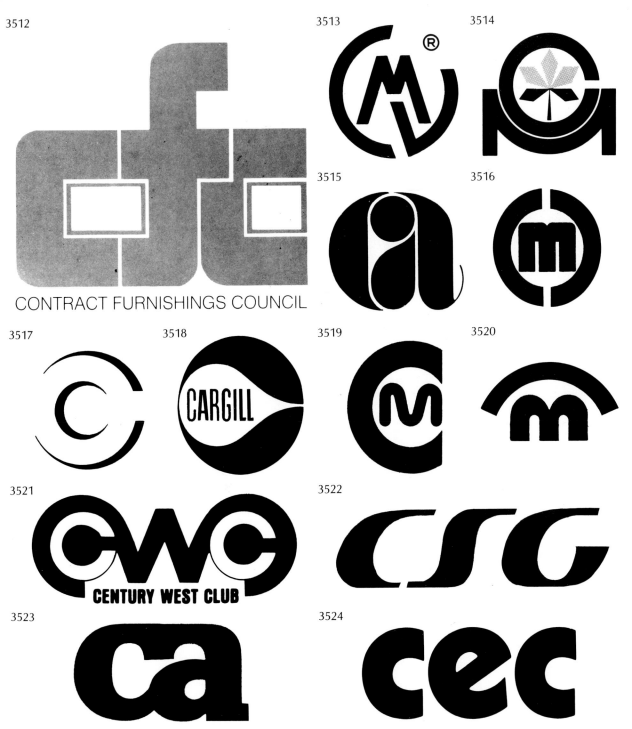

3512

CONTRACT FURNISHINGS COUNCIL

3513

3514

3515

3516

3517

3518

CARGILL

3519

3520

3521

CWC

CENTURY WEST CLUB

3522

3523

3524

3512 AD) Contract Furnishings Council,
Whitney Publications, Inc.
A Division of Billboard Publications
130 East 59th St., New York,
NY 10022 USA

C) Publishing

3513 AD) Costruzioni Meccaniche Varie s.r.l.
Piazza Carducci, 7 40125 Bologna
ITALY

3514 AD) Canadian Meter Co. Ltd.
(A subsidiary of The Singer Company)
9199 65th Ave., Edmonton, Alta.
T6E OLI CANADA

3515 AD) Communication Arts, Inc. Head Office-
USA; In Canada: Kingsway Film
Equipment Ltd., 821 Kipling Ave.,
Toronto, Ont., CANADA

3516 AD) Canada Manpower Centre, Dept. of
Manpower & Immigration CANADA

3517 AD) Cyrus Company, Industrie dell'arredamento. Sede: 20020 Magnago
(Milano), ITALY

3518 AD) Cargill, Minneapolis, MN, USA

3519 AD) Cornell Machine Co., 45 Brown Ave.,
Springfield, NJ 07081 USA

3520 AD) Cumis Insurance Society, CANADA

3521 AD) Century West Club,
ABC Entertainment Center,
2040 Ave. of the Stars, Los Angeles,
CA 90067 USA

3522 AD) Certain-Teed / Saint Gobain,
Textile Glass Fiber Div.
3000 Chrysler Rd., Kansas City,
KS 66115 USA

3523 AD) Commercial Alliance Corporation,
770 Lexington Ave., New York,
NY 10021 USA

3524 AD) Carbonisation Entreprise et Céramique, 4, Place des États-Unis,
92-Montrouge, FRANCE

3525

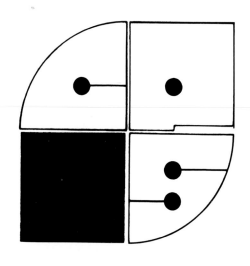

3526

Citizens' Coalition

3527

3528

SINCE 1829

3529

CAM

3530

3531

christie

3532

3533

Canadex

3534

CAUFFIEL
MACHINERY

3535

3536

CEL

3525   AD)   Canadian Premium / Incentive Show,
               481 University Ave., Toronto, Ont.
               M5W 1A7   CANADA
3526   AD)   Citizens' Coalition   Canada
3527   AD)   Castur, Zurich, SWITZERLAND
        DES/A)   Hansruedi Scheller
3528   AD)   Canton Company, Canton House,
               P.O. Box 447, Baltimore, MD   21203
               USA
3529   AD)   The Canadian Advertising & Market-
               ing (Personnel Bureau)   CANADA
3530   AD)   Citterio, Sirone Como
3531   AD)   Christie Chemical Co. Ltd.
3532   AD)   Capital Iron & Metal, 2nd Line West,
               P.O. Box 53, Brampton, Ont.
               L6V 2K7   CANADA
3533   AD)   Canadex Auto Centres Ltd.,
               80 Richmond St. West,
               Toronto, Ont.   M5H 2B6   CANADA
3534   AD)   Cauffiel Machinery, 1400 Hastings
               Ave., Toledo, OH   43606   USA
3535   AD)   Canadian Construction Materials Ltd.,
               330 Wentworth St. North,
               Hamilton, Ont.   L8L 5W2   CANADA
3536   AD)   Criterion Engineering Ltd.,
               465 Vanguard Rd., Richmond,
               B.C.   V6X 2P7   CANADA

3537 AD) Cleveland Trust, Cleveland, OH   USA
C) Banking

3538 AD) Camden State Bank, USA
DES/A) Steve Skaggs
C) Banking

3539 AD) College / University Corporation,
Indianapolis, IN   USA

3540 AD) Contract Interiors, Inc.
Chicago, IL, USA

3541 AD) Concept Industries Corp. USA
DES/A) Gordon Gutke Advertising Agency

3542 AD) Casigliani Import
DES/A) Pisa-Marina

3543 AD) Citizens Savings, 700 Wilshire Blvd.,
Los Angeles, CA, USA
C) Banking

3544 AD) Continental Imports,
Philadelphia, PA   19127   USA

3545 AD) Chemiquip of Canada Ltd., 5165 Queen
Marry Rd., Montreal, Que. CANADA

3546 AD) Ceramica Florence - Pavimenti E
Rivestimenti - 50038 Scarperia-Firenze
ITALY

3547 AD) Bank of The Commonwealth,
Detroit, MI, USA

3548 AD) Bank Cantrade, Zurich,
SWITZERLAND
DES/A) Atelier E.U.M. Leuz
C) Bank

3549 AD) Connecticut General Life Insurance
Co., Hartford, CT, USA
C) Insurance

3550 AD) Credit Card Graphics,
French Banking Group, FRANCE
DES/A) Daniel Maurel

3551 AD) Chemico, Chemical Construction
Corp., One Penn Plaza, New York,
NY   10001   USA

3552 AD) Champlain Productions Ltd.,
405 Ogilvy, Montreal, Que.
H3N 1M4   CANADA

C-17

3553 AD) Canadian Standards Association,
178 Rexdale Blvd., Rexdale, Ont.
M9W 1R3   CANADA

3554 AD) Carl Freudenberg Helia-Werk,
694 Weinheim /Bergstrasse,
GERMANY

3555 AD) Controls, Inc., Box 701 Oneonta,
AL   35121   USA

3556 AD) Cremona Nuova Cremona, ITALY
DES/A)   Franco Grignani

3557 AD) Contraves AG Zurich,
Contraves Italiana S.p.A. Rome,
ITALY

C) Military Equipment

3558 AD) Cattadori Actualform,
via fiammenghini 32, Cantu, ITALY

3559 AD) Commercial Tape & Label,
17 Paton Road, Toronto, Ont.
M6H 1R7   CANADA

3560 AD) Chimney Hill Corp., Wilmington,
VT, USA
DES/A)   Edward Deniega, Jr.

3561 AD) Co-operative Fire & Casualty Co.,
1920 College Ave., Regina, Sask.
CANADA

3562 AD) Crain Books, 740 Rush St., Chicago,
IL   60611   USA

3563 AD) Castur, Zurich, SWITZERLAND
DES/A) Hansruedi Scheller

3564 AD) Canadian Engineering Publications
Ltd., 46 St. Clair Ave. E., Toronto,
Ont., CANADA

C) Trade Publications

3565 AD) Closet Maid Corporation,
720 South West 17th St., P.O. Box 304,
Ocala, FL   32670   USA

3566 AD) Conti Commodity Services Inc.,
Board of Trade Bldg., Chicago,
IL   60604   USA

C-18

3567

3568

3569   3570   3571   3572

3573   3574

CRANZ CANADA CORPORATION

CUMINI
le cucine personalizzate

3575   3576

CARDKEY
TOTAL CONCEPT ACCESS CONTROL

cabot 36

3567	AD)	C.B.C. / Canadian Broadcasting Corp., CANADA
	ST)	Burton Kramer Associates
3568	AD)	Nuclear Pacific Inc. of Seattle Seattle, WA, USA
3569	AD)	Canadian Steel Service Centre Institute, 55 York St., Toronto, Ont. CANADA
3570	AD)	Conant Controls, Inc., 427 Riverside Ave., Medford, MA 02155 USA
3571	AD)	Clecon Incorporated, 2909 E. 79th St., Cleveland, OH 44104 USA
3572	AD)	Centro Consulenza Arredamento Cucine RB
3573	AD)	Cranz (Canada) Corporation, Head Office: 2671 Main St., Buffalo, NY 14214 USA
3574	AD)	Cumini S.p.A - 33010 Cassacco (Udine)
3575	AD)	Cardkey Systems, A Division of Greer Hydraulics, Inc., 20339 Nordhoff St., Chatsworth, CA 91311 USA
3576	AD)	Cabotcraft Industries Ltd., 23 Prince Andrew Pl., Don Mills, Ont. M3C 2H2 CANADA
	C)	Boat Builder

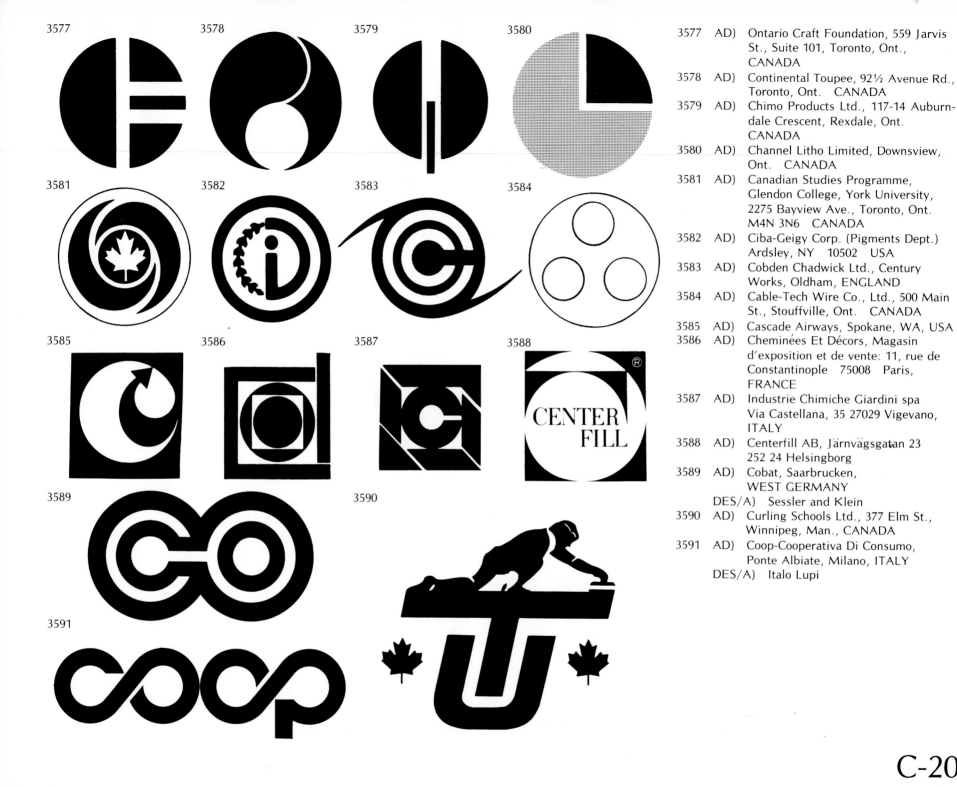

3577 AD) Ontario Craft Foundation, 559 Jarvis St., Suite 101, Toronto, Ont., CANADA

3578 AD) Continental Toupee, 92½ Avenue Rd., Toronto, Ont. CANADA

3579 AD) Chimo Products Ltd., 117-14 Auburndale Crescent, Rexdale, Ont. CANADA

3580 AD) Channel Litho Limited, Downsview, Ont. CANADA

3581 AD) Canadian Studies Programme, Glendon College, York University, 2275 Bayview Ave., Toronto, Ont. M4N 3N6 CANADA

3582 AD) Ciba-Geigy Corp. (Pigments Dept.) Ardsley, NY 10502 USA

3583 AD) Cobden Chadwick Ltd., Century Works, Oldham, ENGLAND

3584 AD) Cable-Tech Wire Co., Ltd., 500 Main St., Stouffville, Ont. CANADA

3585 AD) Cascade Airways, Spokane, WA, USA

3586 AD) Cheminées Et Décors, Magasin d'exposition et de vente: 11, rue de Constantinople 75008 Paris, FRANCE

3587 AD) Industrie Chimiche Giardini spa Via Castellana, 35 27029 Vigevano, ITALY

3588 AD) Centerfill AB, Järnvägsgatan 23 252 24 Helsingborg

3589 AD) Cobat, Saarbrucken, WEST GERMANY
DES/A) Sessler and Klein

3590 AD) Curling Schools Ltd., 377 Elm St., Winnipeg, Man., CANADA

3591 AD) Coop-Cooperativa Di Consumo, Ponte Albiate, Milano, ITALY
DES/A) Italo Lupi

C-20

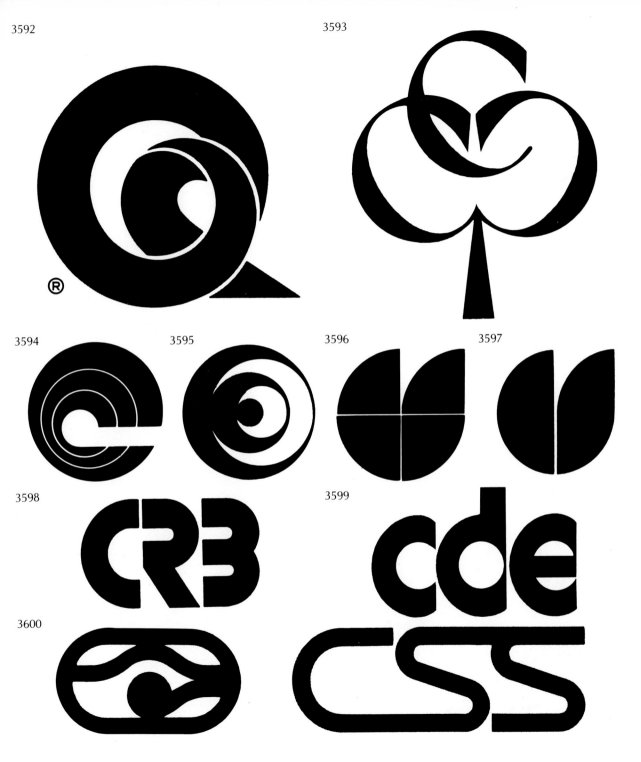

3592 AD) Codima Poliuretani, Consorzio
Divulgazione Marchio di Qualità
Poliuretani Espansi

3593 AD) Cumberland Capital Corp.,
144 Davenport Rd., Toronto,
Ont. M5R 1J2 CANADA

3594 AD) Combined Communications Corp.,
P.O. Box 25518, Phoenix, AZ
85002 USA

DES/A) Barry Wickliffe

ST) Jennings & Thompson Advertising

3595 AD) Cablecasting Ltd., 45 Charles St., E.,
Toronto, Ont. CANADA

3596 AD) Commercial Studios Ltd.,
260 Richmond Street W., Toronto,
Ont. M5V 1W5 CANADA

3597 AD) Cincom Systems of Canada Ltd.,
55 City Centre Drive,
Mississauga, Ont. CANADA

3598 AD) C.R.B. S.p.A., Bagnolo Mella
(Brescia)

3599 AD) CDE, Au 6 de la rue Volney, Paris 2e,
FRANCE

3600 AD) CSS - Compagnia Servizi di Sicurezza
S.p.A., ITALY

3601

3602

3603

3604

3605

3606

3607

Casco

3608

3609

3610 CROWN

CENTAUR

3601 AD) Canada Savings Bonds, Dept. of Federal Revenue, Ottawa, Ont. CANADA
S) Abstract design, Buy Canada Savings Bonds
3602 AD) Canada Design '67
S) Award of Excellence - Canada Design Council, Ottawa, Ont., CANADA
DES/A) Allan R. Fleming
3603 AD) Canada Valve Ltd., 353 Manitou Dr., Kitchener, Ont. N2C 1L5 CANADA
3604 AD) Viajes Cristal, s.a., Palma de Mallorca Ibiza, 17 SPAIN
C) Tour Operators
3605 AD) Ceramiche Italiane, riconosci la buona ceramica, ITALY
3606 AD) Crystal Shores, Crystal Bay, NV, USA
3607 AD) Casco, Industrilim, Box 11010, 100 61 Stockholm 11, SWEDEN
3608 AD) Canadian Imperial Bank of Commerce, Commerce Court West, Toronto, Ont. M5L 1A2 CANADA
3609 AD) Centaur Manufacturing Co. Ltd., 57 Newkirk Rd., Richmond Hill, Ont. L4C 3G4 CANADA
3610 AD) Crown Controls Inc., New Bremen, OH 45869 USA

C-22

3611   AD)   Ceramica Europea S.p.A,
                   42013 Casalgrande (Reggio Emilia)
                   ITALY

3612   AD)   Cascade Electric, Tacoma, WA, USA

3613   AD)   Canada West Insurance Co.,
                   10603-107 Ave., Edmonton, Alta.
                   CANADA

       C)   Insurance

3614   Editor's note: origin of Mark misfiled
                   at time of publication.

3615   AD)   The Caldwell Partners,
                   50 Prince Arthur Ave., Toronto,
                   Ont.   M5R 1B5   CANADA

3616   AD)   Compagnie Française De L'Orient Et
                   De La Chine, Glauco Ceresa 26 V.
                   Borgognona, Roma, ITALY

3617   AD)   Continental Conveyor & Machine
                   Works Ltd., 470 St. Alphonse St. E.,
                   Thetford Mines, Que.,
                   G6G 3V8   CANADA

3618   AD)   Continental Telephone Corporation,
                   P.O. Box 400, Merrifield, VA   22116
                   USA

3619   AD)   Cook Paint & Varnish Co., P.O. Box
                   389, Kansas City, MO   64141 USA

3620   AD)   Crown Center Hotel, Kansas City,
                   MO, USA
                   (Crown Center Redevelopment Corp.,
                   wholly owned subsidiary of Hallmark
                   Cards, Inc.)

3621   AD)   Crown Products, Division Economy
                   Color Card Company, Inc. USA

3622   AD)   Chicago O'Hare International Trade
                   Center, 9400 West Foster Ave.,
                   Chicago, IL   60656   USA

3623   Editor's Note: origin of Mark misfiled
                   at time of publication.

3624   AD)   Ciba-Geigy Canada Ltd.,
                   205 Bouchard Blvd., Dorval,
                   Que.   H9S 1B1   CANADA

       S)   Product Use

3625   AD)   Curling Club Basel, Basel
      DES/A)   Jürg Spahr

3626   AD)   Cacharel, Paris, FRANCE
      DES/A)   Albert Boton
      DES/S)   Delpire-Advico Paris

3627 AD) Chimetal s.r.1., Milano, ITALY
C) Equipment for chemical, metal and ceramics industries
DES/A) Massiho Dradi
3628 AD) Central Bank, Oakland, CA, USA
C) Banking
3629 AD) Corporate Lithographing, Toronto, Ont., CANADA
DES/A) Carl Brett
ST) Hiller Rinaldo Associates
3630 AD) Curtis Products Ltd., 495 Ball St., Cobourg, Ont. K9A 4P9 CANADA
3631 AD) Cosmos Bank, Zürich, SWITZERLAND
DES/A) Stephen Onken
ST) William Douglas McAdams
3632 AD) Compesca S.A., Cia. Brasileira de Pesca, São Paulo, BRAZIL
C) Fishery
DES/A) Alexandre Wollner
ST) Programação Visual Ltda.
3633 AD) CESP - Centrais Eléctricas de São Paulo S.A. São Paulo, BRAZIL
C) Production & distribution of electric power.
DES/A) João Carlos Cauduro & Ludovico Martino
3634 AD) The Center for Technical Development Inc., 2876 Culver Ave., Dayton, OH 45429 USA
3635 AD) Caribbean Communications Ltd., Bridgetown, Barbados, WEST INDIES
C) Promotion of Investment, Business & Trade
DES/A) Heiner Hegemann
ST) Chermayeff & Geismar Associates
3636 AD) Computer Terminal Corporation, USA
ST) Raymond Loewy & William Snaith, Inc.
3637 AD) Cement Ltd., Dublin, IRELAND
DES/A) George Daulby
ST) BDMW Associates Ltd.
3638 AD) The Cove Condominium, USA
DES/A) Elaine M. Lyerly
ST) Monte J. Curry Marketing, NC, USA
3639 AD) Chan Plumbing, USA
DES/A) Mike Quon, CA, USA
3640 AD) Cygnet Canada Ltd., Box 29, Woodstock, N.B. CANADA
3641 AD) Compressor Engineering Corporation, Houston, TX, USA

C-24

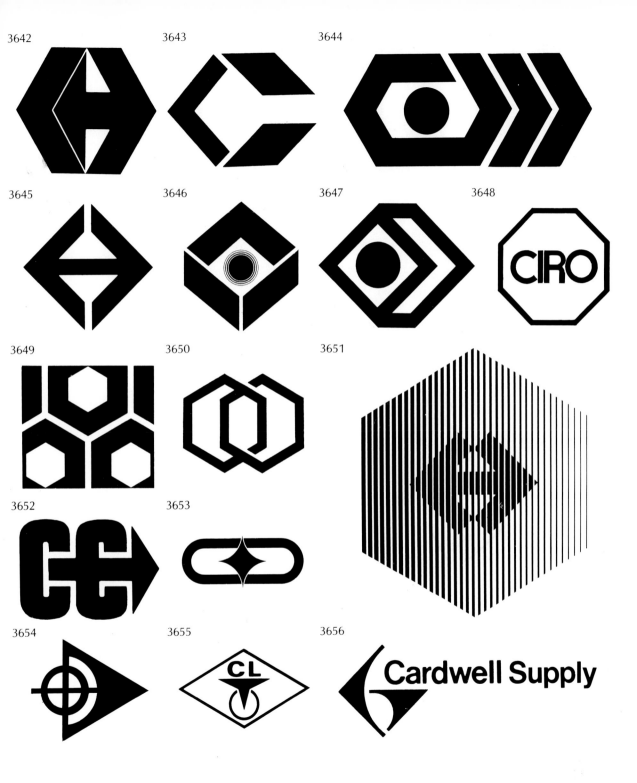

3642 AD) Chemdorff, Barcelona, SPAIN
DES/A) Francisco Marcó Vilar
ST) Grupo de Diseno S.A.

3643 AD) Charlier, Antwerpen, BELGIUM
DES/A) Paul Ibou

3644 AD) Canadian Cablesystems Ltd.,
120 Adelaide St. W., Toronto, Ont.
CANADA

3645 AD) Credit Card Exchange, USA
DES/A) Don Primi

3646 AD) The California State Exposition,
Sacremento, CA, USA
ST) Saul Bass & Associates

3647 AD) Video Security Systems, USA
ST) The Company

3648 AD) CIRO, 711 Fifth Ave., New York,
NY 10022 USA

3649 AD) Ceramiche della Robbia S.p.A.
Casalgrande, Reggio Emilia, ITALY
DES/A) Andrea Rossi

3650 AD) Centralny Zarzad Spótdzielczos'ci
Pracy, Warsaw, POLAND
C) Foreign trade in handicraft products
DES/A) Štefan Sledziński

3651 AD) Canadian Telecommunications
Carriers Assoc., 1 Nicholas St.,
Ottawa, Ont. K1N 7B7 CANADA
C) Promote development of telecommunications in all its forms. Encourage
study and provisions of complete tele-
communications services to meet business and social needs within Canada
and the rest of the world.

3652 AD) Clarke Chapman Ltd., International
Combustion Division, Sinfin Lane,
Derby DE29J ENGLAND

3653 AD) Canada Chain & Forge Co., Ltd.,
Granville Island, Vancouver, B.C.
V611 3M8 CANADA

3654 AD) Canadian Graphic Arts Show,
481 University Ave., Toronto, Ont.
M5W 1A7 CANADA

3655 AD) Creusot-Loire, Département De La
Mécanique Spécialisée, 15, rue
Pasquier 75383 Paris, FRANCE

3656 AD) Cardwell Supply, Div. of Bow Valley
Industry Supplies Ltd., 1200-630 6th
Ave. S.W. Calgary, Alta.,
T2P OS8 CANADA

3657

3658

3659

3660

3661

3662

3663

3664

3665

3666

CAMINITI

3667

3668

COUNTRY PLACE

3657 AD) CanDel, One Calgary Place,
330-5th Ave., S.W., Calgary, Alta.,
T2P OL4   CANADA
3658 AD) L'Association des Fabricants de Cidre
du Quebec Inc., 9 Rue Miami, Parc
Rémillard, Route Rurale no. 2,
Laprairie, Que., CANADA
3659 AD) Contrôle Qualtiss, Paris, FRANCE
DES/A) Gerard Ifert
3660 AD) Canadian Film Institute,
Ottawa, Ont., CANADA
C) Film distributors
DES/A) Georges Beaupré
3661 AD) Chicago City Centre/Holiday Inn,
Chicago, IL, USA
SM) The symbol, based on the three 'Cs' of
the name, will appear on all signage
throughout the hotel, including the
patterns for bedspreads and wallpaper.
DES/A) Charles Sleichter & Fred Wolf
ST) Image Response, Chicago, IL, USA
3662 AD) Cumberland Furniture Corp.
C) Furniture Manufacturers
DES/A) Rudolph de Harak
ST) Corchia, de Harak, Inc.
3663 AD) Cristallerie Antonio Imperatore
150, corso Malta - 80141 Napoli, ITALY
3664 AD) Cultural Exchange Association, Tokyo,
JAPAN
C) Cultural Exchange
DES/A) Kamekura Yusaku
3665 AD) Central National Bank, Chicago, IL,
USA
C) Banking
DES/A) Stephen Dunne
ST) Unimark International
3666 AD) Caminiti, Catania, ITALY
C) Leather goods & perfumery articles
DES/A) Ennio Lucini
3667 AD) Counterweight Industries Limited,
133 Richmond St. West, Toronto,
Ont., CANADA
C) Weight-Watching product
manufacturer
3668 AD) Country Place Subdivision, USA
DES/A) Wyatt L. Phillips, GA, USA

3669

3670

**BRECHT om
undtagelsen og reglen**

Dansk Skolescene

3671

3672

VESTSJÆLLANDSCENTRET

3673

3674

modern living'73

Designer Artist Profile/ ERIK P. CHRISTENSEN,
IDD, Graphic Designer, Vestergade 6, DK-1456
Copenhagen K

Own design office in partnership with
Ib K. Olsen IDD.
Works from 1968-73.
Trademarks, brochures, packaging, posters,
book jackets and exhibitions.

(Ref: Mobilia, Feb./74)
(World of Logotypes File No. 187)

3669   AD)   Gladsaxe Teater, Copenhagen,
                DENMARK
3670   AD)   Poster Graphic Design
3671   AD)   The Newspaper in Education,
                DENMARK
        S)   Danish Press Information Council
3672   AD)   Vestsjaellands Shopping Center,
                Slagelsa, DENMARK
3673   AD)   Lyngby Shopping Center,
                Copenhagen, DENMARK
        S)   Proposed logo design
3674   AD)   Bella Centre, Copenhagen,
                DENMARK
        S)   Logo for Conference

CLAUDE NEON LIMITED

AD)   Claude Neon Industries Ltd.,
        Head Office: 250 Bloor St. E.,
        Toronto, Ont., M4W 1G3 CANADA
C)   Nation-wide Outdoor Advertising
        Sign Firm
DES/A)   Stuart Ash, Fritz Gottschalk, Fredy
        Jaggi
ST)   Gottschalk & Ash Ltd.,
        Graphic Design Consultants,
        322 King St. W., Toronto, Ont.,
        CANADA

(Ref: World of Logotypes File No. 121)

CLAUDE NÉON LIMITÉE

Reference:

Claude Neon Vehicle Identification Manual
Symbol—Illustrated are the five (5) variations of the
Claude Neon symbol. All the variations of the sym-
bol are based on a square. (Page C29)
Name Style—The name style "CLAUDE NEON
LIMITED" and "CLAUDE NÉON LIMITÉE" must
always appear in three lines reading vertically from
bottom upward. (Page C28)

Variation I

C-28

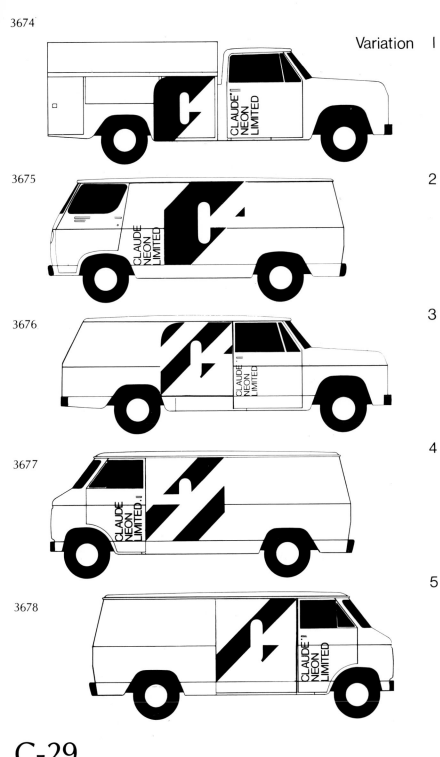

The symbol for Claude Neon represents the philosophy of boldness coupled with good design. It incorporates 5 different abstract shapes emanating from the letter "C", 6 colors are used singly and in every possible combination, giving a total of 90 different logo symbols for use on the various company applications, such as trucks, stationery, calling cards, billboards, brochures. The 90 variations are used at random and are not coded to divisions or job functions. Reproduced here are only 5 of the 90 variations. "A symbol as big, and colorful—and changing—as the world of outdoor advertising itself." For example, each of the company's 100 salesmen are given personalized calling cards carrying 60 different versions of the graphic program.

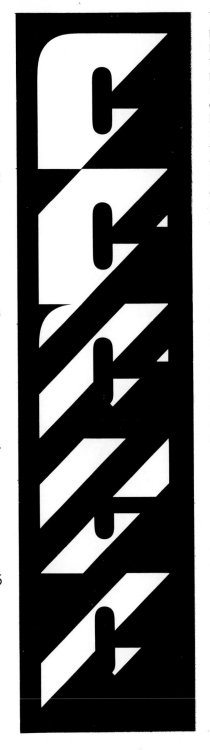

The symbol embraces the merging of major Claude Neon subsidiaries into one Canada-wide communications service group. The companies adopting the name Claude Neon Industries Ltd., are E.L. Ruddy, Universal Signs, Posters Ltd., Outdoor Advertising Sales Ltd., and Market Place Advertising. These subsidiaries will be combined with the parent company's existing operations, Canada-wide. The main products of the new, combined company are electrical signs, billboards, painted bulletins, in cities and shopping mall kiosks.

President Gould of Claude Neon, says the idea of a symbol with a multitude of variants may appear to be out-of-step with the more fashionable single identifying mark, but it works beautifully for our purposes. The multi-logo-matrix is ever changing, it "tells the story that our products, the ads themselves, are also constantly different from one another and constantly changing". Under the program, different variations of the logo will be used throughout areas that can be identified with the company name and symbol.

Illustrated Figures 3674, 3675, 3676, 3677, 3678

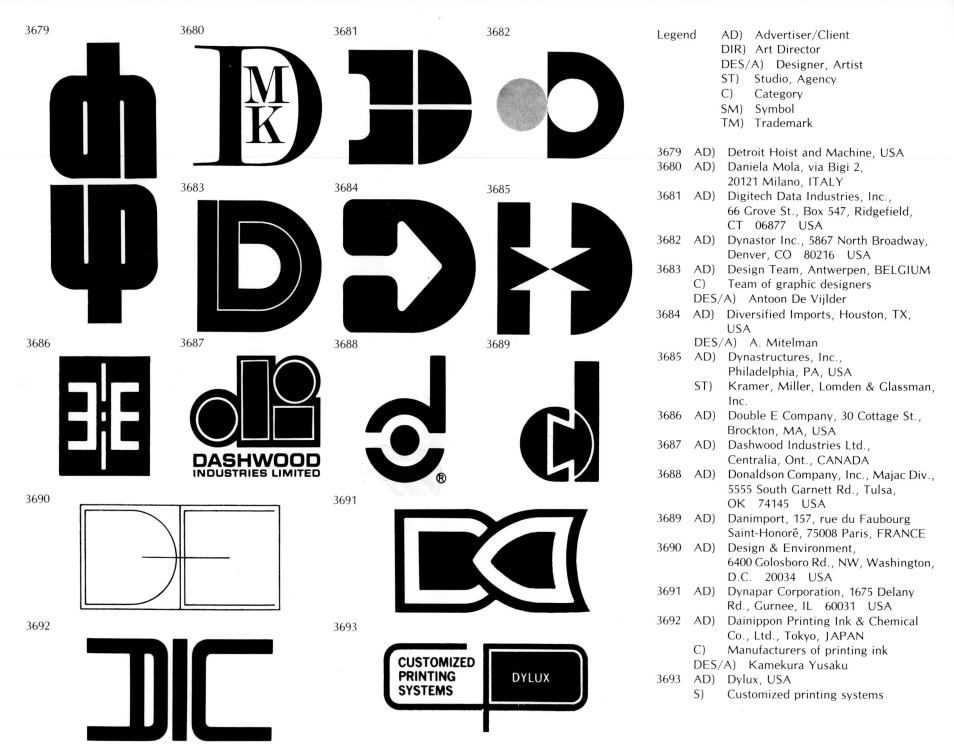

3679

3680

3681

3682

3683

3684

3685

3686

3687

DASHWOOD
INDUSTRIES LIMITED

3688

3689

3690

3691

3692

3693

CUSTOMIZED
PRINTING
SYSTEMS

DYLUX

Legend　　AD)　Advertiser/Client
　　　　　DIR)　Art Director
　　　　　DES/A)　Designer, Artist
　　　　　ST)　Studio, Agency
　　　　　C)　Category
　　　　　SM)　Symbol
　　　　　TM)　Trademark

3679　AD)　Detroit Hoist and Machine, USA
3680　AD)　Daniela Mola, via Bigi 2,
　　　　　　20121 Milano, ITALY
3681　AD)　Digitech Data Industries, Inc.,
　　　　　　66 Grove St., Box 547, Ridgefield,
　　　　　　CT 06877 USA
3682　AD)　Dynastor Inc., 5867 North Broadway,
　　　　　　Denver, CO 80216 USA
3683　AD)　Design Team, Antwerpen, BELGIUM
　　　　C)　Team of graphic designers
　　　　DES/A)　Antoon De Vijlder
3684　AD)　Diversified Imports, Houston, TX,
　　　　　　USA
　　　　DES/A)　A. Mitelman
3685　AD)　Dynastructures, Inc.,
　　　　　　Philadelphia, PA, USA
　　　　ST)　Kramer, Miller, Lomden & Glassman,
　　　　　　Inc.
3686　AD)　Double E Company, 30 Cottage St.,
　　　　　　Brockton, MA, USA
3687　AD)　Dashwood Industries Ltd.,
　　　　　　Centralia, Ont., CANADA
3688　AD)　Donaldson Company, Inc., Majac Div.,
　　　　　　5555 South Garnett Rd., Tulsa,
　　　　　　OK 74145 USA
3689　AD)　Danimport, 157, rue du Faubourg
　　　　　　Saint-Honoré, 75008 Paris, FRANCE
3690　AD)　Design & Environment,
　　　　　　6400 Golosboro Rd., NW, Washington,
　　　　　　D.C. 20034 USA
3691　AD)　Dynapar Corporation, 1675 Delany
　　　　　　Rd., Gurnee, IL 60031 USA
3692　AD)　Dainippon Printing Ink & Chemical
　　　　　　Co., Ltd., Tokyo, JAPAN
　　　　C)　Manufacturers of printing ink
　　　　DES/A)　Kamekura Yusaku
3693　AD)　Dylux, USA
　　　　S)　Customized printing systems

3694

3695

3696

3697

3698

3699

3700

3701

3702

3703

3704

3705

3707

DATUM

dpi

3706

DALMAU

dimension & plywood inc.

3694   AD)   Danish Furniture Makers Control, DENMARK

3695   AD)   Dai-ichi Kangyo Bank, 6-2, Marunouchi 1-chome, Chiyoda-ku, Tokyo 100, JAPAN

3696   AD)   De Dietrich

3697   AD)   Dustex (subsidiary of American Precision Industries Inc.) 2777 Walden Ave., Buffalo, NY 14225 USA

3698   AD)   The Southwest Metroplex, North Texas Commission, 600 Ave. H, E., Suite 101, Dept. 0405, Arlington, TX 76011 USA

3699   AD)   Dainichi Kinzoku Kogyo Co.

3700   AD)   Design Centre, Milano, ITALY
DES/A)   Bob Nooroa
ST)   Unimark International, Milano, ITALY

3701   AD)   D & D Industries, 204 Wildcat Rd., Downsview, Ont., CANADA

3702   AD)   Dow Chemical of Canada, Ltd., Modeland Rd., P.O. Box 1012, Sarnia, Ont., N7T 7K7 CANADA
SM)   Packaging product graphics

3703   AD)   Davis Mfg. Co., P.O. Box 1067, Chattanooga, TN 37401 USA

3704   AD)   Dilo-Gesellschaft Drexler & Co., 8943 Babenhausen, Frundsberg-strasse 36-38, GERMANY

3705   AD)   Datum Structures Engineering Inc., Dallas, TX, USA
DES/A)   Crawford Dunn

3706   AD)   Dalmau, Barcelona, SPAIN
DES/A)   Perez Sanchez

3707   AD)   Dimension & Plywood, Inc. 127 Avondale Dr., P.O. Box 586, High Point, NC 27261 USA

3708

3709

3710

3711

3712

3713

3714

3715

3716

3717

3718

3719

3720

3708 AD) Davis Custom Packaging, Div. of Davis Gelatine, P.O. Box 96, Station "A", Scarborough, Ont., M1K 5B9 CANADA

3709 AD) Dutch Craft Ltd., 29 Peter St., Port Hope, Ont., CANADA

3710 AD) Hallo Partner, Danke Schön

3711 AD) Deminex, D-4000 Düsseldorf, Immermannstrasse 40, WEST GERMANY

3712 AD) Dura-Fiber, 2300 Arrowhead Dr., Carson City, NV 89701 USA

3713 AD) D & R Enterprises, Inc., 8900 Penn Ave. S., Suite 200, Minneapolis, MN 55431 USA
   SM) Graphic animated trademark

3714 AD) Doherty McCuaig Ltd., The Simpson Tower, Suite 3000, Toronto, Ont. CANADA
   C) Stock Brokers

3715 AD) Diamond International Corp., 733 Third Ave., New York, NY 10017 USA
   C) Forest Products, Packaging & Printing, Consumer Products, Building Materials and Home Supplies, Machinery Systems

3716 AD) David Hicks Collection, Miami, FL USA
   SM) Designers tile international in Miami

3717 AD) Dikkers, 1912A Avenue Rd., Toronto, Ont. M5M 4A1 CANADA

3718 AD) Delta Sonics Inc., 14290 S. Main St., Gardena, CA 90248 USA

3719 AD) Deca-Dry by Chart-Pak, Inc., 2200 River Rd., Leeds, MA, USA

3720 AD) Do-Rel Products Ltd., 705 Progress Ave., Unit 15, Scarborough, Ont. CANADA

D-15

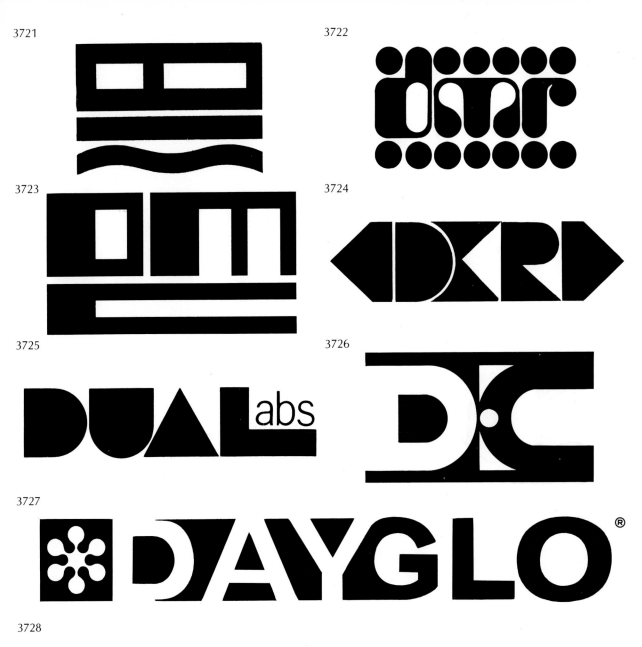

3721

3722

3723

3724

3725

3726

3727

3728

3721 AD) Dampcoursing Ltd., London, ENGLAND
DES/A) Richard Downer
3722 AD) Ducros, Meilleur, Roy & Assoc., Ltd., P.O. Box 259, Place Bonaventure, Montreal, Que. H5A 1B2 CANADA
C) Management Consultants
3723 AD) Drummond, McCall & Co., Ltd., 5205 Fairway St., Lachine, Que. CANADA
3724 AD) DKR Delivery Service Ltd., Toronto, Ont., CANADA
3725 AD) Dual ABS, Arlington, VA, USA
DES/A) Christine L. Stansbury
3726 AD) Distribuzione, Bologna, ITALY
3727 AD) Day-Glo, 4732 St. Clair Ave., Cleveland, OH 44103 USA
3728 AD) Data-file, 25 Howden Rd., Scarborough, Ont. M1R 3C8 CANADA

3729

3730

dunhill

DAVID

3731

david's

3732

3733

Dunlop

Dietzco

3734

3735

DECISION

dynaco

3736

DARIUS

3729 AD) Alfred Dunhill Ltd., 30 Duke St., St. James's, London, ENGLAND

3730 AD) David Manufacturing Co., 1600 12th St., N.E., Mason City, IN 50401 USA

DES/A) David M. Murphy

3731 AD) David's Carpet Distributors Inc., 2560 Linden Blvd., Brooklyn, NY 11208 USA

3732 AD) Dunlop Footwear Ltd., London, ENGLAND

DES/A) Kenneth Lamble

ST) Design Research Unit

3733 AD) Dietzco, Div. of the Entwistle Co., Bigelow St., Hudson, MA 01749 USA

3734 AD) Decision, Inc., 5601 College Ave., Oakland, CA 94618 USA

3735 AD) Dynaco, Div. of Tyco Laboratories, Box 88, Blackwood, NJ 08012 USA

3736 AD) Darios Photography, Crawley, Sussex, ENGLAND

ST) Talmadge Drummond & Partners

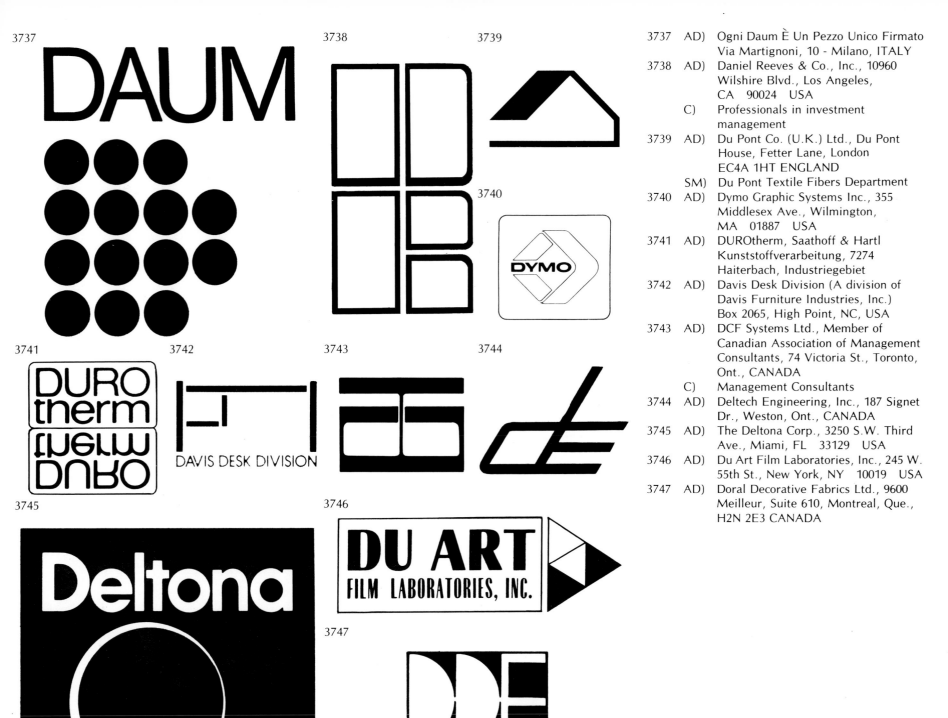

3737

3738

3739

3740

3741

3742

3743

3744

3745

3746

3747

3737 AD) Ogni Daum È Un Pezzo Unico Firmato
Via Martignoni, 10 - Milano, ITALY
3738 AD) Daniel Reeves & Co., Inc., 10960
Wilshire Blvd., Los Angeles,
CA 90024 USA
C) Professionals in investment
management
3739 AD) Du Pont Co. (U.K.) Ltd., Du Pont
House, Fetter Lane, London
EC4A 1HT ENGLAND
SM) Du Pont Textile Fibers Department
3740 AD) Dymo Graphic Systems Inc., 355
Middlesex Ave., Wilmington,
MA 01887 USA
3741 AD) DUROtherm, Saathoff & Hartl
Kunststoffverarbeitung, 7274
Haiterbach, Industriegebiet
3742 AD) Davis Desk Division (A division of
Davis Furniture Industries, Inc.)
Box 2065, High Point, NC, USA
3743 AD) DCF Systems Ltd., Member of
Canadian Association of Management
Consultants, 74 Victoria St., Toronto,
Ont., CANADA
C) Management Consultants
3744 AD) Deltech Engineering, Inc., 187 Signet
Dr., Weston, Ont., CANADA
3745 AD) The Deltona Corp., 3250 S.W. Third
Ave., Miami, FL 33129 USA
3746 AD) Du Art Film Laboratories, Inc., 245 W.
55th St., New York, NY 10019 USA
3747 AD) Doral Decorative Fabrics Ltd., 9600
Meilleur, Suite 610, Montreal, Que.,
H2N 2E3 CANADA

D-18

3748

3749

3750

3751

3752

3753

3754

3755

3756

3757

3758

3759

3748 AD) Delwood Furniture Co., Inc.,
United Chair Division, P.O. Box 96,
114 Churchill Ave., N.W., Leeds,
AL 35094 USA

3749 AD) Data Products Corp., 6219 De Soto St.,
Woodland Hills, CA 91364 USA

3750 AD) Diesse Atelier D'Interni

3751 AD) Decorative Components (Div. of
Polysar Plastics, Inc.) P.O. Box 688,
Forest City, NC 28043 USA
DES/A) Elaine M. Lyerly
ST) Monte J. Curry Marketing

3752 AD) Daymond Vinyl Siding (Subsidiary of
Redpath Ind. Ltd.) 2105 Midland
Ave., Scarborough, Ont., CANADA

3753 AD) Dearborn, Texas Tubular Div.,
TX, USA

3754 AD) Darbert Machinery Co., Ltd., 829
Kipling Ave., Toronto, Ont., CANADA
SM) International Darbert TM

3755 AD) The D.E. Stearns Co., P.O. Box 1234,
Shreveport, LA 71163 USA

3756 AD) Dallas City Police, TX, USA
DES/A) Crawford Dunn

3757 AD) Direction Technique des Constructions
Navales, 2, Rue Royale, 75200 Paris
Naval, FRANCE
C) Naval Ship Builder

3758 AD) Del Monte Lodge at Pebble Beach
Pebble Beach, CA 93953 USA

3759 AD) Design-a-Desk Corp., 320 Taunton
Ave., East Providence, RI 02914
USA

3760

3761

3762

3763

3764

3765

3766

3767

3768

3760 AD) Design Tex Fabrics, 27 5th Ave.,
New York, NY 10001 USA
3761 AD) Distinctive Designs
DES/A) Marie Martel
3762 AD) Deuta-Werke, 0507 Bergisch
Gladbach, Postfach 70, GERMANY
3763 AD) Demonte Bouw, Weert,
THE NETHERLANDS
DES/A) Jan Jaring
3764 AD) Dept. of Health & Social Security,
London, ENGLAND
DES/A) Woudhuysen Ltd.
3765 AD) Design Objectives Ltd., Croydon,
Surrey, ENGLAND
DES/A) Alan Fletcher
ST) Pentagram Design Partnership
3766 AD) Durox Building Units Ltd., Linford,
Essex, ENGLAND
DES/A) Woudhuysen Ltd.
3767 AD) Dalami, Bénélux,
Sa Etersol 9328 Schoonaarde,
PORTUGAL
3768 AD) The Dorset Corp., P.O. Box 491,
Pawtucket, RI 02862 USA
C) Golf Equipment

3769 AD) Delfim S.A.-Indústria E Comercio Da Pesca, Santos, BRAZIL
DES/A) João Carlos Caudro & Ludovico Martino
3770 AD) Dansk Droge Import, Herlev, DENMARK
DES/A) Morten Peetz-Schou
3771 AD) Design Mart, San Francisco, Ice House, 151 Union St., San Francisco, CA, USA
3772 AD) Design Communications, Los Angeles, CA USA
ST) Roger Johnson & Huerta Design
3773 AD) Diffusion Industrielle Á Céramique, FRANCE
DES/A) Serge Defradat
3774 AD) Design Workshops, London, ENGLAND
DES/A) Philip Sharland
3775 AD) Dialogue/Communications, 276 St. James St., Montreal, Que. H2Y 1N3 CANADA
3776 AD) Dimplex Ltd., Southampton, ENGLAND
DES/A) Graham Rhooda
3777 AD) Delta Hydraulic Power Ltd., 8223 Davies Rd., Edmonton, Alta. T6E 4N1 CANADA
3778 AD) Dingles of Plymouth Co., Ltd., Plymouth, ENGLAND
DES/A) Kennith Hollick
3779 AD) Damas & Smith Ltd., Calgary, Edmonton, Winnipeg, Toronto, London, Ottawa, CANADA
C) Urban Development Programs
3780 AD) Dansilar, Milano, ITALY
DES/A) Hanns Lohrer
3781 AD) DAQ Electronics, Inc., 43 Commerce St., Springfield, NJ 07081 USA
3782 AD) Direct Marketing International (World Headquarters) Olive at Twelfth St., Los Angeles, CA, USA
3783 AD) Damson Oil Corporation, New York, NY, USA
The Intermar Organization
DES/A) Flavian Cresci
3784 AD) Datum Inc., 1363 State College Blvd., Anaheim, CA 92806 USA

D-21

3785
3786
3787
3788
3789
3790
3791
3792
3793
3794
3795
3796
3797
3798

Dodge
Dodge Trucks

DRI-PRINT FOILS INC.

DGS

DAVIDSON SAIL

3785 AD) Dodge, Truck Division
3786 AD) McDonald Products Corp., USA
       SM) Duk-it, TM
3787 AD) Design Garamond
       C)   Industrial design
       DES/A) Jacques Garamond
3788 AD) Peter Doehler, Munchen,
            WEST GERMANY
       C)   Marketing Consultants
       DES/A) Phan Phu Oanh
3789 AD) The Platt Brothers & Co.,
            Waterbury, CT, USA
3790 AD) Des Plaines National Bank, Des
            Plaines, IL, USA
       ST) Al Burlini & Tom Morris, Inc.
3791 AD) Del Amo Marine, Los Angeles, CA,
            USA
       ST) The Company
3792 AD) Digi Data Corp., 8580 Dorsey Run Rd.,
            Jessup, MD, USA
3793 AD) Diano Corp., Optical Systems Div.,
            P.O. Box 346, 75 Forbes Blvd.,
            Mansfield, MD, USA
3794 AD) Dumaurier, USA
       C)   Tobacco
3795 AD) Decorators' Mart (Canada) Inc.,
            Montreal, Que., CANADA
3796 AD) Dri-Print Foils Inc., USA
3797 AD) DGS Group, Secretarial & Clerical Div.
            Toronto, Ont., CANADA
       C)   Office Staff Placement Service
3798 AD) Davidson Sail, Toronto, Ont.,
            CANADA
       C)   Sailboat Builder

D-22

3799

3800

3801

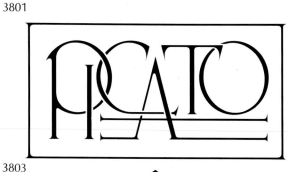

Designer Artist Profile / Michael Doret
Graphic Designer
106 Lexington Avenue,
New York, NY 10016 USA
(Ref: World of Logotypes File No. 114)

Michael Doret is from New York City and attended The Cooper Union For The Advancement Of Science And Art. After graduation in 1967 he held a series of short term staff positions as designer and art director for various companies, while pursuing his passion for lettering related graphics in free-lance projects. By 1972 he had built up enough of a client following to open his own studio. He has been working for himself ever since.

Some of his clients have been; N.W. Ayer Inc., Clinton E. Frank, Inc., Wells, Rich & Greene, Inc., Lee King & Partners, Inc., The Singer Co., Atlantic Records, Columbia Records, Esquire Magazine, National Lampoon, The New York Times Magazine, Time Inc., Viva Magazine, West Magazine and Random House.

Michael has exhibited in both Graphis and Communications Art Annuals, The Art Directors Club of Los Angeles and the Type Directors Club shows, the Creativity Shows, '73 through '77, and in the American Institute of Graphic Arts Shows-Communications Graphics, Mental Picture, Cover Show and Learning Materials.

3802

3803

3804

3805

3806

3799 AD) National Lampoon's "RADIO HOUR"
     DIR) Mike Salisbury
3800 AD) Barry Smith
     C) Illustrator
3801 AD) Picato
     C) Line of women's clothing
     DIR) Tom Hecht
3802 AD) Lee King & Partners Inc.
     DIR) Frank Biancalana
3803 AD) Michael Doret Logo for the designer artist
3804 AD) Starz
     C) Rock and Roll Group
     DIR) Dennis Woloch
3805 AD) Zardoz
     C) Feature Film
     DIR) Murray Smith
3806 AD) Auto Eroticism
     C) Feature article in West Magazine
     DIR) Mike Salisbury

Legend

AD) Advertiser/Client
DIR) Art Director
DES/A) Designer, Artist
ST) Studio, Agency
C) Category
SM) Symbol
TM) Trademark

3807 AD) Espoir
3808 AD) Eurosllo, S.L., Avenida, Portugal 8; Valencia 9, SPAIN
3809 AD) Edward Earl Associates
     C) Corporate Recruiters
        1455 Peel St., Montreal, Que., CANADA
3810 AD) Electronic Laboratories, Inc., 3726 Dacoma St., Houston, TX 77018 USA
3811 AD) Etc Graphics, 1682A Victoria Park, Scarborough, Ont. M1R 1P7 CANADA
3812 AD) Etobicoke Board of Education, Etobicoke Civil Centre, Etobicoke, Ont. M9C 2B3 CANADA
3813 AD) Equal Opportunities, 2 Bloor St. W., Suite 501, Toronto, Ont. M4W 3E2 CANADA
3814 AD) Encyclopedia Fotos e Fotos, SPAIN
     C) Cultural Magazine
     DES/A) Pinto Ziraldo
3815 AD) Emhart Manufacturing, USA
     DES/A) Lester Beall
3816 AD) Elkay Manufacturing Co., 2700 S. 17th Ave., Broadview, IL 60155 USA
3817 AD) Electronic Memories, 1621 Chadron Ave., Hawthorne, CA 90250 USA
        A division of Electronic Memories of Magnetics Corporation.
3818 AD) Dearborn Chemical Division, Chemed Cororation, Lake Zurich, IL 60047 USA
     SM) Ecomation TM
3819 AD) Mico Y Estelles, S.A.
        C/dels Traginers, 7, Poligono Industrial Vara de Cuart, Valencia-14, SPAIN

E-12

3820

3821

3822

3823

3824

3825

3826

3827

3828

3829

3830

3831

EDSON

emulsion
stripping

EXHIBIT
DESIGNERS &
PRODUCERS
ASSOCIATION

3820   AD)   Edmonton Public Schools,
              Edmonton, Alta., CANADA
3821   AD)   Edson / Marr's Marine Ltd., 1470
              Willson Place, Winnipeg, Man.
              R3T 3N9   CANADA
3822   AD)   Eliograf artigrafiche, s.r.l., Roma,
              ITALY
       DES/A)   Sergio Salaroli
3823   AD)   Etinor As, Blommenholm, NORWAY
       DES/A)   Ove Engström
3824   AD)   Estexa S.A., Buenos Aires,
              ARGENTINA
       DES/A)   Carlos Alberto Méndez Mosquera
3825   AD)   Elektroimpex, Sofia, BULGARIA
       DES/A)   Stephan Kantscheff
3826   AD)   Eaton's Business Centre,
              Eaton's Department Stores, CANADA
3827   AD)   Electronic Associates, Inc., West Long
              Branch, NJ   07764   USA
3828   AD)   Electronic Associates of Canada Ltd.,
              4401 Steeles Avenue, W., Downsview,
              Ont. M3N 2S4 CANADA
3829   AD)   Emulsion Stripping (TM), 1133 Leslie
              St., Don Mills, Ont., CANADA
3830   SM)   Eye and Ear Hospital of Pittsburgh,
              USA
       DES/A)   Dennis Ichiyama
3831   AD)   Exhibit Designers & Producers Associ-
              ation, 521 Fifth Ave., New York, NY
              USA
       C)   Public Relations Committee for EDPA
              Association.

E-13

3832

3833

3834

3835

3836

3837

3838

3839

3840

3841

3842

3843

3844

3845

3846

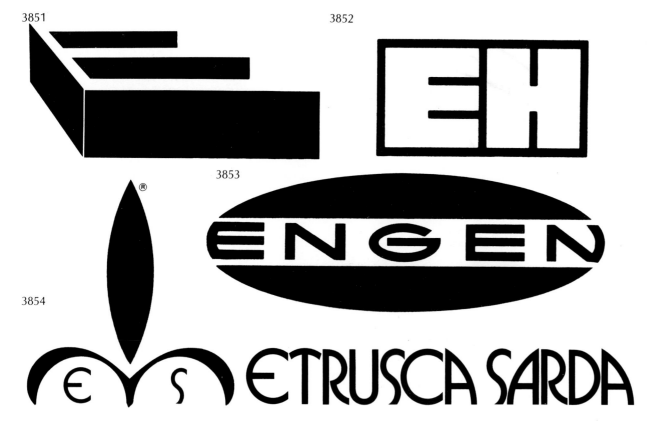

3847

EBONY
PLASTIQUES INDUSTRIELS LTÉE/INDUSTRIAL PLASTICS LTD.

3848

EMERY

3849

Elliott

3850

ENGEL

3851

3852

EH

3853

ENGEN

3854

ETRUSCA SARDA

3847 AD) Ebony Plastiques Industriels Ltée/
Industrial Plastics Ltd., 1487 Begin St.,
St. Laurent, Que. H4R 1V8   CANADA
3848 AD) Emery Industries Ltd., 365 Evans
Ave., Toronto, Ont. M8Z 1K2
CANADA
C) Chemicals Group
3849 AD) Elliot Machine Tool Group, 476 Evans
Ave., Toronto, Ont.   M8W 2T9
CANADA
3850 AD) Ludwig Engel Canada Ltd., 50 Crimea
St., Guelph, Ont.   N1H 2Y6
CANADA
3851 AD) Elementos Decoratiuos S.A.
Barcelona, SPAIN
DES/A)   José Pla Narbona
3852 AD) Empire Hotel, Rio De Janeiro,
BRAZIL
DES/A)   Aloisio Magalhães
3853 AD) AB Engens Fabriker,
28601 Örkelljunga Sverige
3854 AD) Etrusca Sarda, Industria Mobili
56010 Lugnano, Pisa, ITALY

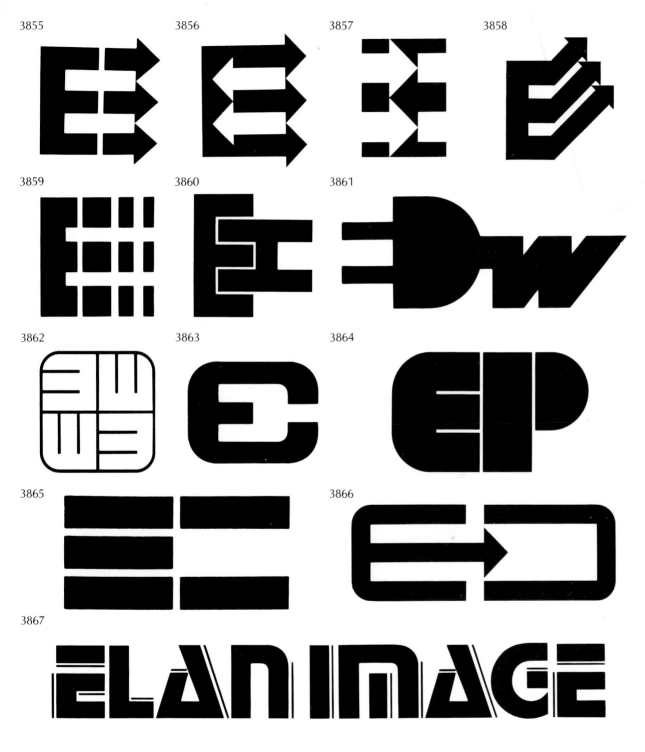

3855

3856

3857

3858

3859

3860

3861

3862

3863

3864

3865

3866

3867

3855 AD) Emhart Manufacturing Co., USA
  DES/A) Lester Beall (Also see #3815)
3856 AD) Euromar, Milano, ITALY
  DES/A) Armado Milani
3857 AD) E. Evensen, Elverum, NORWAY
  DES/A) Per Einar Eggen
3858 AD) Educating Systems Inc.,
  ST) Peterson & Blyth Associates Inc.
3859 AD) Elektronika, Sofia, BULGARIA
  DES/A) Stephan Kantscheff
3860 AD) Electric Harvest Stores, NJ, USA
  DES/A) Félix Beltrán
3861 AD) Electro-Walser, Basel,
  SWITZERLAND
  DES/A) Ulrich Schenker
3862 AD) Emme Edizioni, Milano, ITALY
  DES/A) Salvadore Gregorietti
3863 AD) Electrical Contractor Magazine
  National Electrical Contractors Assoc.,
  Inc., 7315 Wisconsin Ave.,
  Washington, D.C. 20014 USA
  C) Publisher
3864 AD) Engineering Products of Canada Ltd.,
  Boucherville, Que., CANADA
  C) Heating appliance Manufacturers
  DES/A) Jacques Roy
  ST) Jacques Guillon Designers Inc.
3865 AD) Cuban Exhibition Dept., CUBA
  DES/A) Félix Beltrán
3866 AD) East Dayton Tool & Die Co., Dayton,
  OH, USA
  DES/A) J. Budd Steinhilber
3867 AD) Elan Image / Introcol Publishing Co.
  Ltd., 23 McNider, Outremont, Que.
  H2V 3X4 CANADA

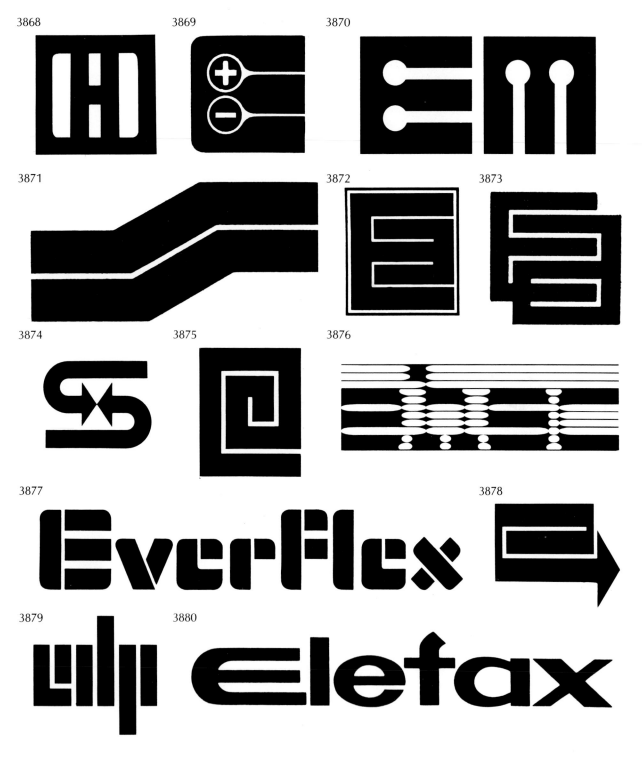

3868 AD) Energy Industries Ltd., 4303 11th St.,
N.E., Calgary, Alta., CANADA

3869 AD) Division of Eldon Industries of Canada
Inc., 50 Prince Andrew Pl., Don Mills,
Ont., M3C 2Y7 CANADA
SM) Elpower Batteries

3870 AD) Electronic Memories Inc., Hawthorne,
CA, USA
C) Computers and Memory Systems
DES/A) Ken Parkhurst

3871 AD) Les Entreprises Transport Provincial
Ltd., Montreal, Que., CANADA
C) Bus Services
DES/A) Jean Morin & Tony Hobbs
ST) Girard, Bkruce et Associés, Ltée.

3872 AD) Eldon Industries of Canada Inc., 50
Prince Andrew Pl., Don Mills, Ont.,
M3C 2Y7 CANADA

3873 AD) Editorial Arte S.A., Caracas,
VENEZUELA
DES/A) John Lange

3874 AD) State Testing Laboratories,
So. Norwalk, CT, USA
DES/A) Ted Trinkaus

3875 AD) Euronolte

3876 AD) European Home Study Council,
Haslum, SWEDEN
DES/A) Carl Steinherr

3877 AD) EverFlex, USA
DES/A) Stan Brod

3878 AD) Executronics Ltd., Toronto, Ont.,
CANADA
C) Management Consultants
ST) J. & A. Breukelman Design Associates

3879 AD) EDP Technology Inc., WA, USA
C) Computer Software & Programming
DES/A) Arnold Saks Inc.

3880 AD) Elefax, 500 King Street West,
Toronto, Ont., CANADA

E-17

3881   AD)   Elma Louise Johnston, P.O. Box 3395, Station B., Saint John West, N.B. CANADA

3882   AD)   Electrozad Supply Co. Ltd., 314 Giles Boulevard E., Windsor, Ont., CANADA
        C)   Wholesale electrical supply business

3883   AD)   Eurographic Limited, Hull, ENGLAND
        C)   Graphic Designers & Consultants
     DES/A)   Eurographic Limited

3884   AD)   Edger Limited, 2363, 43ième Ave., Lachine, Que., CANADA

3885   AD)   E. Tal & Associates Ltd., 30 Levontin, Tel Aviv, ISRAEL
        C)   Advertising, Public Relations, Sales Promotions

3886   AD)   Evans Gallery, 122 Scollard St., Toronto, Ont., CANADA

3887   AD)   Eval, Via Fiorentina/50052 Certaldo Firenze, ITALY

3888   AD)   Wm. Ewart & Son Ltd., Belfast, IRELAND
        C)   Irish linen manufacturers
     DES/A)   Silvia Sewell
       ST)   Allied International Designers Ltd.

3889   AD)   The Electricity Council, London, ENGLAND
     DES/A)   Nicholas Jenkins

3890   AD)   Erwin Communications, 3308 S. Manor Dr., Lansing, IL 60408 USA
     DES/A)   Dale DeYoung
       ST)   Erwin Communications

3891   AD)   The Electric Chain Company of Canada Ltd., 86 Bathurst St., Toronto, Ont., CANADA
        C)   Jewelry

3892   AD)   Elmhurst Cream & Milk Co., Elmhurst, IL, USA
        C)   Dairy Products Distributors
     DES/A)   Bill Wayman

3893   AD)   E + P Gruppe Michel, Rechbergweg 57, 7900 Ulm (Donau) GERMANY

3894   AD)   Erlau AG
           Prospekte und Angebote von Erlau AG, 7505 Ettlingen, Postfach 1204, GERMANY

3895

3896

3897

3898

3899

EMI

3901

3900

3902

3895   AD)   Cominco Ltd., 200 Granville Square,
                 Vancouver, B.C.
                 V6C 2R2   CANADA
       SM)   Elephant Brand
3896   AD)   Emco Wheaton U.K. Ltd.
                 Westwood, Margate, Kent
                 CT9 4JR   ENGLAND
3897   AD)   Eidopor Inc., USA
       ST)   Chermayeff & Geismar Assoc.
3898   AD)   EB Electronics, 49-53 Pancras Rd.,
                 London NW1 2QB   ENGLAND
3899   AD)   EMI (North America) Inc.,
                 100 Research Dr., Glenbrook,
                 CT   06906   USA
3900   AD)   Electric-Aire Corp., 16941 State
                 St., South Holland, IL, USA
       C)   Dryers Manufacturers
3901   AD)   Energine, USA
       ST)   Norma Updyke/Jack O'Rourke
                 River Glen, Studio 26
3902   AD)   Toledo Edison, Edison Plaza,
                 Toledo, OH   43652   USA

E-19

3903 AD) Electro Tec Corporation
             1600 N. Main, Blacksburg,
             VA 24060 USA
3904 AD) Electrical Contractors Association,
             USA
      ST) Donald Mclean, George N. Sepetys &
             Assoc.
3905 AD) Erawan Garden Hotel, Indian Wells,
             CA, USA
3906 AD) Electrical Contractors Association of
             Northern California, San Francisco,
             CA, USA
      C)   Electrical Construction Work
     DES/A) Robert Pease
3907 AD) Energy Systems, American Gas
             Association, 1515 Wilson Blvd.,
             Arlington, VA 22209 USA
3908 AD) John Edginton Exhibitions Ltd.,
             London, ENGLAND
     DES/A) Kenneth Hollick
3909 AD) Edward J. Smith Assoc.
      C)   Advertising, USA
     DES/A) Anita Soos
3910 AD) Cape Eleuthera, 7880 Biscayne Blvd.,
             Miami, FL 33138 USA
3911 AD) Electrochimie Ugine, Levallois,
             FRANCE
      C)   Chemical Products
     DES/A) Philippe Gentil
3912 AD) Eurostile, Via della Spiga, 48, Milano,
             ITALY
3913 AD) Elections Canada, CANADA
3914 AD) Euro Survey, Paris, FRANCE
      C)   Advice on organization
     DES/A) Philippe Gentil

E-20

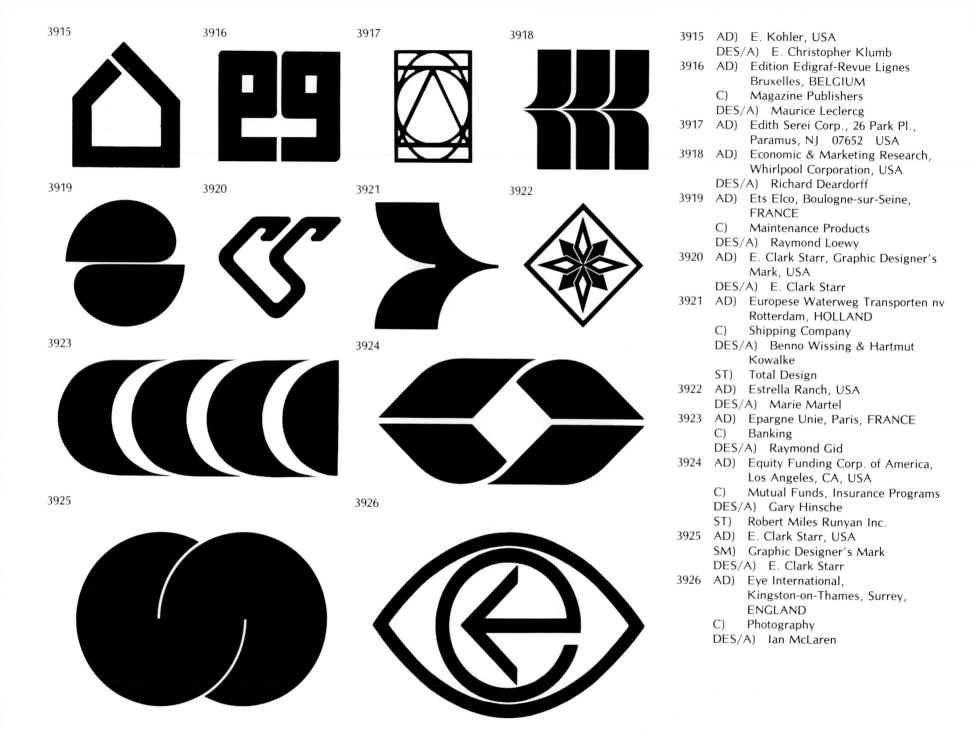

3915 AD) E. Kohler, USA
      DES/A) E. Christopher Klumb
3916 AD) Edition Edigraf-Revue Lignes
           Bruxelles, BELGIUM
      C) Magazine Publishers
      DES/A) Maurice Leclercg
3917 AD) Edith Serei Corp., 26 Park Pl.,
           Paramus, NJ 07652 USA
3918 AD) Economic & Marketing Research,
           Whirlpool Corporation, USA
      DES/A) Richard Deardorff
3919 AD) Ets Elco, Boulogne-sur-Seine,
           FRANCE
      C) Maintenance Products
      DES/A) Raymond Loewy
3920 AD) E. Clark Starr, Graphic Designer's
           Mark, USA
      DES/A) E. Clark Starr
3921 AD) Europese Waterweg Transporten nv
           Rotterdam, HOLLAND
      C) Shipping Company
      DES/A) Benno Wissing & Hartmut
           Kowalke
      ST) Total Design
3922 AD) Estrella Ranch, USA
      DES/A) Marie Martel
3923 AD) Epargne Unie, Paris, FRANCE
      C) Banking
      DES/A) Raymond Gid
3924 AD) Equity Funding Corp. of America,
           Los Angeles, CA, USA
      C) Mutual Funds, Insurance Programs
      DES/A) Gary Hinsche
      ST) Robert Miles Runyan Inc.
3925 AD) E. Clark Starr, USA
      SM) Graphic Designer's Mark
      DES/A) E. Clark Starr
3926 AD) Eye International,
           Kingston-on-Thames, Surrey,
           ENGLAND
      C) Photography
      DES/A) Ian McLaren

3927

3928

3929

3930

3931

3932

3933

3934

3935

3936

3937

3938

3939

3940

3927 AD) Envirotech Corp., Menlo Park, CA, USA
3928 AD) Enviromental Measurements Inc., San Francisco, CA, USA
3929 AD) Euromercato
       ST) Landor Associates
3930 AD) Educational Systems, Inc.
       DES/A) David Leigh
3931 AD) Empire Cybernetics Inc.
       ST) Jack Schecterson Associates
3932 AD) Printing Company, GERMANY
       DES/A) Anton Stankowsky
3933 C)   Advertising
       ST) Easons Advertising Service
3934 AD) The Exdon Co., Tonawanda, NY, USA
       ST) Selame Design
3935 AD) Elastikana, POLAND
       DES/A) Andrzej Bertrandt
3936 AD) Equitable Life Insurance Co. of Iowa, USA
       DES/A) Des Moines
3937 AD) Eden Isles, USA
       DES/A) Joe Schulte, Charles Dolce
3938 AD) Eastern Business Systems
       DES/A) James N. Maccaroni
3939 AD) Englewood (Symbol of City) USA
       DES/A) Kay Ritta
3940 AD) A.T. Euster Furniture Co., Miami, FL, USA

E-22

Legend AD) Advertiser/Client
DIR) Art Director
DES/A) Designer, Artist
ST) Studio, Agency
C) Category
SM) Symbol
TM) Trademark

3941 AD) Friedberg & Co. Ltd., 347 Bay St.,
Toronto, Ont. M5H 2R7 CANADA
3942 AD) Film Fonts, Los Angeles, CA, USA
Facsimile fonts & fototype
3943 AD) Flammersheim & Steinmann
5000 Köln 51 - Höninger Weg 106,
GERMANY
3944 AD) Factory Mutual Systems
3945 AD) Circle F Industries, Box 591,
Trenton, NJ 08604 USA
C) Manufacturers of Wiring Devices
Engineered for Safety
3946 AD) Furness Withy & Co. Ltd., 1 Yonge
St., Toronto, Ont., CANADA
3947 AD) Furniture Components, Inc., 248 Pine
St., P.O. Box 560, Pawtucket,
RI 02862 USA
3948 AD) Foreign Tours, Inc.
3949 AD) FF Gate Valves & Swing Check Valves
3950 AD) Fluid Metering, Inc., 48 Summit St.,
Oyster Bay, NY 11771 USA
3951 AD) Floating Point Systems, 3160 S.W.
87th Ave., Portland, OR 97225 USA
3952 AD) Famur, Katowice, POLAND
DES/A) Tadeusz Grabowski
3953 AD) Fanini Fain S.p.A., Ascoli Piceno,
ITALY
DES/A) Ennio Lucini
3954 AD) Fultron Plastics Inc., 7 Eleventh St.
N.W., Hickory, NC 28601 USA

3955

3956

3957

3958

3959

3960

FOGH

3961

3962

3963

3964

3965

3966

FMC

3967

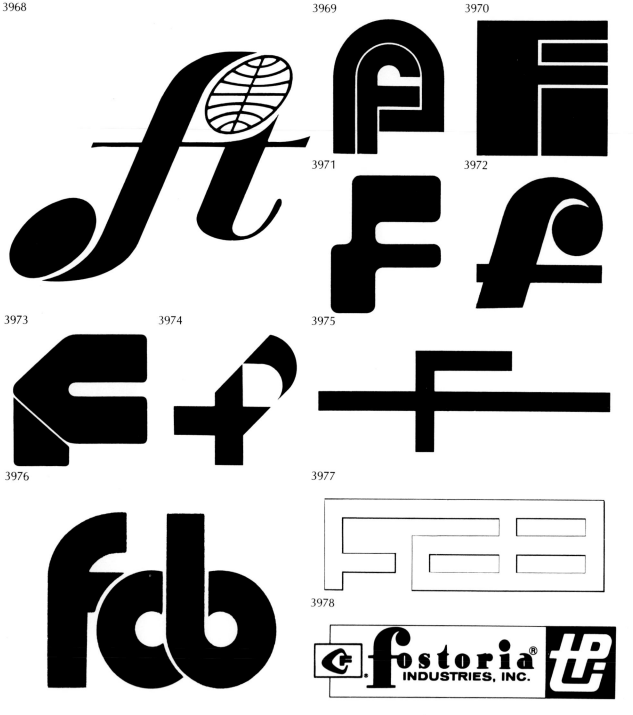

3968

3969

3970

3971

3972

3973

3974

3975

3976

3977

3978

3968 AD) Finlay Travel Ltd., Suite 4203,
Toronto-Dominion Centre,
Toronto, Ont., CANADA
C) Travel Agency

3969 AD) Fotofonts, Inc., Hollywood, CA, USA
C) Photo-type composition
DES/A) Michel Duttel

3970 AD) Fiação Indiana S.A., BRAZIL
DES/A) Alexandre Wolluer

3971 AD) Funkito, Helsinki, FINLAND
DES/A) Eero Syvanoja

3972 AD) Finlandia Travel Agency Ltd., London,
ENGLAND
DES/A) Stan Krol
C) Travel Agency

3973 AD) C. Fulla, Barcelona, SPAIN
DES/A) Tomás Vellvé

3974 AD) Fairchild Publishing Inc., New York,
NY, USA
DES/A) Phillip Franznick
C) Publisher

3975 AD) Finaldi Vigevand, Pavia, ITALY
DES/A) AG Fronzoni

3976 AD) Fives-Cail Babcock, 7 Rue Montalivet,
Paris, Seine, FRANCE

3977 AD) Figli di Angelo, Bonacina Meda,
Milano, ITALY
DES/A) Ilio Negri

3978 AD) Fostoria Industries Inc., 1500 N. Main
St., Fostoria, OH 44830 USA

3979

3980

3981

3982

3983

Freed's

3984

FLEXFORM

3985

FELDMAN

3979 AD) Fulmer & Company, USA
      DES/A) Anita Soos
3980 AD) Fisher & Spellman Architects, USA
      DES/A) Crawford Dunn
      ST) RYA Graphics Inc., Two Lemmon Park
            E., 3619 Howell St., Dallas,
            TX 75204 USA
3981 AD) Fine Fare Limited, ENGLAND
      ST) John Harris Design Assocs., Ltd.
3982 AD) Fort Worth Chamber of Commerce
            Fort Worth, TX, USA
      DES/A) Crawford Dunn
3983 AD) Freed's Stores, USA
      DES/A) L.S. Krispinsky
      C) Retail Clothing
      ST) Second Dimension Studio
3984 AD) Flexform, USA
      C) Furniture Manufacturers
      DES/A) Pino Tovaglia
3985 AD) The Feldman Co., St. Louis, MO, USA
      C) Lighting, Residential & Commercial

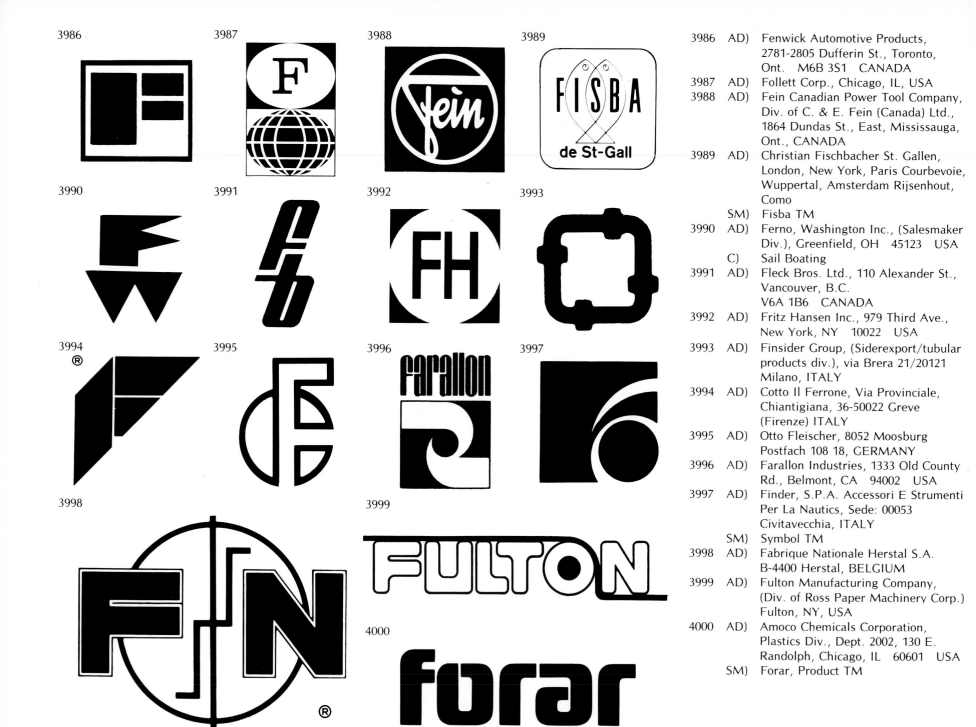

3986

3987

3988

3989

3990

3991

3992

3993

3994

3995

3996

3997

3998

3999

4000

3986 AD) Fenwick Automotive Products, 2781-2805 Dufferin St., Toronto, Ont.   M6B 3S1   CANADA

3987 AD) Follett Corp., Chicago, IL, USA

3988 AD) Fein Canadian Power Tool Company, Div. of C. & E. Fein (Canada) Ltd., 1864 Dundas St., East, Mississauga, Ont., CANADA

3989 AD) Christian Fischbacher St. Gallen, London, New York, Paris Courbevoie, Wuppertal, Amsterdam Rijsenhout, Como

SM) Fisba TM

3990 AD) Ferno, Washington Inc., (Salesmaker Div.), Greenfield, OH   45123   USA

C) Sail Boating

3991 AD) Fleck Bros. Ltd., 110 Alexander St., Vancouver, B.C. V6A 1B6   CANADA

3992 AD) Fritz Hansen Inc., 979 Third Ave., New York, NY   10022   USA

3993 AD) Finsider Group, (Siderexport/tubular products div.), via Brera 21/20121 Milano, ITALY

3994 AD) Cotto Il Ferrone, Via Provinciale, Chiantigiana, 36-50022 Greve (Firenze) ITALY

3995 AD) Otto Fleischer, 8052 Moosburg Postfach 108 18, GERMANY

3996 AD) Farallon Industries, 1333 Old County Rd., Belmont, CA   94002   USA

3997 AD) Finder, S.P.A. Accessori E Strumenti Per La Nautics, Sede: 00053 Civitavecchia, ITALY

SM) Symbol TM

3998 AD) Fabrique Nationale Herstal S.A. B-4400 Herstal, BELGIUM

3999 AD) Fulton Manufacturing Company, (Div. of Ross Paper Machinery Corp.) Fulton, NY, USA

4000 AD) Amoco Chemicals Corporation, Plastics Div., Dept. 2002, 130 E. Randolph, Chicago, IL   60601   USA

SM) Forar, Product TM

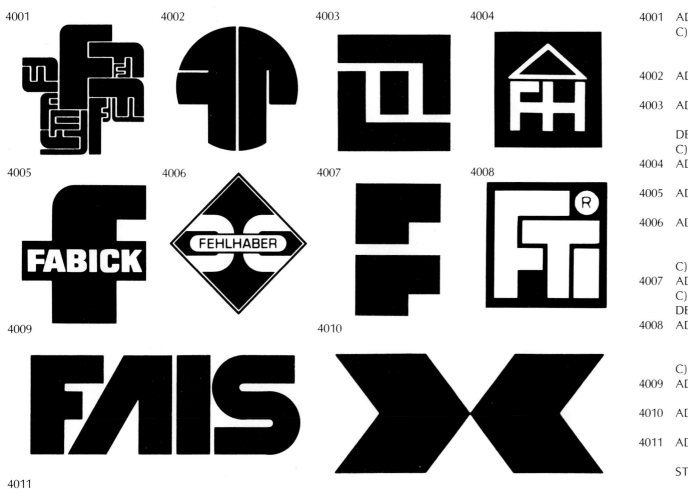

4001 AD) Fortress Inc., USA
C) Manufacturers of Furniture of the Highest Standard in Design and Execution.

4002 AD) Felice Rossi & C., 21011 Casorate S. ne (VA)

4003 AD) Franklin Interiors, Pittsburgh, PA, USA
DES/A) Philip Seefeld
C) Interior Decorator

4004 AD) The Form House, Inc., 5200 W. 26th St., Cicero, IL 60650 USA

4005 AD) John Fabick Tractor Co., 1 Fabik Dr., Fenton/St. Louis, MO 63026 USA

4006 AD) Fehlhaber Associates, Inc., 3201 S.W. State Rd. 84Y, Ft. Lauderdale, FL 33312 USA
C) Yacht Brokers

4007 AD) Donald Forrest
C) Chartered Architect
DES/A) David J. Plumb

4008 AD) Fabri-tek Inc., 5901 South Country Rd. 18, Minneapolis, MN 55436 USA
C) Computer Systems

4009 AD) Fais, Esposizione: Via Folla di Sotto 8, Uffici: Via Bernardo da Pavia 11

4010 AD) First Exchange National Bank of Virginia, USA

4011 AD) Flagship Banks Inc., 111 Lincoln Rd. Mall, Miami Beach, FL, USA
ST) Walter Landor Assoc.

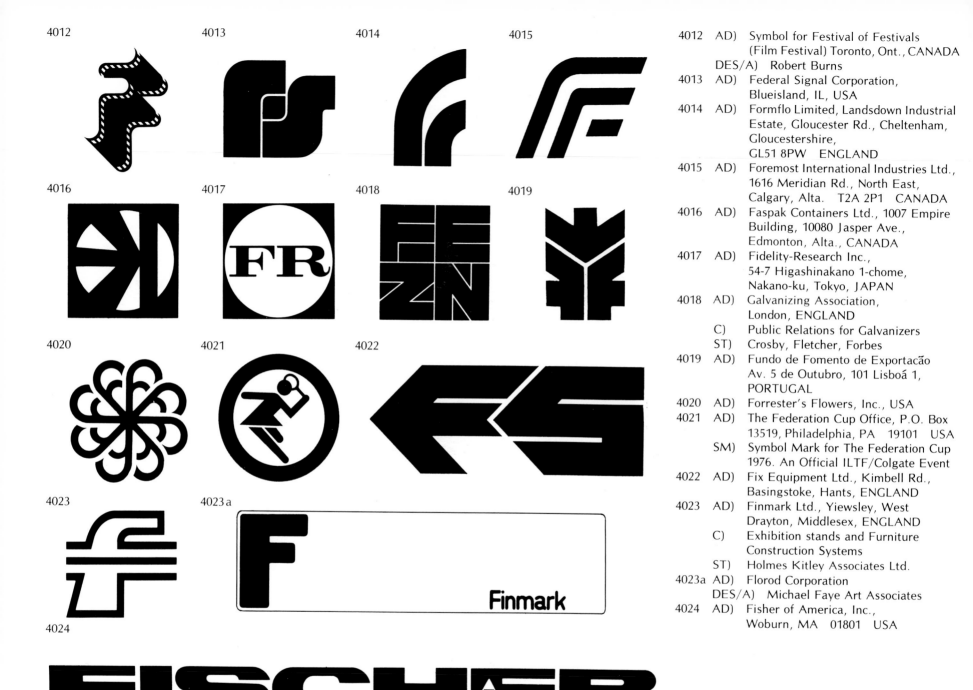

4012

4013

4014

4015

4016

4017

4018

4019

4020

4021

4022

4023

4023a

Finmark

4024

FISCHER
Made in Austria

4012 AD) Symbol for Festival of Festivals
(Film Festival) Toronto, Ont., CANADA
DES/A) Robert Burns
4013 AD) Federal Signal Corporation,
Blueisland, IL, USA
4014 AD) Formflo Limited, Landsdown Industrial
Estate, Gloucester Rd., Cheltenham,
Gloucestershire,
GL51 8PW ENGLAND
4015 AD) Foremost International Industries Ltd.,
1616 Meridian Rd., North East,
Calgary, Alta. T2A 2P1 CANADA
4016 AD) Faspak Containers Ltd., 1007 Empire
Building, 10080 Jasper Ave.,
Edmonton, Alta., CANADA
4017 AD) Fidelity-Research Inc.,
54-7 Higashinakano 1-chome,
Nakano-ku, Tokyo, JAPAN
4018 AD) Galvanizing Association,
London, ENGLAND
C) Public Relations for Galvanizers
ST) Crosby, Fletcher, Forbes
4019 AD) Fundo de Fomento de Exportacão
Av. 5 de Outubro, 101 Lisboá 1,
PORTUGAL
4020 AD) Forrester's Flowers, Inc., USA
4021 AD) The Federation Cup Office, P.O. Box
13519, Philadelphia, PA 19101 USA
SM) Symbol Mark for The Federation Cup
1976. An Official ILTF/Colgate Event
4022 AD) Fix Equipment Ltd., Kimbell Rd.,
Basingstoke, Hants, ENGLAND
4023 AD) Finmark Ltd., Yiewsley, West
Drayton, Middlesex, ENGLAND
C) Exhibition stands and Furniture
Construction Systems
ST) Holmes Kitley Associates Ltd.
4023a AD) Florod Corporation
DES/A) Michael Faye Art Associates
4024 AD) Fisher of America, Inc.,
Woburn, MA 01801 USA

4025

4026

4027

4028

4029

4030

4031

4032

4033

4034

4035

4025 AD) Flachglas AG. Delog-Detag, D-8510 Furth/Bayern, Otto Seeling Promenade 2, Bundersrepubilk, DEUTSCHLAND

4026 AD) Foseco-Minsep Ltd., 36 Queen Anne's Gate, London SW1H 9AR ENGLAND

4027 AD) Foudoulaki Jewellers S.A., 106 Sygrou, Athens 404, GREECE

4028 AD) First Boston, Boston, MA, USA
C) Investment Bankers

4020 AD) Fernandec & Rubin, USA
DES/A) Eric Madsen
ST) Thumbnails Inc.

4030 AD) Futura Möbler AB, Box 66, 543 01 Tibro 1
C) Furniture

4031 AD) Fideg Elletronica, Bari, ITALY
C) Electronics
ST) Fronzoni

4032 AD) Field Work s.r.l., Milano, ITALY
C) Marketing Consultants
DES/A) Piero Borca

4033 SM) Symbol for Furniture Manufacturing Control in Norway

4034 AD) Llewellyn Roberts, 445-1900 Richmond Ave., Victoria, B.C., CANADA

4035 AD) Feingolds Mens Wear, USA
DES/A) Doug Powell
ST) Image Group

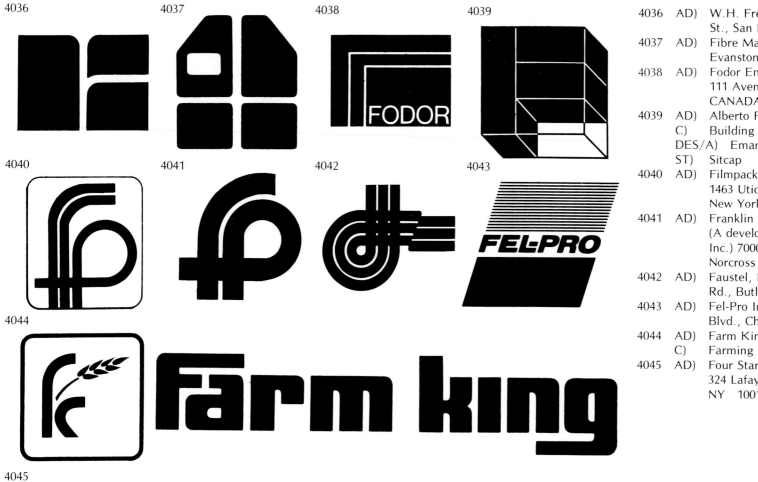

4036

4037

4038

FODOR

4039

4040

4041

4042

4043

FEL·PRO

4044

Farm king

4045

four star typographers inc.

4036　AD)　W.H. Freeman and Co., 660 Market St., San Francisco, CA, USA

4037　AD)　Fibre Mats Envain Corporation, 2205 Evanston, IL, USA

4038　AD)　Fodor Engineering Ltd., 111 Avenue Rd., Toronto, Ont., CANADA

4039　AD)　Alberto Ferrari, ITALY
　　　C)　Building Firm
　　　DES/A)　Emanuele Centazzo
　　　ST)　Sitcap

4040　AD)　Filmpack Plastic Corporation, 1463 Utica Ave., Brooklyn, New York 11234 USA

4041　AD)　Franklin Park Office Community, (A development of Lee Investments Inc.) 7000 Peachtree Industrial Blvd., Norcross Atlanta, GA 30071 USA

4042　AD)　Faustel, Inc., 12801 W. Silver Spring Rd., Butler, WI 53007 USA

4043　AD)　Fel-Pro Inc., 7450 North McCormick Blvd., Chicago, IL, USA

4044　AD)　Farm King, USA
　　　C)　Farming Equipment

4045　AD)　Four Star Typographers Inc., 324 Lafayette St., New York, NY 10012 USA

4046 AD)   Four Seasons Racquet Club,
      DES/A) Wyatt L. Phillips
4047 AD)   Fisher Scientific Co., Ltd., 184 Railside
             Rd., Don Mills, Ont.   M3A 1A9
             CANADA
4048 AD)   Freewheel
      DES/A) Fred Colcer
4049 AD)   Friedrich Grohe Armaturenfabrik
             137, Hauptstrasse, Hemer,
             Westphalia, GERMANY
      C)   Fittings for water supply installations
4050 AD)   Federal Industrial Development
             Authority, Wisma Damansara,
             P.O. Box 618, Kuala Lumpur,
             MALAYSIA
4051 AD)   Oy Finleuy Ab; Helsinki, FINLAND
      C)   Record Company
      DES/A) Jukka Pelinen
4052 AD)   Fujibank, Tokyo, JAPAN
4053 AD)   Finlayson Enterprises Ltd., Toronto,
             Ont., CANADA
      DES/A) Micky Edden
      ST)   Ken Borden Ltd.
4054 AD)   Fibre Glass-Evercoat Co., Inc., 6600
             Cornell Rd., Cincinnati, OH   45242
             USA
4055 AD)   Foremost
4056 AD)   Forbo Betriebs AG, Färbestrasse 6,
             Zurich, SWITZERLAND
      C)   Wallpaper Manufacturers
4057 AD)   Foamcoil Bedding Centres, Toronto,
             Ont., CANADA
      C)   Retail Stores, Bed Furnishings

F-22

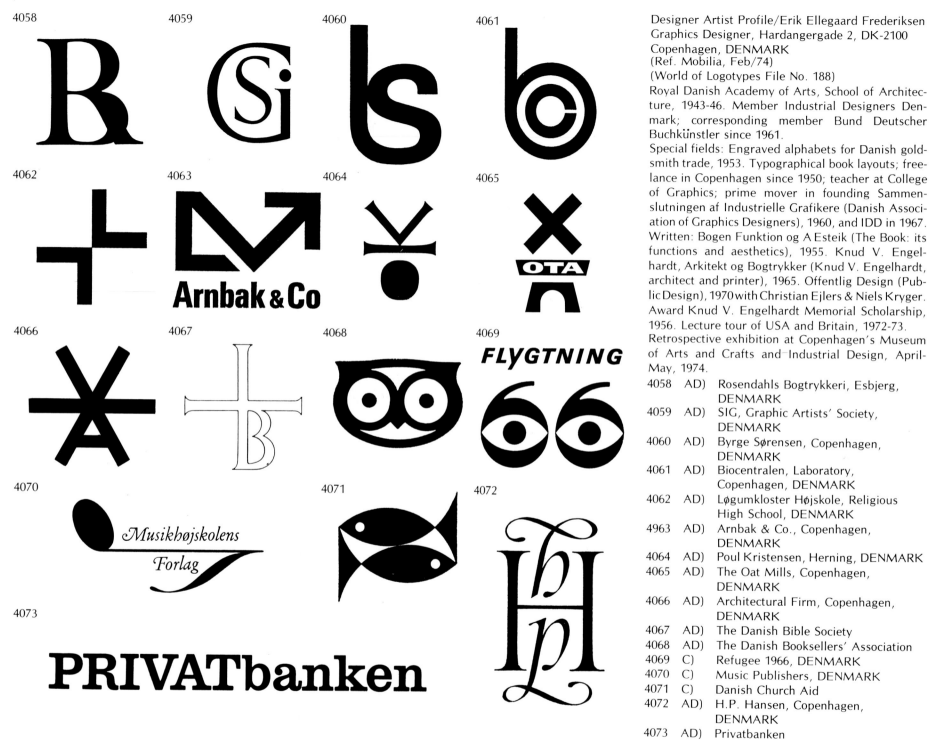

Designer Artist Profile/Erik Ellegaard Frederiksen
Graphics Designer, Hardangergade 2, DK-2100
Copenhagen, DENMARK
(Ref. Mobilia, Feb/74)
(World of Logotypes File No. 188)
Royal Danish Academy of Arts, School of Architecture, 1943-46. Member Industrial Designers Denmark; corresponding member Bund Deutscher Buchkünstler since 1961.
Special fields: Engraved alphabets for Danish goldsmith trade, 1953. Typographical book layouts; freelance in Copenhagen since 1950; teacher at College of Graphics; prime mover in founding Sammenslutningen af Industrielle Grafikere (Danish Association of Graphics Designers), 1960, and IDD in 1967. Written: Bogen Funktion og A Esteik (The Book: its functions and aesthetics), 1955. Knud V. Engelhardt, Arkitekt og Bogtrykker (Knud V. Engelhardt, architect and printer), 1965. Offentlig Design (Public Design), 1970 with Christian Ejlers & Niels Kryger. Award Knud V. Engelhardt Memorial Scholarship, 1956. Lecture tour of USA and Britain, 1972-73. Retrospective exhibition at Copenhagen's Museum of Arts and Crafts and Industrial Design, April-May, 1974.

4058 AD) Rosendahls Bogtrykkeri, Esbjerg, DENMARK
4059 AD) SIG, Graphic Artists' Society, DENMARK
4060 AD) Byrge Sørensen, Copenhagen, DENMARK
4061 AD) Biocentralen, Laboratory, Copenhagen, DENMARK
4062 AD) Løgumkloster Højskole, Religious High School, DENMARK
4963 AD) Arnbak & Co., Copenhagen, DENMARK
4064 AD) Poul Kristensen, Herning, DENMARK
4065 AD) The Oat Mills, Copenhagen, DENMARK
4066 AD) Architectural Firm, Copenhagen, DENMARK
4067 AD) The Danish Bible Society
4068 AD) The Danish Booksellers' Association
4069 C)   Refugee 1966, DENMARK
4070 C)   Music Publishers, DENMARK
4071 C)   Danish Church Aid
4072 AD) H.P. Hansen, Copenhagen, DENMARK
4073 AD) Privatbanken

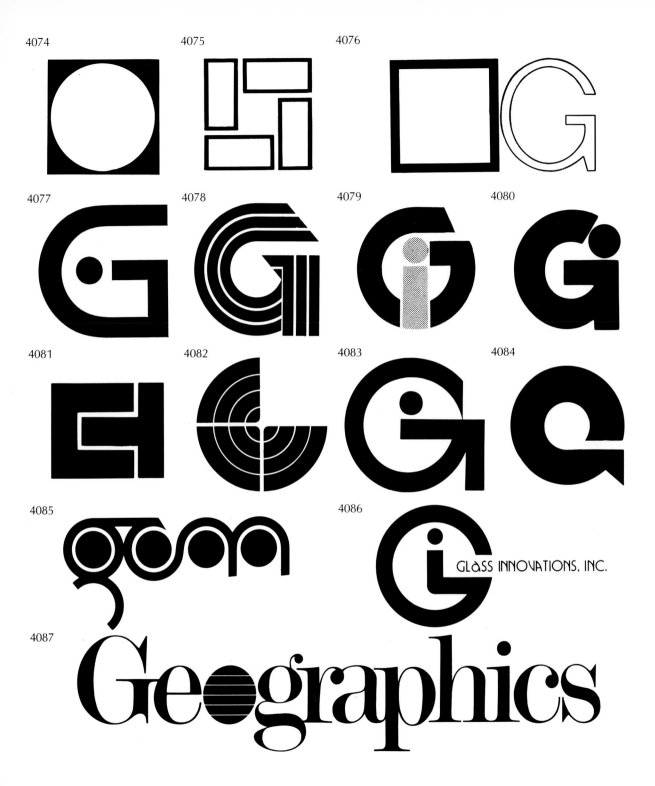

Legend

AD)	Advertiser/Client
DIR)	Art Director
DES/A)	Designer, Artist
ST)	Studio, Agency
C)	Category
SM)	Symbol
TM)	Trademark

4074   AD)   Greta, Via L. da Vinci, 36, 20090 Trezzano sui Naviglio, ITALY

4075   AD)   Gold Metal Folding Furniture Co., Dept. 300, 1704 Packard Ave., Racine, WI, USA
       SM)   Gold Metal
       C)   Folding Furniture Company

4076   AD)   Germa srl Industria Per L'Arredamento, 33050 Risano-Udine, ITALY

4077   AD)   Gilcodan, Copenhagen, DENMARK
       DES/A)   Adam Moltke

4078   AD)   The Getz Corp., San Francisco, CA, USA
       DES/A)   Nancy Kraft, Dave Alcorn, Primo Angeli
       ST)   Primo Angeli Graphics

4079   AD)   Gauges International, Inc., 1418 Roy St., Houston, TX 77007 USA

4080   AD)   Gidon Industries Inc., 22 Iron St., Rexdale, Ont., CANADA

4081   AD)   Gustin-Bacon Group (Div.), TM of Certain-teed Products Corp., Box 15079, Kansas City, KA 66110 USA
       C)   Mechanical Pipe Couplings

4082   AD)   Gazette Printing Co., Ltd., Montreal, Que., CANADA
       DES/A)   William J. Campbell

4083   AD)   Rex Granby Studios, Warrington, Lancashire, ENGLAND
       DES/A)   Anthony Douglas Forster

4084   AD)   Gore-Tex, W.L. Gore & Assoc., Inc., RFD #5, Box 513, Elkton, MD 21921 USA

4985   AD)   Graphic Communication Month
       DES/A)   Victor Di Cristo

4086   AD)   Glass Innovations, Inc.

4087   AD)   Geographics Inc., Cheyenne, WY, USA

G-12

4088

4089

4090

4091

4092

4093

4094

4095

4096

4097

4098

4099

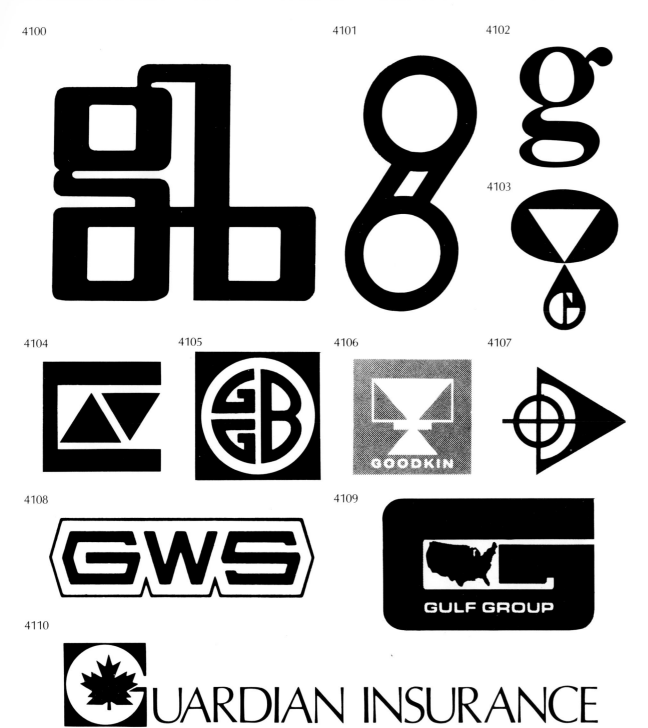

4100

4101

4102

4103

4104

4105

4106

4107

4108

4109

4110

GOODKIN

GWS

GULF GROUP

GUARDIAN INSURANCE

4100	AD)	Gejervall & Broo, Tibro
4101	AD)	G & B Automated Equipment Ltd., 580 Supertest Rd., Downsview, Ont. M3J 2M7 CANADA
4102	AD)	Gordon Securities Ltd., Suite 1960, Place du Canada, Montreal, Que., CANADA
4103	AD)	Gessner & Co., GmbH, D-8206 Bruckmühl, WEST GERMANY
4104	AD)	George Brown College of Applied Arts and Technology, Toronto, Ont., CANADA
	SM)	Technical School Symbol
4105	AD)	Gordon G. Brown & Co., Ltd., Vancouver, Toronto, Montreal, CANADA
4106	AD)	The M.P. Goodkin Co., 140-146 Coit St., Irvington, NJ 07111 USA
4107	AD)	Graphic Arts Industries Association, Canadian Graphic Arts Show, 481 University Ave., Toronto, Ont. M5W 1A7 CANADA
4108	AD)	GWS Ltd., 45 St. Clair Ave. W., Toronto, Ont., CANADA
4109	AD)	Gulf Insurance Group, Gulf Insurance Co., Atlantic Insurance Co., Select Insurance Co., Insurance Co. of The Pacific Coast, Executive Offices, P.O. Box 1711, Dallas, TX, USA
4110	AD)	Guardian Insurance Co. of Canada

4111 AD) Plum Creek Lumber Co., Columbia Falls, MT 59912 USA
SM) Glacier Edge, Product Line
C) Fine Printing Papers
4112 AD) Gulf Stream Yacht Brokers, Inc., 7800 Red Rd., South Miami, FL 33143 USA
4113 AD) Richard Gratopp, 42 Holmcrest Trail, West Hill, Ontario, M1C 1V5 CANADA
SM) Graphic Designer own identity mark
4114 AD) Golf Enterprises Limited
4115 AD) Getex Consult AG. Chur.
DES/A) Werner Hartz
4116 AD) Geodel Systems, 232 Guelph St., Georgetown, Ont., CANADA
4117 AD) Gomer & Anderson, SWEDEN
C) Estate Consultants
DES/A) Ove Engström
4118 AD) G & L Services, Inc., P.O. Box 767, Cambridge, OH 43725 USA
4119 AD) J. Geißler, 8 München 22, Maximilianstrasse 45, GERMANY
4120 AD) Gateco Products, 1711 Langley Ave., Irvine Industrial Complex, CA 92705 USA
4121 AD) G & H Industries, Chapel Rd., Smallfield, Horley, Surrey RH6 9NT ENGLAND
4122 AD) Gummed Papers of America, 1001 W. Van Buren St., Chicago, IL, USA
4123 AD) Gibbs Wire & Steel Co., Inc., Burlington, Ont., CANADA

G-15

4124 AD) Gozlan Brothers Ltd., 60 Apex Rd., Toronto, Ont. M6A 1A6 CANADA

4125 AD) The Gallery, Dept. 9042, Amsterdam, NY 12010 USA

4126 AD) General Atomic Co., P.O. Box 81608, San Diego, CA 92138 USA
A Gulf and Royal Dutch/Shell Co.

4127 AD) Gifford-Hill & Co., Inc., P.O. Box 47127, Dallas, TX 75247 USA

4128 AD) Selections AB Gösta Westerberg Pipersgatan 26, 112 28 Stockholm, SWEDEN

4129 AD) Gratton Productions, 1440 St. Catherine St. West, Suite 407, Montreal, Que., CANADA

4130 AD) Glaverbel Société Anonyme, Chausée de La Hulpe 166, B-1170 Bruxelles, BELGIUM

4131 AD) Geolograph Service Ltd., 5730-103 A St., Edmonton, Alta., CANADA

4132 AD) Go Magazine, USA

4133 AD) Granada T.V. Rentals, Toronto, Ont., CANADA

4134 AD) Goodwill/Vézina French Services Ltd., Suite 402, 696 Yonge St., Toronto, Ont. M4Y 2A7 CANADA
C) French Translators

4135 AD) Greer Olaer Products, 5930 W. Jefferson Blvd., Los Angeles, CA 90016 USA
Div. of Greer Hydraulics, Inc.

4136 AD) Great Western Federal Saving, Los Angeles, CA, USA
DES/A) Sergio Privitera
ST) P & T
C) Banking

4137 AD) Grady-White Boats by National Boat Works Inc., P.O. Box 1527, Greenville, NC 27834 USA
C) Sail Boat Builders

4138 AD) Goertz Mantelhaus,
            WEST GERMANY
      DES/A) Hans Ulrich Alleman
4139 AD) Gomen Co. Ltd., Osaka, JAPAN
      DES/A) Ohtaka Takeshi
4140 AD) The Golden Fleet
      C) Sea Cruise
4141 AD) Gould Marketing Co. Ltd., 9429 Côte
           De Liesse Rd., Dorval, Que.,
           CANADA
4142 AD) Gipron, Milano, ITALY
      DES/A) Studio GSZ
4143 AD) Giardini S.p.A., Milano, ITALY
      DES/A) G & R Associati
4144 AD) General Signal Appliances Ltd.,
           201 Major St., Welland, Ont.,
           CANADA
4145 AD) Gendai Geijutsu Kenkyu-Jo, Tokyo,
           JAPAN
      DES/A) Kamekura Yusaku
4146 AD) Givaudan AG, Dübendorf,
           SWITZERLAND
      DES/A) Hans Hurter
4147 AD) Gardner Industrial Electric Ltd., 36
           Highview Ave., Scarborough, Ont.
           M1N 2H3   CANADA
4148 AD) Goes Lithographing Co., 42 W. 61st
           St., Chicago, IL   60621   USA
4149 AD) A B Gerdins Stansknivfabrik, Box 113
           870-31 Mjällom
4150 AD) Geddes, Brecher, Qualls &
           Cunningham, Philadelphia, PA, USA
      ST) Kramer, Miller, Londen, Glassman,
           Inc.

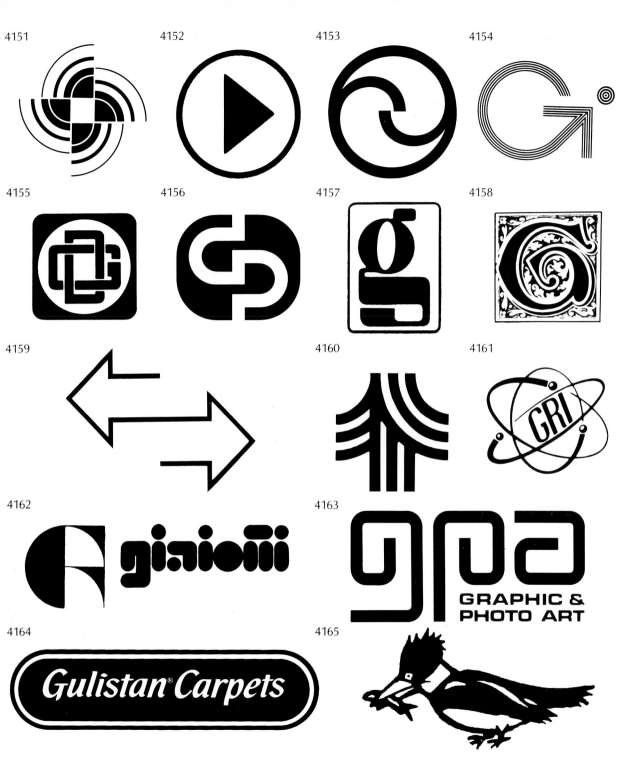

4151
4152
4153
4154
4155
4156
4157
4158
4159
4160
4161
4162
4163
4164

gpa
GRAPHIC &
PHOTO ART

Gulistan® Carpets

4165

4151   SM)   Detroit Suburban Network,
                 Detroit, MI, USA
           DES/A)   William Davis
4152   AD)   Dictaphone Corporation Ltd., 103
                 Rivalda Rd., Weston, Ont.,
                 M9M 2M6   CANADA
4153   AD)   Formus, Paris, FRANCE
           C)   Publication on furniture
           DES/A)   Bruno Pfäffli
           ST)   Atelier Frutiger
4154   AD)   National Giro, Great Britain
           DES/A)   FHK Henrion
4155   AD)   Gardner-Denver Co. (Canada) Ltd.,
                 406 Western Union Building,
                 640 8th Ave., S.W., Calgary, Alta.
                 CANADA
4156   AD)   General Paper Corporation,
                 Pittsburgh, PA, USA
           DES/A)   Francis R. Esteban
4157   AD)   Gregson Manufacturing Co., Liberty,
                 NC, USA
4158   AD)   J. Arthur Grimes, 3335 Yonge St.,
                 Toronto, Ont., CANADA
4159   AD)   J.C. Hovey & Associates, 1440 Ste.
                 Catherine St. W., Suite 306,
                 Montreal, Que., H3G 1R8   CANADA
           SM)   Gordon Hovey Group Limited
4160   AD)   Great Northern Nekoosa Corporation,
                 75 Prospect St., Stamford,
                 CT   06901   USA
4161   AD)   Gam Rad, Inc., 16825 Wyoming Ave.,
                 Detroit, MI   48221   USA
4162   AD)   Giaiotti (TM) Divisione Legno S.A.S.
                 33043 Cividale del Friuli, ITALY
4163   AD)   Graphic & Photo Art, Salt Lake City,
                 UT, USA
           DES/A)   Peter J. Rabe
4164   AD)   J.P. Stevens & Co. Inc., 1185 Ave. of
                 Americas, New York, NY   10036
                 USA
           SM)   Gulistan Carpets (TM) by J.P. Stevens
4165   AD)   The Garcia Corp., 329 Alfred Ave.,
                 Teaneck, NJ   07666   USA
           SM)   Product Symbol

G-18

4166 | AD) | Graphic Productions
| ST) | Cutro Associates
4167 | AD) | Gazocean, Paris, FRANCE
4168 | AD) | Gruen Watch Co. of Canada Ltd., The Gruen Building, 315 Bering Ave., Toronto, Ont.   M8Z 3A5   CANADA
4169 | AD) | Gentil Plastics Ltd.
| DES/A) | Burton Kramer
4170 | AD) | A B Gustaf Kahr, SWEDEN
4171 | AD) | Garvey Labelmatic, 11550 Adie Rd., Maryland Heights, MO, USA A Consolidated Foods Company
| SM) | Product Trademark
4172 | AD) | Gateway Aviation Ltd., Hangar 11, Edmonton Municipal Airport, Edmonton, Alta.   CANADA
4173 | AD) | Glaxo Laboratories, A Glaxo Canada Limited Company, 1 Dorchester Ave., Toronto, Ont.   M8Z 4W1   CANADA
4174 | AD) | Gepetod, 330 Montpellier Blvd., Ville St. Laurent, Que.   H4N 2G7   CANADA
4175 | AD) | Gateway Products, 1711 Langley Ave., Irvine, CA, USA
4176 | AD) | Gatx Corporation, 120 South Riverside Plaza, Chicago, IL, USA
4177 | SM) | Graphic Typography for product, fabbrica di tappeti e moquettes-13011 Borgosesia (VC) ITALY
4178 | AD) | Guitar Association, JAPAN
| DES/A) | Yasaburo Kuwayama

G-19

4179

4180

4181

4182

4183

4184

4185

4186

4187

4188

4189

4179 AD) G.W. Furniture Ltd., Montreal, Que., CANADA

DES/A) Jean Mouir & Dennis L'Allier

4180 AD) Pat Gilbert and Associates Ltd., 797 Don Mills Rd., Suite 1005, Don Mills, Ont. M3C 1V1 CANADA

C) Executive Recruiting Consultants

4181 AD) J.R. Geigy AG., SWITZERLAND

DES/A) Jörg Hamburger

4182 AD) Sielding Gäbelbach, Bern, SWITZERLAND

DES/A) Hans Hartman

4183 AD) J.R. Geigy AG., SWITZERLAND

DES/A) Jörg Hamburger

4184 AD) G & L Services, Inc., P.O. Box 767, Cambridge, OH 43725 USA

4185 AD) The Georgian Group, Bramalea, Ont., CANADA

C) Builder, developer of residential homes

4186 AD) Go Camping, Hwy. 7, West of Hwy. 27, Ont., CANADA

C) Camp vehicle rolling equipment

4187 AD) Grubee's International Ltd., 1485 Inkster Blvd., Winnipeg, Man., CANADA

4188 AD) Galleria, 115 E. 57 St. (Park Ave.) New York, NY, USA

C) Office complex

4189 AD) Gérard Martin Ltd., 9600 Meilleur St., Montreal, Que. H2N 2E3 CANADA

4190

4191

4192

4193

4194

4195

4196

4197

Great Smokies
HILTON

4198

Gateco Products

4199

green start

4200

Gideon

4190 AD) The Graphic Statement, Vancouver,
           B.C., CANADA
      DES/A) Michael Pacey
4191 AD) Gulf Atlantic, Houston, TX, USA
      DES/A) Baxter & Korge
4192 AD) Golden Twist Food Ltd., Toronto,
           Ont., CANADA
      DES/A) William Tam
      ST) Ken Borden Limited
4193 AD) Gairloch Gardens Gallery,
           1306 Lakeshore Rd., E., Oakville,
           Ont., CANADA
4194 AD) Girouard Graphics, Nashville,
           TN, USA
      DES/A) Dan Girouard
4195 AD) Great Smokies Hilton,
           Asheville, NC 28802   USA
      C) Hotel
4196 AD) Gallerie Rewolle, Bremen, GERMANY
      DES/A) Sibylle Haase
4197 AD) Griffiths-Kerr Sales, Toronto,
           Ont., CANADA (a division of
           Finlayson Enterprises Ltd.)
      DES/A) Micky Edden
      ST) Ken Borden Limited
4198 AD) Gateco Products, 1711 Langley Ave.,
           Irvine, CA 92705   USA
4199 AD) Heron Cable Industries Ltd., 440
           Phillip St., Waterloo, Ont., CANADA
      SM) Product Wordmark
4200 AD) Gideon Fashion Jewelry

4201

4202

4203

4204

4205

4206

4207

4208

4209

4210

4211

4201 AD) Geron Associates Ltd., 20 Progress Rd., Scarborough, Ont., CANADA

4202 AD) Graphic Center, Opwijk, BELGIUM
DES/A) Robert Geisser

4203 AD) The Greenery, 90 Bloor St. E., Toronto, Ont., CANADA

4204 AD) General Fireproofing Company, Youngstown, OH, USA
DES/A) Ivan Chermayeff

4205 AD) Girec S.A., Bruxelles, BELGIUM
DES/A) Luc Vanmalderen

4206 AD) General Graphics Ltd., Eindhoven, NETHERLANDS
DES/A) Sjoerd Bylsma

4207 AD) Mazda
SM) GLC, Vehicle model series North American Market

4208 AD) Guest Keen & Nettlefold Ltd., London, ENGLAND
DES/A) Abram Games

4209 AD) General Services Administration, Chicago, IL, USA

4210 AD) Groep De Bondt, BELGIUM
DES/A) Rob Buytaert

4211 AD) Garlock Construction Products, Palmyra, NY 14522   USA

G-22

4212

4213

4214

4215

4216

4217

4218

4219

4220

4221

4222

4223

4224

4225

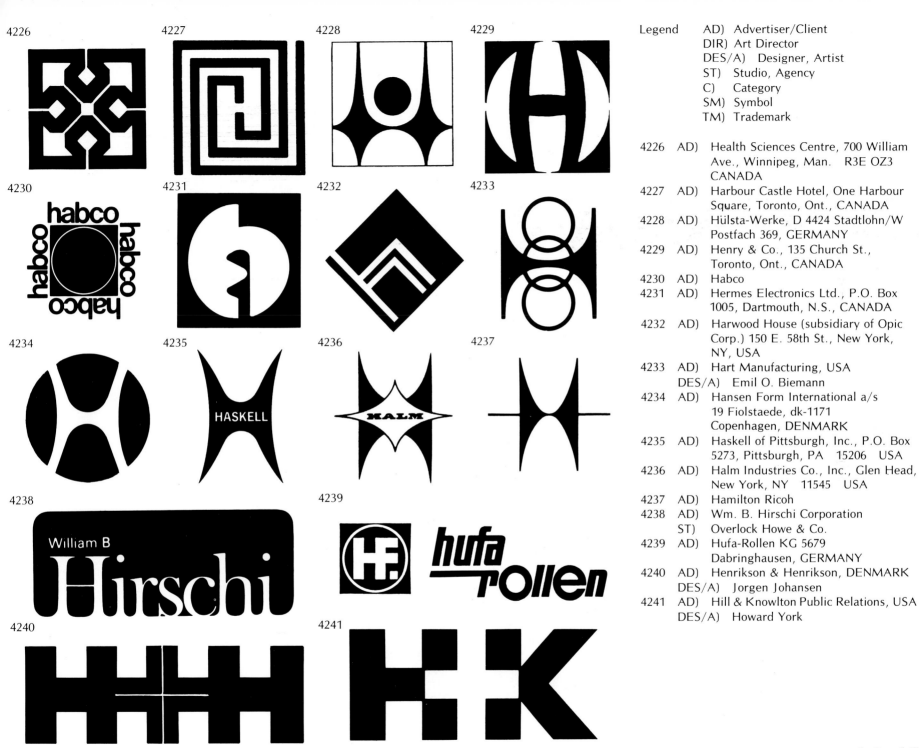

4226

4227

4228

4229

4230

4231

4232

4233

4234

4235

4236

4237

4238

4239

4240

4241

4226 AD) Health Sciences Centre, 700 William
           Ave., Winnipeg, Man.   R3E OZ3
           CANADA

4227 AD) Harbour Castle Hotel, One Harbour
           Square, Toronto, Ont., CANADA

4228 AD) Hülsta-Werke, D 4424 Stadtlohn/W
           Postfach 369, GERMANY

4229 AD) Henry & Co., 135 Church St.,
           Toronto, Ont., CANADA

4230 AD) Habco

4231 AD) Hermes Electronics Ltd., P.O. Box
           1005, Dartmouth, N.S., CANADA

4232 AD) Harwood House (subsidiary of Opic
           Corp.) 150 E. 58th St., New York,
           NY, USA

4233 AD) Hart Manufacturing, USA
      DES/A) Emil O. Biemann

4234 AD) Hansen Form International a/s
           19 Fiolstaede, dk-1171
           Copenhagen, DENMARK

4235 AD) Haskell of Pittsburgh, Inc., P.O. Box
           5273, Pittsburgh, PA   15206   USA

4236 AD) Halm Industries Co., Inc., Glen Head,
           New York, NY   11545   USA

4237 AD) Hamilton Ricoh

4238 AD) Wm. B. Hirschi Corporation
      ST) Overlock Howe & Co.

4239 AD) Hufa-Rollen KG 5679
           Dabringhausen, GERMANY

4240 AD) Henrikson & Henrikson, DENMARK
      DES/A) Jorgen Johansen

4241 AD) Hill & Knowlton Public Relations, USA
      DES/A) Howard York

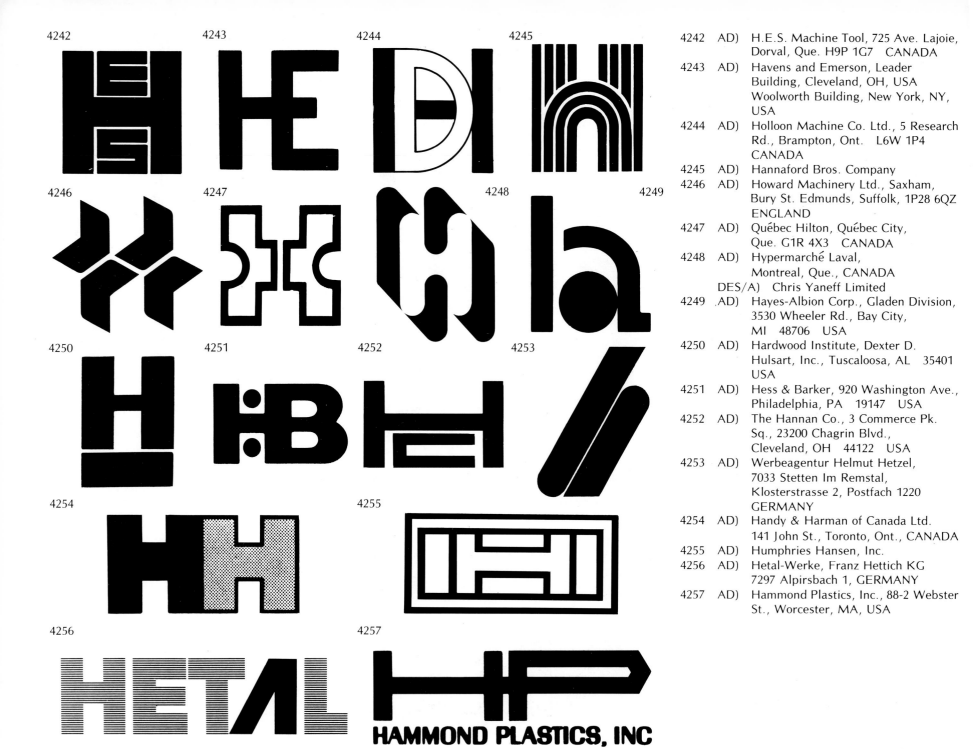

4242 AD) H.E.S. Machine Tool, 725 Ave. Lajoie, Dorval, Que. H9P 1G7   CANADA

4243 AD) Havens and Emerson, Leader Building, Cleveland, OH, USA Woolworth Building, New York, NY, USA

4244 AD) Holloon Machine Co. Ltd., 5 Research Rd., Brampton, Ont.   L6W 1P4 CANADA

4245 AD) Hannaford Bros. Company

4246 AD) Howard Machinery Ltd., Saxham, Bury St. Edmunds, Suffolk, 1P28 6QZ ENGLAND

4247 AD) Québec Hilton, Québec City, Que. G1R 4X3   CANADA

4248 AD) Hypermarché Laval, Montreal, Que., CANADA
DES/A)   Chris Yaneff Limited

4249 .AD) Hayes-Albion Corp., Gladen Division, 3530 Wheeler Rd., Bay City, MI   48706   USA

4250 AD) Hardwood Institute, Dexter D. Hulsart, Inc., Tuscaloosa, AL   35401 USA

4251 AD) Hess & Barker, 920 Washington Ave., Philadelphia, PA   19147   USA

4252 AD) The Hannan Co., 3 Commerce Pk. Sq., 23200 Chagrin Blvd., Cleveland, OH   44122   USA

4253 AD) Werbeagentur Helmut Hetzel, 7033 Stetten Im Remstal, Klosterstrasse 2, Postfach 1220 GERMANY

4254 AD) Handy & Harman of Canada Ltd. 141 John St., Toronto, Ont., CANADA

4255 AD) Humphries Hansen, Inc.

4256 AD) Hetal-Werke, Franz Hettich KG 7297 Alpirsbach 1, GERMANY

4257 AD) Hammond Plastics, Inc., 88-2 Webster St., Worcester, MA, USA

4258

4259

4260 HEXCEL

4261

4262

4263 HASTINGS

4264

4265 HI-LO

4266

4267

4268

4269 HMTC HOUDAILLE

4270 HEMISPHERE

4271 HAYES DANA

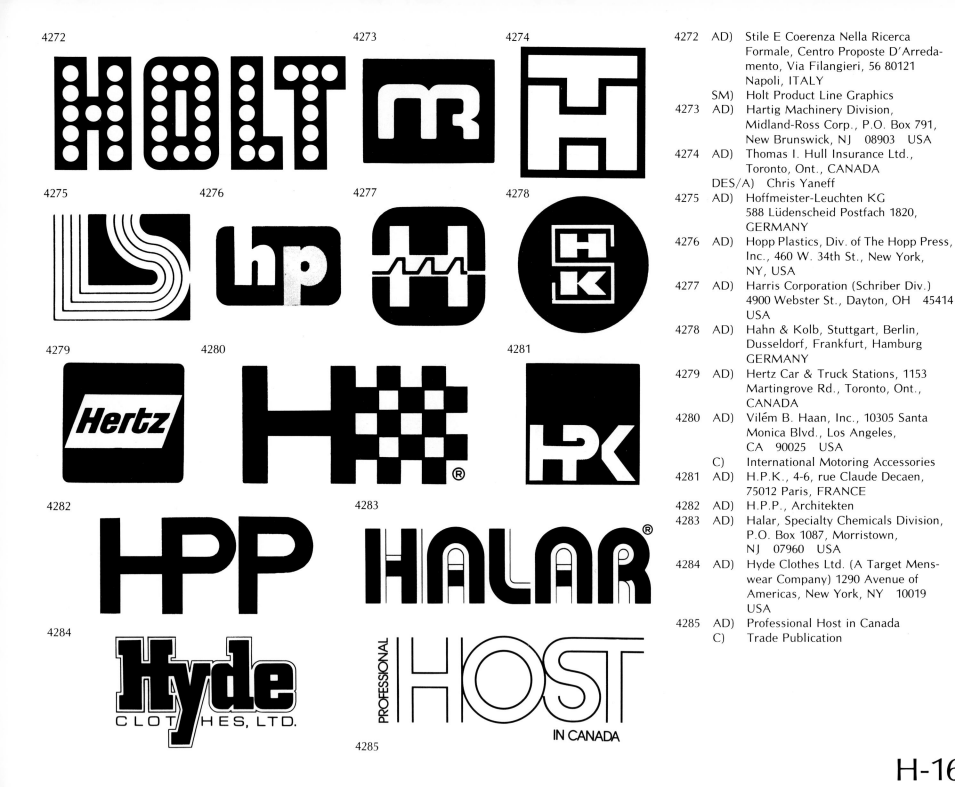

4272 AD) Stile E Coerenza Nella Ricerca Formale, Centro Proposte D'Arredamento, Via Filangieri, 56 80121 Napoli, ITALY

SM) Holt Product Line Graphics

4273 AD) Hartig Machinery Division, Midland-Ross Corp., P.O. Box 791, New Brunswick, NJ 08903 USA

4274 AD) Thomas I. Hull Insurance Ltd., Toronto, Ont., CANADA

DES/A) Chris Yaneff

4275 AD) Hoffmeister-Leuchten KG 588 Lüdenscheid Postfach 1820, GERMANY

4276 AD) Hopp Plastics, Div. of The Hopp Press, Inc., 460 W. 34th St., New York, NY, USA

4277 AD) Harris Corporation (Schriber Div.) 4900 Webster St., Dayton, OH 45414 USA

4278 AD) Hahn & Kolb, Stuttgart, Berlin, Dusseldorf, Frankfurt, Hamburg GERMANY

4279 AD) Hertz Car & Truck Stations, 1153 Martingrove Rd., Toronto, Ont., CANADA

4280 AD) Vilém B. Haan, Inc., 10305 Santa Monica Blvd., Los Angeles, CA 90025 USA

C) International Motoring Accessories

4281 AD) H.P.K., 4-6, rue Claude Decaen, 75012 Paris, FRANCE

4282 AD) H.P.P., Architekten

4283 AD) Halar, Specialty Chemicals Division, P.O. Box 1087, Morristown, NJ 07960 USA

4284 AD) Hyde Clothes Ltd. (A Target Menswear Company) 1290 Avenue of Americas, New York, NY 10019 USA

4285 AD) Professional Host in Canada

C) Trade Publication

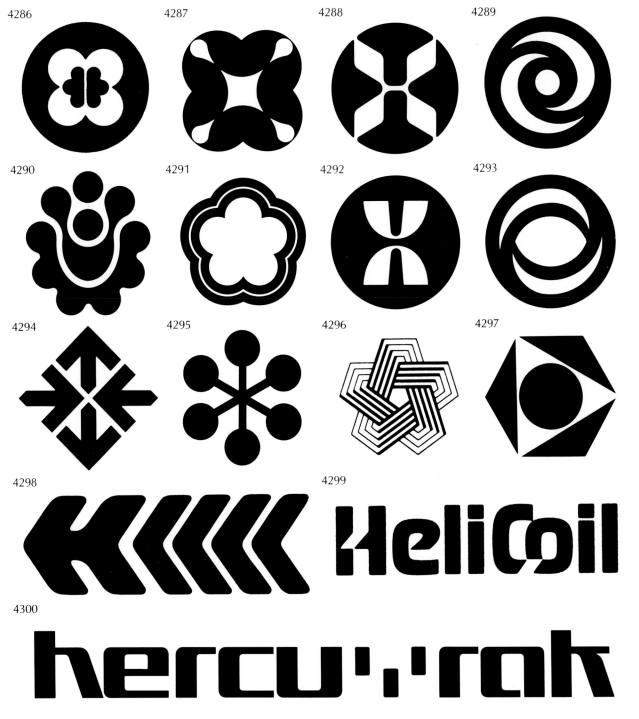

4286 AD) Hyatt Hotel
C) Hotels in US, CANADA and all over the world—Iran, Thailand, Hong-Kong, Israel, Singapore, etc.

4287 AD) Hotel Leamington, Oakland, CA, USA
DES/A) Jerry Berman

4288 AD) Hawaiian Airlines, Honolulu, HI, USA
DES/A) Clarence Lee

4289 AD) Hyspa, Bern, SWITZERLAND
DES/A) Hans Neuburg

4290 AD) Hillside Townhomes, Dallas, TX, USA
ST) The Richards Group

4291 AD) Holiday World Inc., Dallas, TX, USA
DES/A) Patrick Benton

4292 AD) Howard Miller Clock Co., USA
ST) Irving Haper, George Nelson & Co.

4293 AD) Helicon Ltd., Dublin, IRELAND
DES/A) Peter Wildbur

4294 AD) Hillier, Parker, May & Powden, London, ENGLAND
DES/A) Michael Tucker

4295 AD) Hyvon-Kudeneule Oy, Hanko, FINLAND
DES/A) Matti Viherjuuri

4296 AD) Hermes Precisa International Div., Hermes Products Inc., 1900 Lower Rd., Linden, NJ 07036 USA

4297 AD) Hoerner Waldorf Corp., St. Paul, MN, USA

4298 AD) Hudsons Freight, London, ENGLAND
ST) Woudhuysen Limited

4299 AD) Heli-Coil, Insert Products Division, Heli-Coil Corp., Danbury, CT 06810 USA

4300 AD) Metalwork Limited (Makers of Hercu-Rak) (TM) 1200 50th Ave., Lachine, Que. H8T 2V4 CANADA

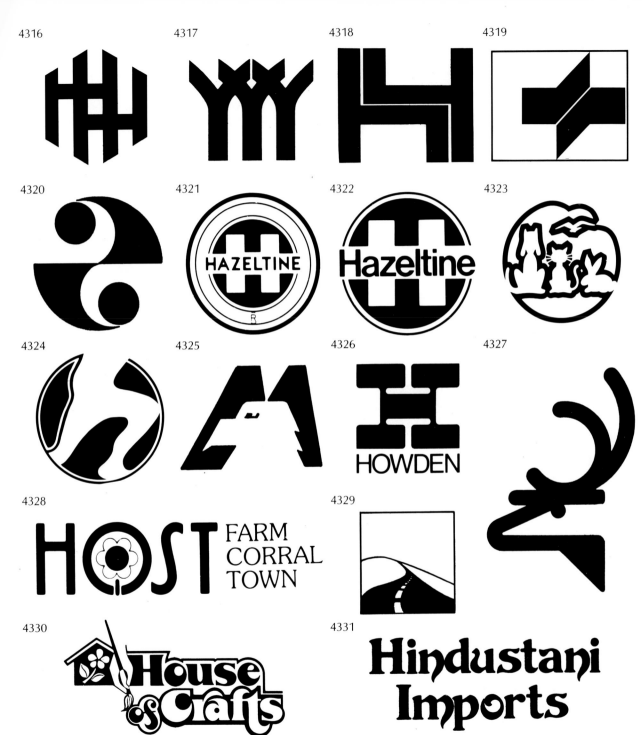

4316 AD) Hutchison House Ltd., Hong Kong
DES/A) Michael Miller Yu

4317 AD) Herman Smith Management
Resources Inc., 47 Colborne St.,
Suite 306, Toronto, Ont.   M5E 1E3
CANADA
C) Executive Placement Service

4318 AD) Hagenbuch Holz, SWITZERLAND
DES/A) Josef P. Grabner
C) Lumber

4319 AD) Handelsblatt-Verlag, Düsseldorf,
GERMANY
DES/A) Arno Ernst Rettig

4320 AD) Supplies (Health & Comfort) Ltd.,
Bowling Green Mills, P.O. Box 23,
Bingley, Yorkshire BD16 4BH
ENGLAND

4321 AD) Hazeltine Corp., Greenlawn, NY, USA
TM) Old

4322 AD) Hazeltine Corp., Greenlawn, NY, USA
TM) New

4323 AD) Humane Society of St. Charles, USA
DES/A) Bob Leu (refined child's design)
ST) Pred Creative Marketing
Communications

4324 AD) Harbour Castle Hotel, A Div. of
Campeau Corp., P.O. Box 450,
Terminal A, Ottawa, Ont., CANADA
SM) Health Club Symbol

4325 AD) H.B. Fuller Co., 2400 Kasota Ave., St.
Paul, MN   55108   USA

4326 AD) D.H. Howden & Co. Ltd., P.O. Box
2485, London, Ont. N6A 4G8
CANADA

4327 AD) Harvey Dodds Ltd., 2270 Moreau St.,
Montreal, Que. H1W 2M6
CANADA

4328 AD) Host Farm Corral Town, 2300 Lincoln
Hwy. E., Lancaster, PA   17602   USA

4329 AD) Hav-a-kar Leasing, 1474 Bathurst St.,
Toronto, Ont., CANADA

4330 AD) House of Crafts, USA

4331 AD) Hindustani Imports, 7893 St.
Lawrence Blvd., Montreal, Que.
CANADA

4332

4333

4334

4335

4336

4337

4338

4339

4340

4341

Hazelton Lanes

4342

Holiday HOUSE®

4343

Halstead Industries Inc

4344

Hytec DIVISION OF OWATONNA TOOL ® COMPANY

4345

THE HIDDEN HINGE

4332   AD)   Hester Industries Inc., Chicago, IL, USA

DES/A)   Randall R. Roth

4333   AD)   Hardacre Real Estate, Chicago, IL, USA

DES/A)   Randall R. Roth

4334   AD)   Hofmann Industries Inc., 3145 Shillington Rd., Sinking Springs, PA, USA

4335   AD)   Hogartel 7; Barcelona, SPAIN

DES/A)   Ernesto Moradell Catala

4336   AD)   Harush Studio, Yitzuv Ltd., ISRAEL

4337   AD)   Hargraves Audio Visual, 204-206 Warbreck Moor, Aintre, Liverpool, ENGLAND

4338   AD)   Hampe Blitzschutzbau, Brannschweig, GERMANY

DES/A)   Klaus Grözinger and Hans Georg Oehring

4339   AD)   Hotel Limmathaus, Zurich, SWITZERLAND

DES/A)   Rudolf Bircher

4340   AD)   Hollywood Motorama Museum, 7001 Hollywood Blvd., Los Angeles, CA, USA

4341   AD)   Hazelton Lanes Ltd., 37A Hazelton Ave., Toronto, Ont., CANADA

4342   AD)   Canadian Travel Advisors Ltd., 25 Adelaide St., E., Toronto, Ont., CANADA

C)   Travel Agency

4343   AD)   Halstead Industries Inc., Zelienpole, PA, USA

4344   AD)   Hytec, (Div. of Owatonna Tool Co.) 191 State Ave., Owatonna, MN, USA

4345   AD)   Southern Tool Mfg. Co. Inc., Winston-Salem, NC, USA

SM)   Product Typography

4346

4347

4348

4349

4350

4351

4352

HEALTHWAYS

4353

4354

4355

4356

HOLMS

4357

HOCKEY
PLAYER

4358

HOUSTON CITIZENS
BOOKSTORE

4346 AD) Henry S. Miller Co., Corporate
Headquarters: 2001 Bryan Tower,
Dallas, TX 75201 USA
C) Realtors
4347 AD) Arts Graphiques Heliogra SA,
SWITZERLAND
DES/A) Roger-Virgile Geiser
4348 AD) Häberli, SWITZERLAND
DES/A) Marcel Wyss
4349 AD) House of Harambee, USA
DES/A) Herb Jackson
4350 AD) Hospital Consortium Inc.,
San Francisco, CA, USA
DES/A) Michael Vanderbyl
4351 AD) Helsingør VÆRFT A/S
3000 Helsingør Denmark
4352 AD) Healthways, P.O. Box 45055,
Los Angeles, CA 90045 USA
4353 AD) Christian Holzäpfel KG 7240
Horb/Neckar
4354 AD) Howard F. Thompson
C) Architect
DES/A) Ernest H. Stedman
4355 AD) Highland House Development
DES/A) Richard Deardorff
4356 AD) Holms, S-570 80 Virserum,
GERMANY
4357 AD) Hockey Player, 240 Eglinton Ave., E.,
Toronto, Ont. M4P 1K8 CANADA
4358 AD) Houston Citizens Bookstore, Houston,
TX, USA
DES/A) Dean Harahara

4356a

4357a

4358a

4359

4360

4361

4362

4363

4364

4365

HENKEL GmbH

4366

HOGG ROBINSON KNOX JOHNSTON

4367

hotsy ®

4368

4369

4370

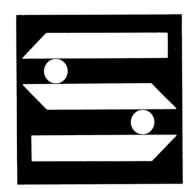

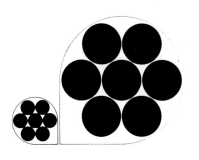

4371

4372

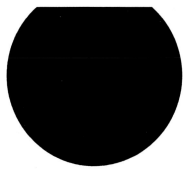

CBC/

CBC/

4373

CBC/Danmark
CBC/Holland
CBC/Norge
CBC/International
CBC/Byggeadministration AS
CBC/Feasibility Studies
CBC/Project Managers
CBC/Quantity Surveyors
CBC/Cost Consultants

Designer Artist Profile/Jørgen Hartzack
Industriel designer IDD
Ref. World of Logotypes File No. 150
ST)   Frederiksgade 12
1265 København K/Denmark

4368 AD) CBC Byggeadministration AS,
            Kokkedal, DENMARK (EDT manage-
            ment in building industry)
            Design: 1973
4369 AD) Svend Schrøder APS, Roedovre,
            DENMARK
      C)   Chemical-electronic apparatures
            Design: 1964
4370 AD) Skaarup & Jespersen, Copenhagen,
            DENMARK
      C)   Architects and planners
            Design: 1973
4371 AD) Jørgen Hartzack, graphic design,
            Copenhagen, DENMARK
      SM) Designer's own mark means ''almost
            complete.''
            Design: 1973
4372 AD) Logotype (outline and bold) fc. ¯3C
            Ref. CBC/Corporate Identity Manual
      SM) Logo stroke with graphic typography
            mix.
            Design: 1973
4373 AD) The Copenhagen Municipality
            Planning Department, DENMARK
            Design: 1969

H-23

4374

4375

4376

4377

4378

4379

4380

4381

4382

4383

4384

4385

4374   AD)   ICSID 1973
        SM)   ICSID '73 Kyoto, Japan
        DES/A)   Yusaku Kamekura, Japan's leading graphic designer, drew the symbol for the 8th ICSID Congress in Japan.

4375   AD)   Illinois Audio, 12 E. Delaware Pl., Chicago, IL   60611   USA

4376   AD)   Innovative Graphics International, Ltd. 304 E. 45th St., New York, NY   10017   USA

4377   AD)   Industries Resistol S.A., Chancery Lane, London, ENGLAND

4378   AD)   Imlac Corp., 150 A St., Needham, MA   02194   USA

4379   AD)   Instrumentation Laboratory Inc., Lexington, MA   02173   USA

4380   AD)   Invo Spline Inc., P.O. Box 7, Warren, MI   48090   USA

4381   AD)   Inter-Ruckversicherungs AG Zurich, SWITZERLAND
        DES/A)   Paul Bühlmann

4382   AD)   Interyacht, 6 Quay St., Woodbridge, Suffolk IP12 1BY ENGLAND

4383   AD)   Industrial and Trade Shows of Canada, 481 University Ave., Toronto, Ont. M5W 1A7   CANADA
        C)   Trade Shows

4384   AD)   International Time Recording Co., Ltd., Beavor Lane, Hammersmith, London W6 9AR, ENGLAND
        C)   Horological and chronometric instruments

4385   AD)   Idomo Furniture International, 760 Supertest Rd., Downsview, Ont., CANADA
        C)   Retail Furniture Mart

I-13

4386 AD) Ilse-Werke KG (Div. of BSB),
Abt. ZH 3418 Uslar, Postfach 30,
GERMANY

SM) Ilse Sauna

4387 AD) Invader Corp., P.O. Box 420,
Giddings, TX 78942 USA

4388 AD) Impruneta, 50023 Impruneta Firenze,
Via Provinciale Chiantigiana 67, ITALY

C) Cottoimpruneta cotto smaltato
ceramica

4389 AD) Industrial Silos Ltd., (a member of The
Weston-Evans Group) Cherry Tree,
Blockburn, Lancashire, ENGLAND

4390 AD) Italvela, 48100 Ravenna,
Viale Trieste 116, ITALY

4391 AD) Interyacht, 6 Dock St., Annapolis,
MA 24104 USA

C) Boating

4392 AD) Intra glas-vertrieb, 741 Reutlingen,
St. Peter-Str. 22, Elke Lukaszewitz,
GERMANY

4393 AD) ISA Headquarters, 400 Stanwix St.,
Pittsburgh, PA 15222 USA

4394 AD) International Warranty Co., Ltd.,
1125B Leslie St., N., Toronto,
Ont. M3C 2J6 CANADA

4395 AD) Industrial Designers Soceity of
America, 1750 Old Meadow Rd.,
McLean, VA 22101 USA

4396 AD) Ipedex International, 140 Avenue Paul-
Doumer, 92500 Rueil-Malmaison,
FRANCE

4397 AD) Ilver-Cantiere Nautico s.r.l.
20035 Lissone (MI) Via C. Cattaneo,
90 Milano, ITALY

4398 AD) Ideal Shirts Co., JAPAN
DES/A) Hiroyuki Miyazaki

4399 AD) International Scientific Systems Ltd.
ST) Crosby/Fletcher/Forbes

4400 AD) Interdéveloppement, Paris, FRANCE
ST) Lonsdale Design
4401 AD) Icomi-Indústria Comércio De Minérios
S.A., Rio De Janeiro, BRASIL
DES/A) Aloisio Magalhães
4402 SM) IST Iupac - conference on physical
organic chemistry, Zurich,
SWITZERLAND
DES/A) Gisela Buomberger
4403 AD) Institut Des Banquiers Canadiens,
Montreal, Que., CANADA
DES/A) Jean Morin
ST) Girard, Bruce et Associés Ltée.
C) Banking
4404 AD) Interspace Inc.
DES/A) Beverly Gilman
ST) Corporate Design System
4405 AD) The Inn & Tennis Club (at Manitou
Island) 821 Eglinton Ave. W.,
Toronto, Ont., CANADA
4406 AD) Interior Products Group, Inc.
850 Third Ave., New York,
NY 10022 USA
4407 AD) Interessengemeinschaft Deutscher
Stutt Garter Ausstellungs GMBH
Stuttgard, WEST GERMANY
DES/A) Peter Wehr
4408 AD) International Minerals & Chemicals
4415 West Harrison St., Hillside,
IL 60162 USA
DES/A) Morton Goldsholl
ST) Morton Goldsholl Design Associates
4409 AD) Industrial Valley Bank,
Philadelphia, PA, USA
ST) Dixon & Parcels Associates, Inc.
4410 AD) Italstat S.p.A. Rome, ITALY
DES/A) Mimmo Castellano
4411 AD) Instituto Brasileiro De Mercado
De Capitais, Rio De Janeiro, BRASIL
DES/A) Luiz Sergio Coelho De Sampaio
4412 AD) Ingliss Ltd., 14 Strachan Ave.,
Toronto, Ont. M6K 1W6 CANADA
ST) D'Arcy, Macmanus & Masius
Advertising
4413 AD) International Laboratories (1972) Ltd.,
490 Rue Des Meurons, Winnipeg,
Man. R2H 2P3 CANADA

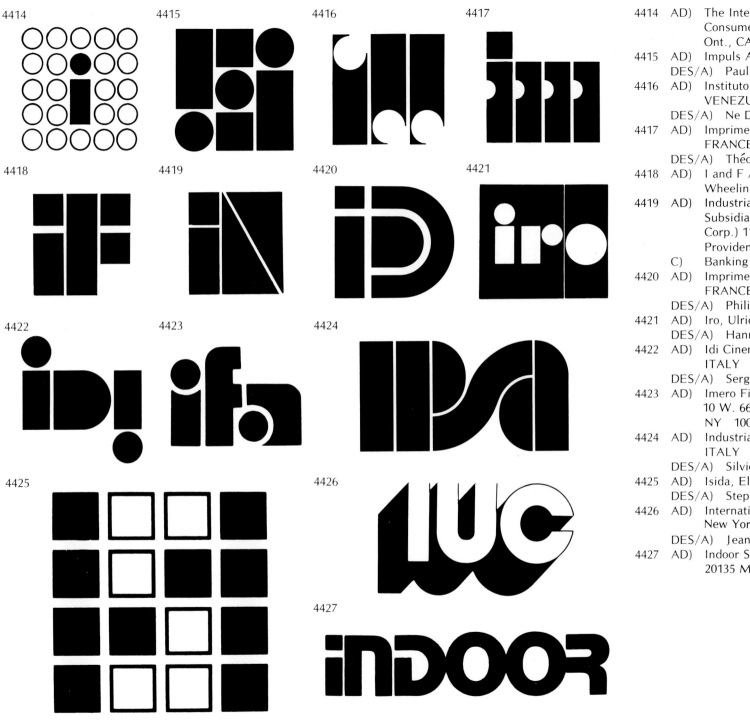

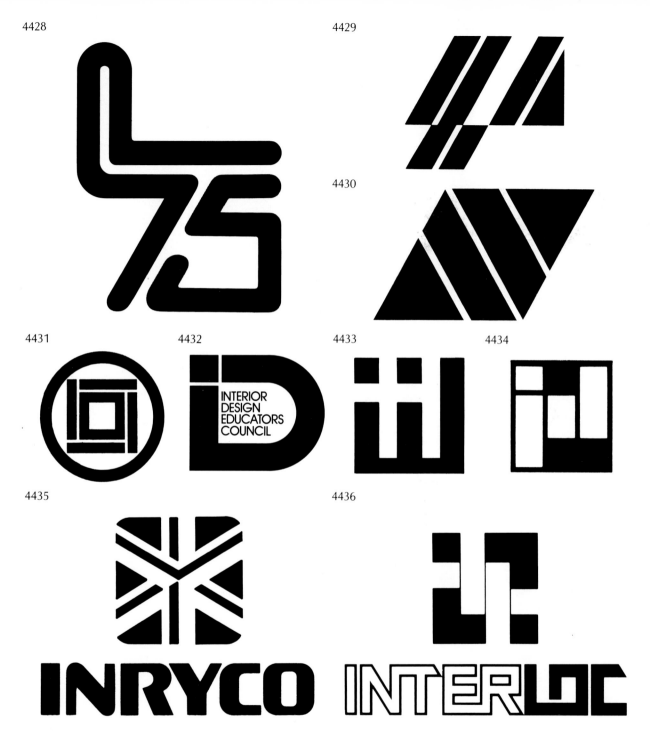

4428

4429

4430

4431

4432

INTERIOR
DESIGN
EDUCATORS
COUNCIL

4433

4434

4435

4436

INRYCO

INTERLOC

4428 AD) BFM Exhibitions Ltd., 17 Berners St., London W1P 4DY ENGLAND
SM) The 1975 International Furniture Show
4429 AD) Istituto Di Studi Di Servizio Sociale Roma, ITALY
DES/A) Michele Spera
4430 AD) International Audio-Visual Technical Centre, Antwerpen, BELGIUM
DES/A) Rob Buytaert
4431 AD) ICIPU Italian Public Statutory Credit Institute, Instituto di Credito per le Imprese di Pubblica Utilita, H.Q. via Q. Sella 2, Roma, ITALY
4432 AD) Interior Design Educators Council, USA & CANADA
DES/A) Catherine Rowe
4433 AD) Interiors International Ltd., 231 E. 55th St., New York, NY 10022 USA
4434 AD) International Research & Development Co., Ltd., Newcastle, ENGLAND
DES/A) David Caplan
4435 AD) Inryco (An Island Steel Co.) Dept. J, 4033 West Burnham, Milwaukee, WI 53201 USA
4436 AD) Interloc Realty Co., New York, NY, USA
DES/A) Don Primi

4437

4438

4439

4440

image impact

4441

4442

4443

4444

4445

4446

4447

4448

4449

4450

4451

4437   AD)   Interprint Co., Ltd., USA
       DES/A)   Michael Miller Yu
4438   AD)   International Vinyl Transfer Ltd.
       DES/A)   Michael Miller Yu
4439   AD)   International Timber Corp., Ltd., P.O.
       Box 118, Carpenters Rd.,
       London E1S 2DY, ENGLAND
       C)   Wood & Non-wood Building Materials
4440   AD)   Image Impact, 410 N. Michigan Ave.,
       Chicago, IL   60611   USA
       DES/A)   Lester J. Galligan, Yim F.W. Wong
4441   AD)   Interpersonal Growth Systems, Inc.,
       Shelard Plaza, 400 S. County Rd. 18,
       Minneapolis, MN, USA
4442   AD)   Insurance Brokers Association,
       Que., CANADA
4443   AD)   Interteam, SWITZERLAND
       C)   Voluntary Organization
     DES/A)   Atelier Stadelmann Bisig
4444   AD)   International Tennis Clubs,
       Wimbleton, ENGLAND; Washington,
       D.C., USA; Toronto, Ont., CANADA
4445   AD)   International Interior Design Show,
       Toronto, Ont., CANADA
4446   AD)   Ibris, 00146 Roma, Vicolo Pian Due
       Torri 65, Roma, ITALY
       C)   For furniture collection ''delta''
4447   AD)   IPI S.p.A., Nerviano, Milano, ITALY
       C)   Prefabricated Construction Units
     DES/A)   Mimmo Castellano
4448   AD)   Interactive Data Services, Waltham,
       MA, USA (Div. of White Weld & Co.)
     DES/A)   Heiner Hegemann
4449   AD)   Institut Pédagogique National,
       Paris, FRANCE
     DES/A)   René Ponot
4450   AD)   I.S.V.E.T., ITALY
     DES/A)   Mimmo Castellano
4451   AD)   Interdomo S.A.S., Desio, Milano,
       ITALY
       C)   Design Objects Manufacturers
     DES/A)   Giulio Confalonieri

4452

4453

4454

4455

4456

4457

4458

4459

4460

4461

4462

4463

4464

4452 AD) Internationale Handwerkerksmesse,
München, GERMANY
DES/A) Harold Heinrichs
ST) Kunstschule Alsterdamm Hamburg
4453 AD) Industrial Instruments Ltd.,
Stanley Rd., Bromley BR2 9JF,
Kent, ENGLAND
4454 AD) International Masonry Institute,
Suite 1001, 823 15th St., N.W.,
Washington, D.C. 20005 USA
4455 AD) IAC Ltd., 45 St. Clair Ave. W.,
Toronto, Ont., CANADA
C) Operation of Chartered Bank
SM) Symbol proposed
4456 AD) Industrial Blueprinting and Supply Co.
Ltd., Don Mills, Ont., CANADA
C) Blueprint and Whiteprint Reproduction
DES/A) Richard Janis
4457 AD) Information et Entreprise, Paris,
FRANCE
C) Public Relations Organization
DES/A) Adrian Frutiger
4458 AD) International Gas Transmission Co.,
(proposed) USA
ST) Overlock Howe & Co.
4459 AD) Isle of Sand Key, 1621 Gulf Blvd.,
Sand Key, Clearwater Beach,
FL 33515 USA
4460 AD) Industrial Safety Equipment Co., Ltd.,
9 Meteor Dr., Rexdale, Ont., CANADA
C) Industrial safety equipment
DES/A) John S. Brown
4461 AD) Inspectronic, Flushing, NY, USA
C) Electrical engineering & testing
DES/A) Jeanette Koumjian
ST) Russell & Minrichs, Inc.
4462 AD) Ikelite Underwater Systems,
3303 N. Illinois St., Indianapolis,
IN 46208 USA
4463 AD) Indicia, USA
C) Mail order company
4464 AD) International Data Corp.,
Waltham, MA, USA

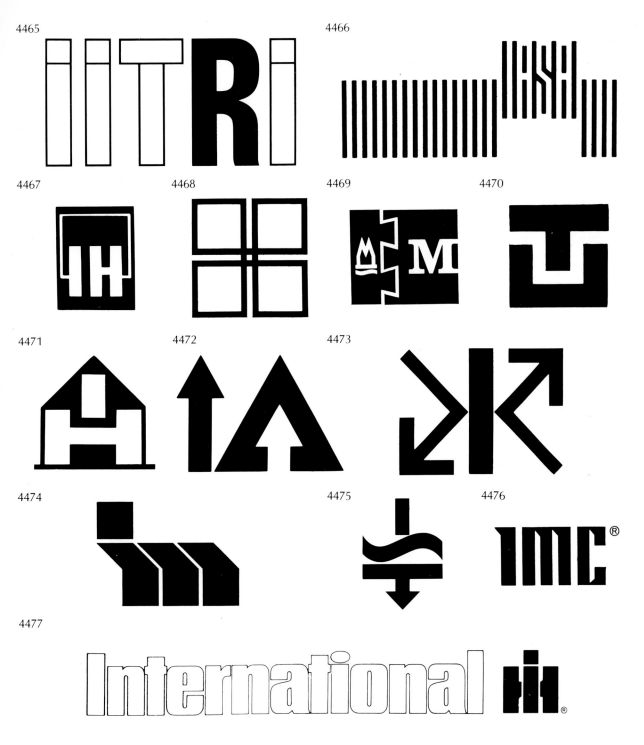

4465

4466

4467 4468 4469 4470

4471 4472 4473

4474 4475 4476

4477

4478

4479 intra VAN DEN BERG

4480

4481

4482 is molas GOLF CLUB

4483

4484

4485

4486

4487 inraum die Küche von becker

4488 intel®

4489

4490 icam

4478 AD) The Imperial Group, 202-283 Portage Ave., Winnipeg, Man. R3B 2B5 CANADA

4479 AD) Intra, P.O. Box 15715, 3528 S. W. Temple, Salt Lake City, UT, USA
C) Leather Furniture

4480 AD) Intranszmas, Budapest, HUNGARY
C) Transport Agency
DES/A) Nándor Gremsperger

4481 AD) Interni Luce apparecchi per l'illuminazione, 20127 Milano, via rovetta 6, ITALY

4482 AD) Is Molas Gold Club, Casella Postale No. 7, Pula (Cagliari), Sardinia, SPAIN

4483 AD) International Motorsport Association of Canada, Islington, Ont., CANADA
DES/A) William Newton & Bill Hedges

4484 AD) Indoor Billboard Corp., Box 3881, 3115 Griffith St., Charlotte, NC 28203 USA

4485 AD) Ingos, Warsaw, POLAND
C) Pen Manufacturing
DES/A) Andrzej Bertrandt

4486 AD) International Coffee Organization London, ENGLAND
DES/A) Aloisio Magalhães
ST) Aloisio Magalhães Programação Visual, Desenho Industrial Ltda.

4487 AD) Inraum die Küche von Becker, Becker Möbelwerk KG, 75 Karlsruhe 41-Stu., GERMANY

4488 AD) Intel Corporation, 3065 Bowers Ave., Santa Clara, CA 95051 USA

4489 AD) The International, USA
C) Apartment Complex
DES/A) Dan Bittman

4490 AD) Icam, Lecco, Como, ITALY
C) Confectionery Manufacturers
DES/A) Amleto Dalla Costa

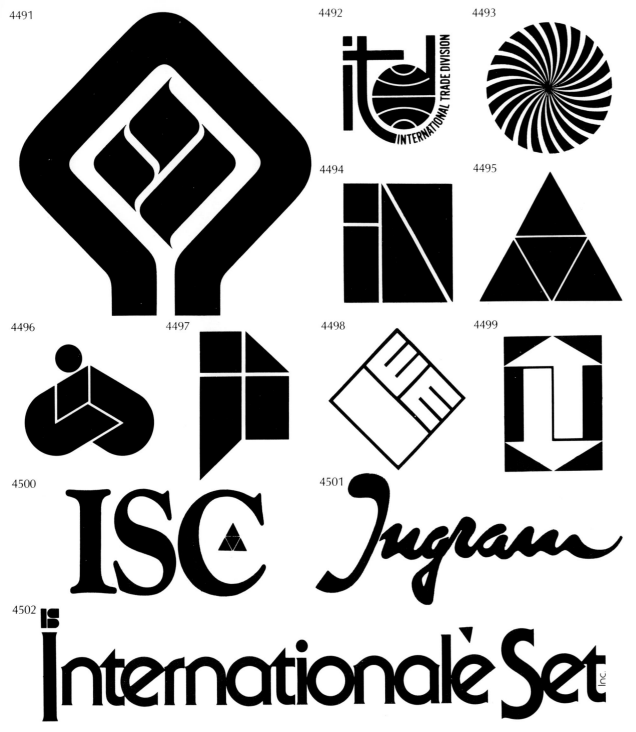

4491

4492

4493

4494

4495

4496

4497

4498

4499

4500

4501

4502

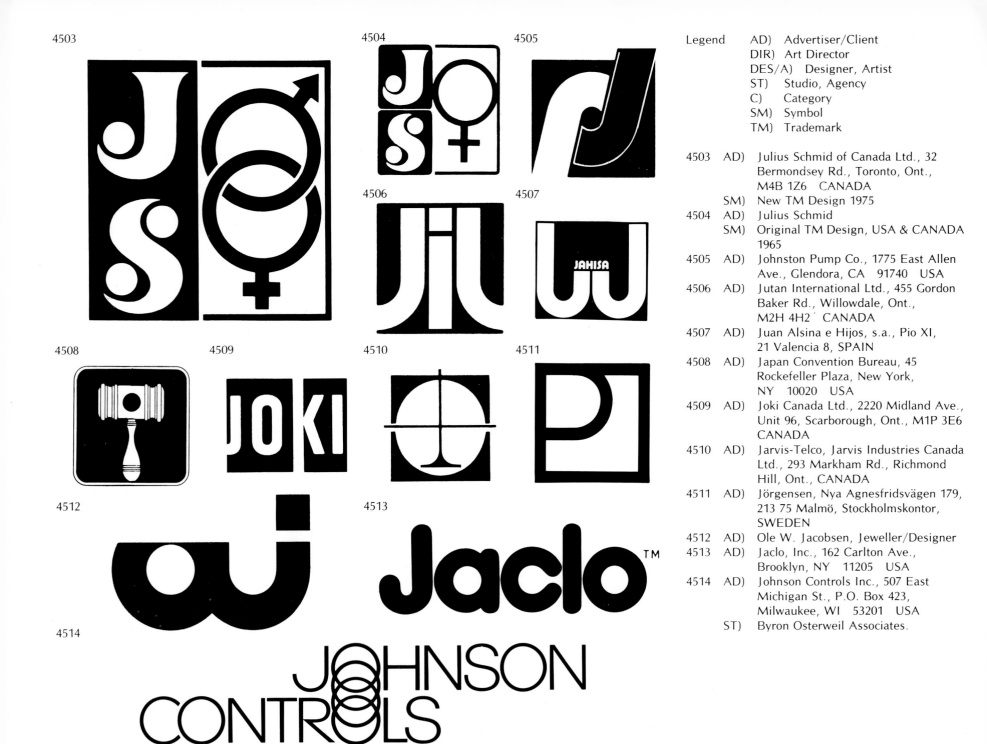

4503

4504

4505

4506

4507

4508

4509

4510

4511

JAHISA

JOKI

4512

4513

Jaclo™

4514

JOHNSON
CONTROLS

Legend AD) Advertiser/Client
        DIR) Art Director
        DES/A) Designer, Artist
        ST) Studio, Agency
        C) Category
        SM) Symbol
        TM) Trademark

4503 AD) Julius Schmid of Canada Ltd., 32
            Bermondsey Rd., Toronto, Ont.,
            M4B 1Z6 CANADA
      SM) New TM Design 1975
4504 AD) Julius Schmid
      SM) Original TM Design, USA & CANADA
            1965
4505 AD) Johnston Pump Co., 1775 East Allen
            Ave., Glendora, CA 91740 USA
4506 AD) Jutan International Ltd., 455 Gordon
            Baker Rd., Willowdale, Ont.,
            M2H 4H2 CANADA
4507 AD) Juan Alsina e Hijos, s.a., Pio XI,
            21 Valencia 8, SPAIN
4508 AD) Japan Convention Bureau, 45
            Rockefeller Plaza, New York,
            NY 10020 USA
4509 AD) Joki Canada Ltd., 2220 Midland Ave.,
            Unit 96, Scarborough, Ont., M1P 3E6
            CANADA
4510 AD) Jarvis-Telco, Jarvis Industries Canada
            Ltd., 293 Markham Rd., Richmond
            Hill, Ont., CANADA
4511 AD) Jörgensen, Nya Agnesfridsvägen 179,
            213 75 Malmö, Stockholmskontor,
            SWEDEN
4512 AD) Ole W. Jacobsen, Jeweller/Designer
4513 AD) Jaclo, Inc., 162 Carlton Ave.,
            Brooklyn, NY 11205 USA
4514 AD) Johnson Controls Inc., 507 East
            Michigan St., P.O. Box 423,
            Milwaukee, WI 53201 USA
      ST) Byron Osterweil Associates.

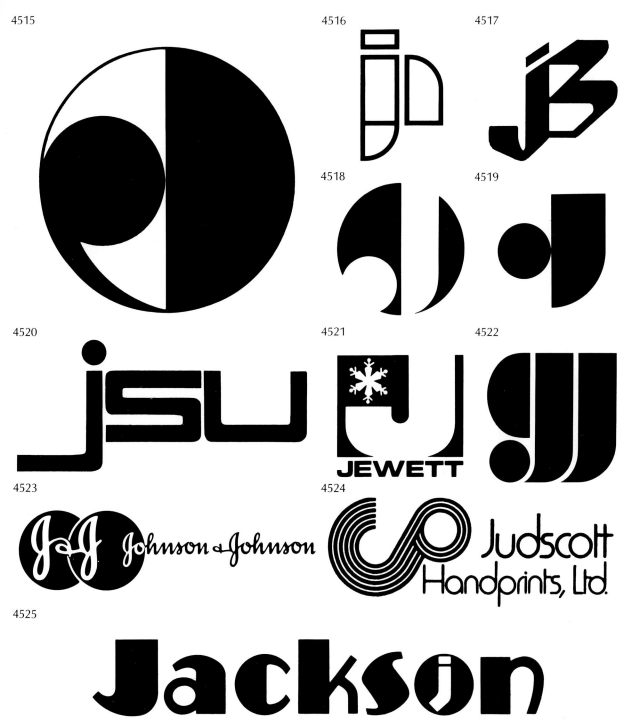

4515

4516

4517

4518

4519

4520

4521

4522

4523

4524

4525

4515 AD) Drozstvo ''Javorina''
Žilina, CZECHOSLOVAKIA
DES/A) Frantisek Boban
4516 AD) Jerome & Norris Ltd., Croydon,
Surrey, ENGLAND
DES/A) David Caplan
4517 AD) J & B Clothes, 82 Spadina Ave.,
Toronto, Ont., CANADA
C) Menswear
DES/A) Al Cooper
ST) Cooper Graphics & Associates Ltd.
4518 AD) Joko Co., Ltd., JAPAN
DES/A) Yoichi Maeno
4519 AD) J'Herrenmode, SWITZERLAND
DES/A) Otto Krämer
4520 AD) JSU Supplies Ltd., 122 Chandos Ave.,
Toronto, Ont., M6H 2E8 CANADA
4521 AD) Jewett Refrigerator, 2 Letchworth St.,
Buffalo, NY 14213 USA
4522 AD) Georg Jensen, Sølvsmedie
Copenhagen, DENMARK
ST) Morton, Peetz-schov and Ulla
Heegaard
4523 AD) Johnson & Johnson, Athletic Division,
New Brunswick, NJ 08903 USA
4524 AD) Judscott Handprints Ltd.,
Office: J.W. Showroom, Inc., 2400
Market St., Philadelphia,
PA 19103 USA
C) Wallcoverings & Matching Fabrics
4525 AD) W.L. Jackson Manufacturing Co., Inc.
P.O. Box 11168, Chattanooga,
TN 37401 USA

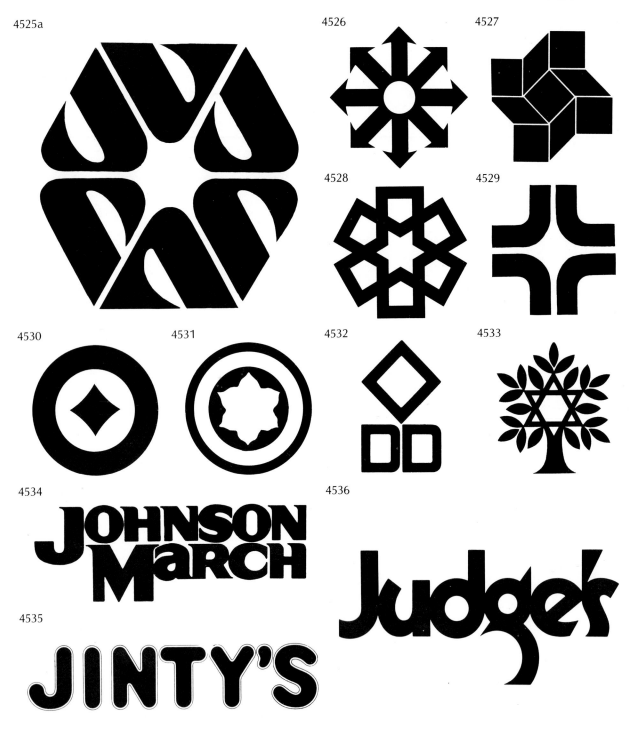

4525a

4526

4527

4528

4529

4530

4531

4532

4533

4534

JOHNSON MARCH

4536

Judge's

4535

JINTY'S

4524a AD) Jacobs Visconsi & Jacobs Co., USA
DES/A) Brandt-Worth
4526 AD) Jacobson Diversified, Phoenix, AZ, USA
DES/A) Marie Martel
4527 AD) Jörn Jörgensen, Oslo, NORWAY
DES/A) Paul Brand
4528 AD) Japan Six cities Trade Exhibition Assoc., Kyoto, JAPAN
DES/A) Nishiwaki Tomoichi & Heda Akisato
4529 AD) Johnson & Johnson, 501 George St., New Brunswick, NJ, USA
4530 AD) Journal of The History of Biology, Cambridge, MA, USA
DES/A) David Ford
4531 AD) Judo Club Jigoro Kano, Milano, ITALY
DES/A) Giancarlo Iliprandi
4532 AD) John Brereton & Co. Ltd., Ashburton Road East, Trafford Park, Manchester M17 1WB   ENGLAND
A subsidiary of Daniel Doncaster & Sons Ltd., Sheffield, ENGLAND
4533 AD) Jewish National Fund, London, ENGLAND
DES/A) Abram Games
4534 AD) Johnson March, 3018 Market St., Philadelphia, PA   19104   USA
4535 AD) Jinty Dresses Ltd., London, ENGLAND
ST) Crosby, Fletcher, Forbes
4536 AD) Judge's Property Management, New York, NY, USA
DES/A) David Leigh

4537

4538

4539

4540

4541

4542

4543

4544

4545

Jayco

4546

Jerry's of Chico

4547

JSI

4548

June-one

4537 SM) Jelen, Beograd, JUGOSLAVIA
      DES/A) Miloš Ciric
4538 AD) Jonneret S.A., Genève,
           SWITZERLAND
      DES/A) Michel Martina
4539 AD) Jahre Line, Sandefjor, NORWAY
      DES/A) Bruno Oldani
4540 AD) International Janitor Ltd., Camberley,
           Surrey, ENGLAND
      DES/A) Ulrich Aaupt
4541 AD) Jack's at the Beach, Santa Monica,
           CA, USA
      C)   Seafood Restaurant
4542 AD) Products distributed in Canada by
           Neil-Hildon Ltd.
      SM) James Neil Tools
           37 Six Point Rd., Toronto,
           Ont., M8Z 2X3   CANADA
4543 AD) Japan Society of Obstetrics &
           Gynecology, Tokyo, JAPAN
      DES/A) Kamekura Yusaku
4544 AD) Jaguar Knitting Mills Ltd., 86 Colville
           Rd., Toronto, Ont., M6M 2Y6
           CANADA
4545 AD) Jayco Inc., P.O. Box 460, Middleburry,
           IN   46540   USA
4546 AD) Jerry's of Chico
      DES/A) Charles Oburn
      ST) Image Group
4547 AD) John Strauss International, 160 East
           Erie St., Chicago, IL 60611   USA
4548 AD) June-one Stores Ltd., 1625 Dublin
           Ave., Winnipeg, Man., CANADA

4549

4550

4551

4552

4553

4554

4555

4556

4557

4558

4559

4560

4561

4562

4549 AD) Japan Restaurant, Köln-Braunsfeld, Melatengürtel 21, GERMANY

4550 AD) Jerusalem Plaza, 47 King George St., Jerusalem, ISRAEL

4551 AD) Jagdish J. Chavda, P.O. Box 336, Oviedo, Fl, USA
DES/A) Jagdish J. Chavda

4552 AD) Jackson Tool & Engineering, P.O. Box 309, Brampton, Ont., CANADA

4553 AD) Charles Jourdan/Paris, 5 Köln 1, Hohe Strasse 166-168, GERMANY

4554 AD) Japhet Bank Ltd., ISRAEL
C) Banking

4555 AD) Johnson & Johnson, 501 George St., New Brunswick, NJ 08903 USA

4556 AD) Jackson Brothers (London) Ltd., Kingsway, Waddon, Croydon CR9 4DG ENGLAND

4557 AD) Japan Industrial Designers Association, Tokyo, JAPAN
DES/A) Kamekura Yusaku

4558 AD) Julien et Mége, Lyon, FRANCE
DES/A) Technès

4559 AD) Jacque Salis, 79 Yorkville Ave., Toronto, Ont. M5R 1C1 CANADA
C) Nail Salon

4560 AD) Abbey Glen Property Corp., 123 Edward St., Toronto, Ont., CANADA
SM) Jolibourg; graphic typography, wordmark & symbol style
C) Country Estate Development

4561 AD) Jato Inc., 214 Avenue St-Sacrement, Quebec City, Que. CANADA

4562 AD) Jagdish J. Chavda, P.O. Box 336, Oviedo, FL, USA
DES/A) Jagdish J. Chavda

4563

4564

4565

4566

4567

4568

4569

4570

INSTRUMENTS

4571

4572

JOTUN

4573

JANO

4574

4575

J.P. Allen

4576

JUG CITY *more than milk*

4577

The Jupiter Ocean & Racquet Club

4563	AD)	Lesna Industrija, Javor, Pivka, JUGOSLAVIA
	DES/A)	Albert Kastelec
4564	AD)	Johnson Fry & Partners Ltd., 54 Grosvenor St., W1X 9FH, London, ENGLAND
4565	AD)	Joint Ethics Committee, P.O. Box 179, Grand Central Stn., New York, NY, USA
4566	AD)	Jerusalem Tower Hotel, 21 Hillel St., Jerusalem, ISRAEL
4567	AD)	Jade Leaf Co., HONG KONG
	DES/A)	Michael Miller Yu
4568	AD)	De Jong Painting Co., USA
	DES/A)	Otto H. Truemann
4569	AD)	C.E. Jamieson Co., 2051 Ambassador Dr., Windsor, Ont., CANADA
4570	AD)	J.J. Lloyd Instruments Ltd., Brook Ave., Warsash, Southampton SO3 6HP ENGLAND
4571	AD)	Jewish National Fund of Canada Montreal, Que. CANADA
4572	AD)	Jotungruppen, Sandefjord, NORWAY
4573	AD)	Sea Gliders Inc., 561 Chemin Champlain, Fabreville, Que., CANADA
	SM)	Jano, Product TM
4574	AD)	Japan Agricultural Co-op Associations, Tokyo, JAPAN
	DES/A)	Hayashi Yoshio
4575	AD)	J.P. Allen, Atlanta, GA, USA
4576	AD)	The Oshawa Group Ltd., 300 The East Mall, Islington, Ont., CANADA
	C)	Convenience Food Shop
	SM)	Jug City, Franchise Stores
4577	AD)	The Jupiter Ocean & Racquet Club Jon Mallard III, 1605 U.S. 1, Jupiter, FL 33458 USA

4578

4579

4580

4581

4582

4583

4584

4585

4586

4587

4588

4589

4590

4591

4592

J-14

Legend
- AD) Advertiser/Client
- DIR) Art Director
- DES/A) Designer, Artist
- ST) Studio, Agency
- C) Category
- SM) Symbol
- TM) Trademark

4593 AD) Wilhelm Knoll. Exquisite Polster-
         möbel, 7160 Gaildorf/Württbg

4594 AD) King Motor Center, East Sunrise
         Blvd., USA

4595 AD) Krautkramer-Branson, NDT North
         America, Subsidiary of SmithKline
         Corp., 76 Progress Dr., Stamford,
         CT 06902 USA

4596 AD) Keystone Park, Bristol Township,
         Bucks County, PA, USA

4597 AD) Kent Cambridge Instrument Co.,
         Div. of Kent Cambridge Corp.,
         80 Doncaster Ave., Thornhill,
         Ont., L3T 1L3 CANADA

4598 AD) Knudsen Creamery Co., Los Angeles,
         CA, USA
     DES/A) Vance Jonson

4599 AD) Klose Kollektion 73, Karl-Heinz
         Klosse-Sitzmöbelfabrik 4471 Herzlake
         Postfach 25, SWEDEN

4600 AD) Klik, Barcelona, SPAIN
     DES/A) Ribast Creus

4601 AD) Kenlin Enterprises, Inc., 1530 Old
         Skokie Rd., Highland Park,
         IL 60035 USA

4602 AD) AB Karl Anderson & Söner
         Möbelfabrik, Huskvarna, SWEDEN

4603 AD) Korea Trade Promotion Corp.,
         I.P.O. Box 1621, Seoul, KOREA

4604 AD) Kailani Building, Honolulu, Miami, USA
     DES/A) Clarence Lee & Claire Trept

4605 AD) Kuhn and Drake; Summit, NJ, USA
     DES/A) James S. Ward and Arnold Saks

4606 AD) Kano Laboratories, 1075 Thompson
         Lane, Nashville, TN 37211 USA

4607 AD) Koppers Products Ltd., 19 Meteor Dr.,
         Rexdale, Ont., CANADA

4608 AD) Koss Ltd., 4112 South Service Rd.,
         Burlington, Ont., L7R 3X5 CANADA
     C) Electronic Fidelty Equipment

4609 SM) Kastilia TM for Quality Control Product

4610 AD) KT Furniture, 20100 South Alameda St., Compton, CA 90220 USA

4611 AD) Keymatch Computer Corp., 20 Sylvan Rd., Woburn, MA 01801 USA

4612 AD) Kem Electronic Corp., (an affiliate of the Intercraft Corp.) 225 Park Avenue S., New York, NY 10003, USA

4613 AD) KT Furniture, 24251 Frampton Ave., Harbor City, CA 90710 USA

4614 AD) Kennedy Data Systems, Inc., 31829 W. La Tienda Dr., Westlake Village, CA, USA

4615 AD) Key Advertising Service Ltd., 99 Doncaster Ave., Willowdale, Ont. CANADA

C) Commercial Printing & Direct Mail Service

4616 AD) Alfred Kill GMBH 7012 Fellbach, Schorndorfer Str. 33, GERMANY

4617 AD) Hans Kaufeld, Polstermöbelfabrik 4805 Brake/Bielefeld

4618 AD) KDI Paragon Inc., 12 Paulding St., Pleasantville, NY 10570 USA

4619 AD) Kasparians, Inc., Los Angeles, CA, USA

ST) The Graphics Studio

4620 AD) Drukkerij a Knijnenberg Nv.

4621 AD) Albert Kraftczyk Industrial Photography, Montreal, Que., CANADA

DES/A) Stuart Ash

ST) Gottschalk & Ash Ltd.

4622 AD) Keen Pipe & Supply Co., Los Angeles, CA, USA
DES/A) Thomas Laufer & Assoc.
4623 AD) Kohlenversorgungs AG., Basel, SWITZERLAND
DES/A) Igildo Biessele
4624 AD) Krengel Machine Co., Inc.
ST) Gordon Gutke Advertising Art
4625 AD) Klein Builders, Inc.
DES/A) Brian Schuiling
4626 AD) Kremer Automation Ltd., Reading, Bucks, ENGLAND
DES/A) Abram Games
4627 AD) Kay Jewelers
DES/A) Christopher Klumb
4628 AD) Kirjalike Oy, Helsinki, FINLAND
DES/A) Alfons Eder
4629 AD) Knechtel Wholesale Grocers Ltd., Kitchener, Ont., CANADA
DES/A) John S. Brown
4630 AD) Kunstoff AG. Reiden-Lucerne, SWITZERLAND
DES/A) Hans Hurter
4631 AD) Kossuth Köntvkiadó, Budapest, HUNGARY
DES/A) Judit Erdély
4632 AD) Bombones Keops-Blanxart, Barcelona, SPAIN
DES/A) Ribas & Creus
4633 AD) Kalin & Co., Winterthur, SWITZERLAND
DES/A) Ruedi Peter
4634 AD) KSB-Klein, Schanzling & Becker Nürnberg, WEST GERMANY
DES/A) Seigfreid Opermatt
4635 AD) W. Kröck, Dülken, WEST GERMANY
DES/A) Klaus Winterhager
4636 AD) Kantscho Kanev Sofia, BULGARIA
DES/A) Kantscho Kanev
4637 AD) Källbo Möbel AB, 280 64 Glimäkra, SWEDEN

K-13

4638

4639

4340

4641

4642

4643

4644

4645

4646

4647

4648

4649

KNOXVILLE

4650

4651

4652

kroy
industries inc.

4638 AD) Kastinger & Co., KG. Sportschuh-
fabrik, Seewalchen, AUSTRIA

4639 AD) Karin Schieber, 624 Indian Rd.,
Toronto, Ont., M6P 2C6   CANADA

4640 SM) K Way
C) Women's Wear Product-giacche e
pantaloni antivento e antipioggia in
vendita nei migliori negozi di articoli
sportivi

4641 AD) Kastle Gesellschaft M.B.H., Reid I/
Innkreis, Oberstereich, AUSTRIA

4642 AD) Koopturist - Sofia, POLAND
C) Travel Agency
DES/A) Stephen Kantscheff

4643 AD) Kruper Pulp & Paper Ltd., (Fine Paper
Division) CANADA
DES/A) Ernest Roch, Montreal

4644 AD) Kundkredit, Box 45103,
Kontorsadress Drottninggatan 97.
104 30, Stockholm, SWEDEN

4645 AD) Kinsho Company, Kyoto, JAPAN
DES/A) Nishiwaki Tomoichi

4646 AD) Karl Kessel, Paris, FRANCE
DES/A) Felix Beltrán

4647 AD) K+L Color Service Inc., K+L
Building, 10 E. 46th St., New York,
NY, USA

4648 AD) Kobayashi Engineering Works Ltd.,
JAPAN

4649 AD) Knoxville University of Tennessee
705 Gay St., Knoxville, TN   37902
USA

4650 AD) Kansas City Art Institute, Kansas
City, MO, USA
ST) Overlockttowe & Co.

4651 AD) Ksan Association, Hazelton, B.C.,
CANADA

4652 AD) Kroy Industries Inc., (Pierce Division)
6238 Oasis Ave. N., Stillwater,
MN   55082   USA

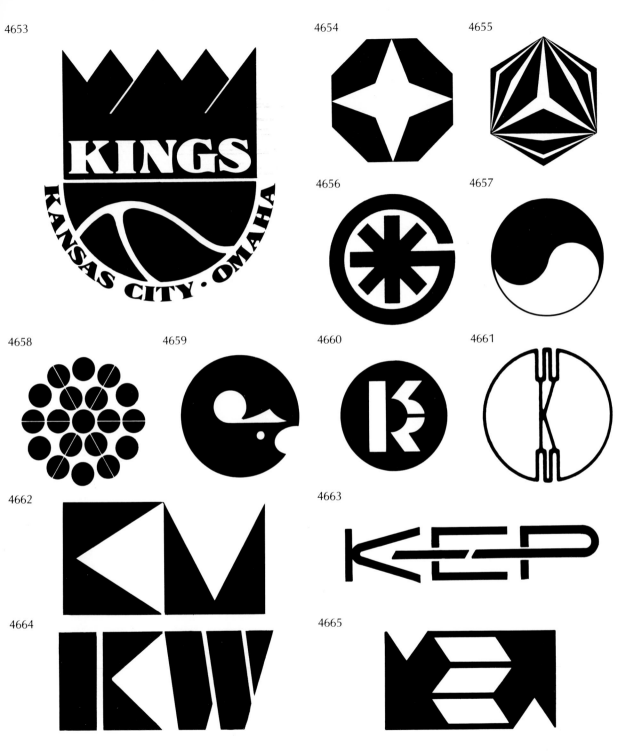

4653   AD)   Kings Professional Basketball Club, Inc., 210 W. 14th St., Kansas City, MO 64105 USA

4654   AD)   Koyo Co., Ltd., Osaka, JAPAN
       DES/A)   Ohtaka Takeshi

4655   AD)   Kyowa Hakko Co., Ltd., Tokyo, JAPAN
       DES/A)   Kamekura Yusako

4656   AD)   Kingston Gifts Ltd., Hull, ENGLAND
       ST)   Eurographic Ltd.

4657   AD)   Korean Construction Industry, Agent to USA: Asia Pacific Capital Corp., Ltd., Managed by Bank of America N.T. and S.A.

4658   AD)   Kosmos, Aalsmeer, NETHERLANDS
       DES/A)   Jan Jaring

4659   AD)   Kölner Aquarium Zoo, Köln, GERMANY

4660   AD)   Kasto Racine, 100 McClue Rd., Monroeville, PA 15146 USA

4661   AD)   Knoll International, 745 Fifth Ave., New York, NY 10022 USA

4662   AD)   Keane Monroe Corp., P.O. Box 1071, Monroe, NC 28110 USA

4663   AD)   Kessler-Ellis Products Co., 120 First Ave., Atlantic Highlands, NJ 07716 USA
       Scarborough, Ont., CANADA

4665   AD)   Kirkup Realty Corp., Toronto, Ont., CANADA

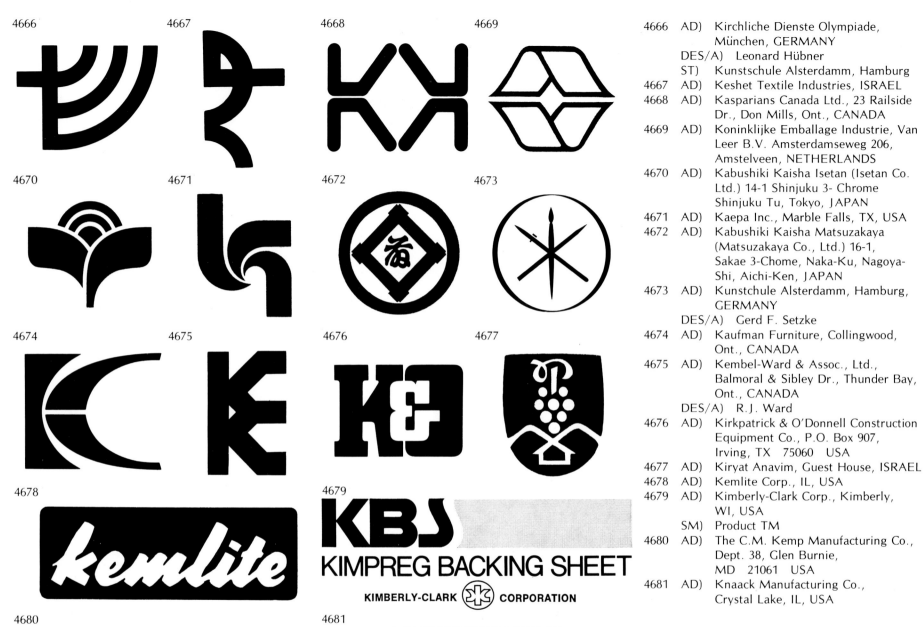

4666

4667

4668

4669

4670

4671

4672

4673

4674

4675

4676

4677

4678

4679

KIMPREG BACKING SHEET

KIMBERLY-CLARK CORPORATION

4680

4681

4666	AD) Kirchliche Dienste Olympiade, München, GERMANY
	DES/A) Leonard Hübner
	ST) Kunstschule Alsterdamm, Hamburg
4667	AD) Keshet Textile Industries, ISRAEL
4668	AD) Kasparians Canada Ltd., 23 Railside Dr., Don Mills, Ont., CANADA
4669	AD) Koninklijke Emballage Industrie, Van Leer B.V. Amsterdamseweg 206, Amstelveen, NETHERLANDS
4670	AD) Kabushiki Kaisha Isetan (Isetan Co. Ltd.) 14-1 Shinjuku 3- Chrome Shinjuku Tu, Tokyo, JAPAN
4671	AD) Kaepa Inc., Marble Falls, TX, USA
4672	AD) Kabushiki Kaisha Matsuzakaya (Matsuzakaya Co., Ltd.) 16-1, Sakae 3-Chome, Naka-Ku, Nagoya-Shi, Aichi-Ken, JAPAN
4673	AD) Kunstchule Alsterdamm, Hamburg, GERMANY
	DES/A) Gerd F. Setzke
4674	AD) Kaufman Furniture, Collingwood, Ont., CANADA
4675	AD) Kembel-Ward & Assoc., Ltd., Balmoral & Sibley Dr., Thunder Bay, Ont., CANADA
	DES/A) R.J. Ward
4676	AD) Kirkpatrick & O'Donnell Construction Equipment Co., P.O. Box 907, Irving, TX 75060 USA
4677	AD) Kiryat Anavim, Guest House, ISRAEL
4678	AD) Kemlite Corp., IL, USA
4679	AD) Kimberly-Clark Corp., Kimberly, WI, USA
	SM) Product TM
4680	AD) The C.M. Kemp Manufacturing Co., Dept. 38, Glen Burnie, MD 21061 USA
4681	AD) Knaack Manufacturing Co., Crystal Lake, IL, USA

K-16

4682 AD) Kay Laboratories Inc., 11675 Sorrento
Valley Rd., San Diego,
CA 92121 USA

C) Kwik Kold TM Product, Cooling
Packages

4683 AD) Kitchen Kompact, Inc., KK Plaza,
Jeffersonville, IN 47130 USA

4684 AD) Boris Kroll Fabrics Inc., D & D
Building, 979 Third Ave. at 58th St.,
New York, NY, USA

4685 AD) Karo, Siedlce, POLAND

C) Knitwear Manufacturer

DES/A) Zbigniew Marjandwski

4686 AD) Kerr-McGee Chemical Corp.,
Kerr-McGee Center, Oklahoma City,
OK 73125 USA

4687 AD) Kusnierz, Łódź, POLAND

C) Fur Manufacturer

DES/A) Ryszard Sidorowski

4688 AD) 'T Koggeschip NV. Amsterdam,
HOLLAND

C) Printers & Publishers

DES/A) Otto Treumann

4689 AD) Kantonsspital, Luzern,
SWITZERLAND

C) School for pre-natal care

DES/A) Mark Zeugin

4690 AD) Kinley, (Product of Coca-Cola),
ISRAEL

ST) Dahaf, Tel Aviv, ISRAEL

4691 AD) Effem Foods Ltd., 920 Yonge St.,
Toronto, Ont., M4W 3C7 CANADA

C) Small domestic utensils and containers

SM) Product TM ''Klix''

4692 AD) Kibbutz Inns, Ayelet Hashahar,
ISRAEL

4693 AD) Drogerie Kohler, Neuenkirch,
SWITZERLAND

DES/A) Atelier Stadelmann Bisig

4694 AD) Display Arts, 74 Niagara St., Toronto,
Ont., M5V 1C5 CANADA

SM) Product TM ''Klem''

4695 AD) Karobes Ltd., Queensway,
Leamington Spa, ENGLAND

C) Sports Equipment

4696 AD) Kruger Pulp and Paper Ltd., 3285
Bedford Rd., Montreal,
Que. H3S 1G5   CANADA
New 1976 C.I. Logo
Prev. C.I. Logo See #4643

4697 AD) Keystone Mortgage Co., Los Angeles,
CA, USA
DES/A) James L. Potocki

4698 AD) K-2 Ski Canada Ltd., 4201 6th St.
S.E., Calgary, Alta., CANADA
C) Ski Equipment

4699 AD) Kewanee National Bank
DES/A) Lawrence E. Pelini

4700 AD) Kuoni Travel Ltd., Deepdene House,
Dorking, Surrey, ENGLAND

4701 AD) Korson's Tree Farm, USA
DES/A) Donald McLean
ST) George N. Sepetys & Associates

4702 AD) The Knack (div. of Ratner Corp.)
730 13th St., San Diego, CA, USA

4703 AD) Kathie Keller, 176 Spring St., New
York, NY   10012   USA
C) Hand tailored clothes for men and
women

4704 AD) Kopp Variators, 75 Densley Ave.,
Toronto, Ont., CANADA

4705 AD) Kenting Exploration Services,
6004 Centre St. S.,
Calgary, Alta., CANADA

4706 AD) Kailua Chamber of Commerce
DES/A) Swatek & Starr
4707 AD) Kraftco Corp., Glenview, IL, USA
4708 AD) Knight Accounting Services,
Toronto, Ont., CANADA
DES/A) Steve Gill
4709 AD) Katimavik Inc., Montreal,
Que., CANADA
DES/A) Yvon Laroche & Pierre Yves
Pelletier
4710 AD) Kuhlman Corp.
DES/A) Thomas H. Pfahlert
ST) Flourney & Gibbs, Inc.
4711 AD) Kyoho Co., Ltd., Kyoto, JAPAN
DES/A) Nishiwaki Tomoichi & Ueda
Akisato
4712 AD) Kopp Bauunternehmung,
SWITZERLAND
DES/A) Hansruedi Scheller
4713 AD) Fr. Koch, SWITZERLAND
DES/A) Klaus Grözinger
4714 AD) Concentro Service Corp., Box 6202,
1815 E. Wendover Ave.,
Greensboro, NC, USA
SM) Kwik-Set TM
4715 AD) Teledyne Taber, 455 Bryant St.,
North Tonawanda, NY, USA
SM) Kenco TM
4716 AD) Kingswell Sports Co., Ltd.,
Cliftonville Rd., Northampton
NN1 5EG ENGLAND

4717 AD) Gebr. Knecht, SWITZERLAND
DES/A) Hans R. Woodtli
4718 AD) Konservative-Christlichsoziale
Volkspartei, St. Gallen,
SWITZERLAND
DES/A) Robert Geisser
4719 AD) Kaneda Ski Manufacturing Co.,
JAPAN
DES/A) Nagai Kazumasa
4720 AD) Kronenberg
DES/A) Atelier Stadelmann Bisig
4721 AD) Kalamazoo Center
DES/A) Richard Deardorff
4722 AD) K-Products, Inc., Industrial Air Park,
Orange City, IA 51041 USA
4723 AD) KTVU Channel 2
DES/A) Michael Vanderbly & Dean Smith
4724 AD) Kickham Boiler and Engineering, Inc.
DES/A) Mel Zimmerman
4725 AD) Kalglo Electronics Co., Inc., P.O. Box
2062, Bethlehem, PA 18001 USA
4726 AD) Eli Lilly and Co. (Canada) Ltd.,
Toronto, Ont., CANADA
SM) Keflex, product TM
C) Pharmaceutical
4727 AD) Kangaroo Campers
ST) James Potocki & Associates

K-20

Legend AD) Advertiser/Client   SM) Symbol
      DIR) Art Director   TM) Trademark
      DES/A) Designer, Artist
      ST) Studio, Agency
      C) Category

4728 AD) Paul L'Anglais Inc., 2200 Yonge St.,
           Toronto, Ont., M4S 2C6 CANADA

4729 AD) Long Term Credit Bank of Japan, Ltd.
           Otemachi, Tokyo, JAPAN

4730 AD) Lear Siegler, Inc., Seymour
           Housewares Co., Seymour,
           IN 47274 USA

4731 AD) Lykes-Pasco Co., Clearwater, FL, USA
      DES/A) Charles MacMurray
      ST) Latham Tyler Jensen Inc.

4732 AD) Hans Kjell Larsen, Oslo, NORWAY
      DES/A) Paul Brand

4733 AD) Lok Box Inc., Boxwood Lane 1 Rd. #9,
           York, PA 17402 USA

4734 AD) Le Page & Son Ltd., 5525 Yonge
           St., Willowdale, Ont., CANADA

4735 AD) Laboratori Cosmochimici S.P.A.,
           Milano, ITALY
      DES/A) Walter Ballmer

4736 AD) Liquid Paper Ltd. of Canada,
           705 Progress Ave., Scarborough,
           Ont., CANADA

4737 AD) Lion Shipping Supplies (Ontario) Ltd.,
           1375 Aimco Blvd., Mississauga,
           Ont., L4W 1B5 CANADA

4738 AD) Lion Yachts, At Yacht Haven West,
           Washington Blvd., Stamford,
           CT 06902 USA

4739 AD) Gage Stationery Co. (a div. of DRG
           Ltd.) Georgetown, Ont./Longueuil,
           Que., CANADA
      SM) Product TM Lion Brand

4740 AD) Lucas Keelavite (Div. Joseph Lucas
           Can. Ltd.) Montreal, Toronto,
           Vancouver, CANADA

4741 AD) Luxor International, industrieterrein
           B-3660 Opglabbeek

4742 AD) Livingston Industries, 14550 W. 99th
           St., Lenexa, KS 66215 USA
           (New Wordmark & Logo)

4743 AD) Livingston Industries, 14550 W. 99th
           St., Lenexa, KS 66215 USA
           (Old Typography Name & Logo)

4744	AD) Lantana Boatyard, Inc., 808 N. Dixie Hwy., Lantana, FL 33460 USA
4745	AD) L & L Machinery, P.O. Box 190, North Wilkesboro, NC 28659 USA
4746	AD) La Salle Paper, 215 W. Colorado Ave., Las Vegas, NV 89102 USA
4747	AD) Pneumatic GmbH., D-5 Köln 1, Ubierring 11, Fed. Rep. GERMANY
4748	AD) Charles R. Lister International, Inc. 30 Rockefeller Plaza, Suite 1917, New York, NY 10020 USA
4749	AD) Limestone Products Corp. of America, Newton, NJ, USA
4750	AD) AB Lindåsbeslag, Box 21, 331 01 Värnamo, GERMANY
4751	AD) Leeds & Northrup, North Wales, PA 19454 USA
4752	AD) Lapponia Jewelry Ltd., Helsinki, FINLAND
	DES/A) Eka Lainio
4753	AD) Laresco, 900 Ave. Jean-Marchand, Lauzon, Que., CANADA
4754	AD) Gunther Lambert Import, Dusseldorf, GERMANY
	C) Importers
	DES/A) F.K. von Oppeln
4755	AD) Karl Thomas KG, 2140 Bremervörde Postfach 83, GERMANY
	SM) Lattoflex, product TM
	C) Gutschein fur eine umfassende Systemdokumentation
4756	AD) Leisuretron, 132 W. 31st St., New York, NY 10001 USA
4757	AD) Parke, Davis & Co., Ltd., Montreal, Que., H4L 4Y7 CANADA
	SM) Loestrin TM
4758	AD) New York's Lighting Gallery, 417 Bleecker St., New York, NY 10014 USA
4759	AD) Leicht, via larga; P. 2A S. Stefano 5, Milano, ITALY

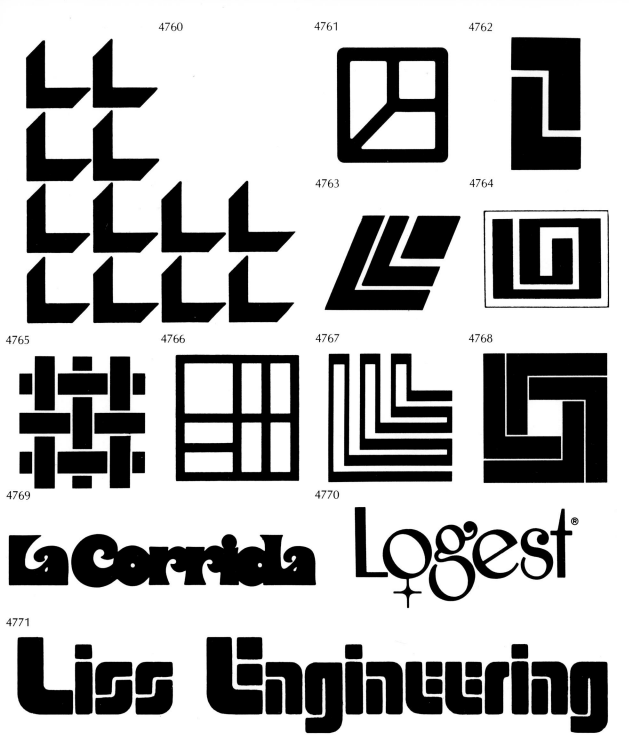

4760

4761

4762

4763

4764

4765

4766

4767

4768

4769

4770

4771

4760 AD) Lehndorff Corp., Suite 700, 360 Bay St., Toronto, Ont., M5H 2V6 CANADA

4761 AD) C.H. Leavell & Co., 13612 Midway Rd., Suite 600, Dallas, TX 75240 USA
A subsidiary of The Leavell Co.

4762 AD) Laidlaw Lumber Co., Ltd., Weston, Ont., CANADA
DES/A) Rudy Eswarin (also see #4828)
ST) Stewart & Morrison Ltd.

4763 AD) Lake Chemical Co., 250 N. Washtenaw Ave., Chicago, IL 60612 USA

4764 AD) University of Lethbridge, 4401 University Dr., Lethbridge, Alta., T1K 3M4 CANADA

4765 AD) Jach Lenor Larsen, New York, NY, USA
DES/A) Arnold Saks & James S. Ward
ST) Ward & Saks, Inc.

4766 AD) Light Metal Founders Association, Birmingham, ENGLAND
DES/A) Roger O. Denning

4767 AD) Loomloft Designs Ltd., Toronto, Ont. CANADA
DES/A) Jean Morin & Karen Bulow

4768 AD) Leo Loser, Hard, AUSTRIA
DES/A) Othmar Motter
ST) Vorarlberger Graphic

4769 AD) La Corrida, 3536 N. Federal Hwy., Fort Lauderdale, FL, USA

4770 AD) Cyanamid of Canada Ltd., P.O. Box 1039, Montreal, Que. H3C 2X4 CANADA
SM) Lederle Products Department

4771 AD) Liss Engineering, 1366-H Logan Ave., Costa Mesa, CA 92626 USA

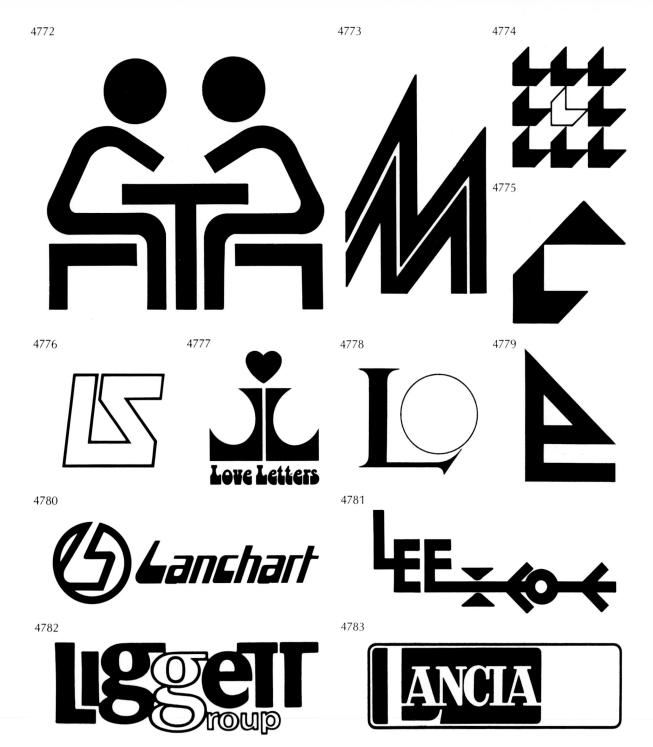

4772

4773

4774

4775

4776

4777

Love Letters

4778

4779

4780

Lanchart

4781

LEE

4782

Liggett **Group**

4783

LANCIA

4784

4785

4786

4787

4788

4789

4790

4791

4792

4793

4794

4795

4796

4784 AD) Löw and Manz, Loma-Bausystem,
Basel, SWITZERLAND
DES/A) Igildo Biesele
4785 AD) La Barge Inc., 20 S. Fourth St.,
St. Louis, MO 63102 USA
4786 AD) Leidschenhge Nv, Leidschendam,
HOLLAND
DES/A) Benno Wissing
4787 AD) Laboratories Goupil, Cachan, FRANCE
ST) Lonsoale Design
4788 AD) Lipa, Silistra, BULGARIA
DES/A) Stephan Kantscheff
4789 AD) A. Long Products Ltd., Harbour Rd.,
Rye, East Sussex TN31 7TE
ENGLAND
4790 AD) Lea Valley Regional Park Authority,
Enfield, ENGLAND
DES/A) David Lock
4791 AD) Luís López & Guillermo Sáez,
Barcelona, SPAIN
DES/A) Ribas & Creus
4792 AD) Landesverband Bayerischer
Bauinnungen, Munich, GERMANY
DES/A) Wolf D. Zimmermann
4793 AD) Lawron Industries Ltd., Toronto,
Ont., CANADA
DES/A) René Demers
4794 AD) Lucidity Inc., New York, USA
DES/A) A. Mitelman
4795 AD) Lever Data Processing System,
New York, USA
DES/A) Dominick Sarica
4796 AD) Ladybug Magazine, Philadelphia,
PA, USA
DES/A) Jay Dillon

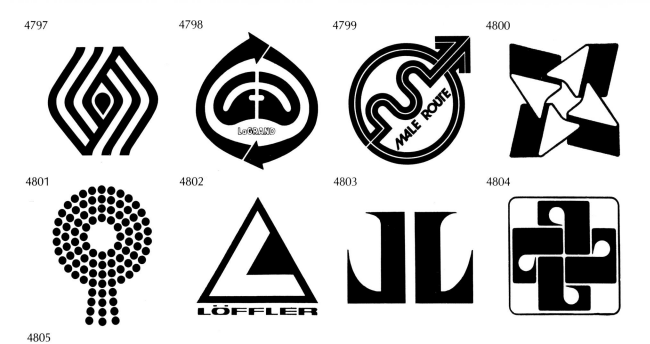

4797   **4798**   **4799**   **4800**

4801   **4802**   **4803**   **4804**

4805

LAVAL THE GROWING CITY

4806   **4807**

Leland Tube

LEPAGE'S Gel CONTACT CEMENT

4808   **4809**

LAKEHAVEN

LUNG MEI TRADING COMPANY

4797	AD)	Lantern Festival '75, HONG KONG
	DES/A)	Michael Miller Yu
4798	AD)	Lagrand Chain Corp., 4000 North West St., Helens Rd., Portland, OR, USA
4799	AD)	Lewis Shoes Ltd., 4900 Bourg St., Montreal, Que., CANADA
	SM)	Product TM
4800	AD)	Lambert Frères & Compagnie, 27, rue de Lisbonne, Paris 75008, FRANCE
4801	AD)	Lutheran Fraternal Organizations, Appleton, WI, USA
4802	AD)	Elfriede Loffler Gesellschaft m.b.H., Südtirolerstrasse 41, A-4910 Ried im Innkreis, AUSTRIA
4803	AD)	Lord Label Co., 268 Main St., Hackensack, NJ 07601 USA
4804	AD)	The Landmark Inn, 4150 Albert St. S., Regina, Sask., CANADA
4805	AD)	Laval—''The Growing City'' Development Commissioner, 1 Place du Souvenir, Laval, Que., CANADA
4806	AD)	Leland Tube Co., 20 Harmich Rd., South Plainfield, NJ 07080 USA
4807	AD)	Lepage's Ltd., 50 West Dr., Bramalea, Ont. L6T 2J4 CANADA
	C)	Contact Cement
	SM)	Gel TM
4808	AD)	Lakehaven, USA
	ST)	Unicom
4809	AD)	Lung Mei Trading Co., 584 Bank St., No. 2, Ottawa, Ont. K1S 3T3 CANADA

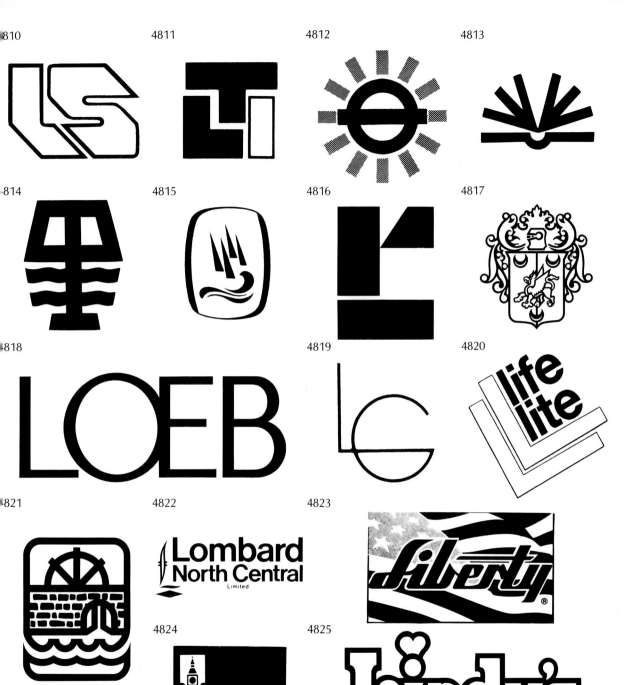

4810
4811
4812
4813

4814
4815
4816
4817

4818
4819
4820

4821
4822
4823

4824
4825

4810 AD) Lamson & Sessions of Canada Ltd., 20 Rangemore Rd., Toronto, Ont., CANADA
4811 AD) L.T.I. Corp., USA
4812 AD) London Transport Coach Tours, London, ENGLAND
4813 AD) Board of Education, City of London, London, ENGLAND
4814 AD) Lake Ontario Cement Ltd., 2 Carlton St., Toronto, Ont., CANADA
4815 AD) Lanier Islands Rentals, P.O. Box 1213, Buford, GA 30518 USA
4816 AD) Lan Ron Inc., Pasedena, CA, USA
       DES/A) Frank R. Cheatham
       ST) Porter & Goodman Design
4817 AD) The Lindenwood Colleges, St. Charles, MO, USA
       C) Sesquincentennial Redesign of College Coat of Arms
       ST) PR & D Creative Marketing Communications
4818 AD) Loeb Department Store, Berne, SWITZERLAND
4819 AD) Lev Gard Properties, Inc., Atlanta, GA, USA
4820 AD) William Scully Ltd., 2090 Moreau, Montreal, Que., H1W 2M3   CANADA
4821 AD) Lowell, MA, USA
       DES/A) Marya Kraus
       ST) Fly Specks Inc.
4822 AD) Lombard North Central Ltd., 2 Purley Way, Croydon CR9 3BL   ENGLAND
4823 AD) Liberty Trouser Co., 2301 First Ave., N., Birmingham, AL, USA
4824 AD) London Tourist Board, London, ENGLAND
4825 AD) Lindy's of Flamingo Hotel
       C) Dining
       DES/A) Mike Miller
       ST) Graphic Art Services

L-19

4826

4827

4828

4829

4830

4831

4832

4833

4834

4835

4836

4837

LINCOLN
WELDERS

4838

LUMAX®
PULSED XENON LIGHT

4839

Landmark Banks

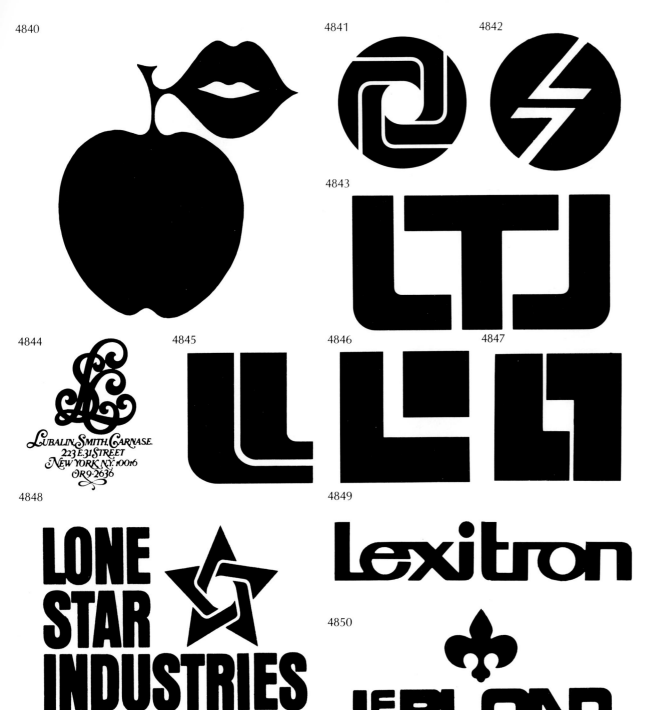

4840

4841

4842

4843

4844

4845

4846

4847

4848

4849

4850

4851

4852

4853

4854 **LAIRD**

4855

4856

4857 Loch Highland

4858 THE LOBSTER TRAP

4859

4860

4861

4862 LE CHÂTEAU

4863 *Lister*

4851 AD) LeFeure Studios Inc., Rochester NY, USA
ST) LeFeure Studios
4852 AD) LeBlanc & Royle Communications Towers Ltd., 514 Chartwell Rd., Oakville, Ont., CANADA
4853 AD) Leybold-Heraeus Vacuum Products Inc., 200 Seco Rd., Monroeville, PA 15146 USA
4854 AD) Camimel Laird & Co., Birkenhead, ENGLAND
DES/A) Geoffrey Gibbons
4855 AD) Lucas Industries Canada Ltd., Fluid Power Div., Montreal, Toronto, Vancouver, CANADA
SM) Lucas fluid power TM
4856 AD) Logan & Associates, USA
DES/A) Melville M. Drake
4857 AD) Loch Highland Subdivision, USA
DES/A) Wyatt L. Phillips
4858 AD) The Lobster Trap, 1962 Avenue Rd., Toronto, Ont., CANADA
C) Seafood Restaurant
4859 AD) Larson, Raikko & Weaver Inc.
DES/A) Anita Soos
4860 AD) Leisure Distributors, Inc.
DES/A) Don Primi
4861 AD) Herb Lubalin, 223 E. 31st St., New York, NY 10016 USA
C) Graphic Designer
DES/A) Herb Lubalin (also see #4844)
4862 AD) Chateau Stores Ltd., 1237 St. Catherine St. W., Montreal, Que., CANADA
4863 AD) R.A. Lister & Co. Ltd., Dursley, Gloucestershire, ENGLAND
C) Div. of Hawker Siddeley Group supplies mechanical, electrical and aerospace equipment
SM) Lister Diesels TM

4864

4865

4866

4867

4868

4869

louis
poulsen

4870

LaSalle
Steel

4871

4872

4873

CENTRE D'AFFAIRES
LE LOUVRE

4874

LILY
OF FRANCE

4864   AD)   Laguna Niguel Corp., CA, USA
4865   AD)   Lake City Bank, USA
        DES/A)   Bob Pilce
        ST)   Waldbilling & Besteman
        C)   Banking
4866   AD)   LaMair-Mulock-Condon Co., USA
        ST)   The Graphic Corporation
4867   AD)   Lucas Creek Park, USA
        DES/A)   Everett Forbes
4868   AD)   Linder Plaza
        DES/A)   Stan Hutchinson, Skip Morrow,
              Selje, Bond & Steward
4869   AD)   Louis Poulsen, USA
4870   AD)   La Salle Steel, Hammond, IN, USA
        ST)   Goldsholl Associates
4871   AD)   Lundwig & Co., WEST GERMANY
        DES/A)   Erich Unger
4872   AD)   Leslie Salt Co., San Francisco, CA,
              USA
        ST)   Walter Landor Associates
4873   AD)   LeLouvre, 2, Place du Palais Royal,
              BP 115, Paris, FRANCE
4874   AD)   Lily of France
        SM)   Product TM
        ST)   Stan Kovics Advertising Inc.

4875 AD) Burt Manion Interior Design Ltd., 20 Hazelton Ave., Toronto, Ont., CANADA

4876 AD) Mitchell/Mann, 125 N. Robertson Blvd., Los Angeles, CA 90048 USA

4877 AD) Mattew McAvan Enterprises Ltd., 211 Signet Dr., Toronto, Ont., CANADA
DES/A) William Tam
ST) Ken Borden Ltd.

4878 AD) Marr Electric Ltd., 2555 Hensall St., Mississauga, Ont., CANADA
DES/A) Brenda Langerfield
ST) Whitehead, Titherington & Bowyer Ltd.

4879 AD) Mariner Electronics, P.O. Box 51, Southampton S09 7DR ENGLAND

4880 AD) Merrill Manufacturing Corp. Merrill, WI, USA

4881 AD) Minter Homes Corp., Huntington, WV, USA

4882 AD) Morris Museum of Arts & Sciences, Morristown, NJ, USA

4883 AD) Muirhead Systems Ltd., 50 Galaxy Blvd., Rexdale, Ont., CANADA

4884 AD) Mid American Pipeline System, 1437 S. Boulder Ave., Tulsa, OK 74119 USA
DES/A) William Fritz
ST) Creswell, Munsell, Schubert & Zirbel Inc.

4885 AD) Marshall & Williams Co., 46 Baker St., Providence, RI 02905 USA

4886 AD) Metro/Kalvar, Inc., 745 Post Rd., Darien, CT 06820 USA

4887 AD) Marvel Kitchens, Inc., 1150 Wyoming Ave., Wyoming, PA 18644 USA

4888 AD) Mim Pompes, S.A. MIM, 44 rue Chanzy, 75011 Paris, FRANCE

4889 AD) Midwest Automation, Inc., 7940 Chicago Ave., S., Minneapolis, MN 55420 USA

4890 AD) Moyer Diebel Ltd., Queen Elizabeth Way, Jordan Station, Ont., CANADA

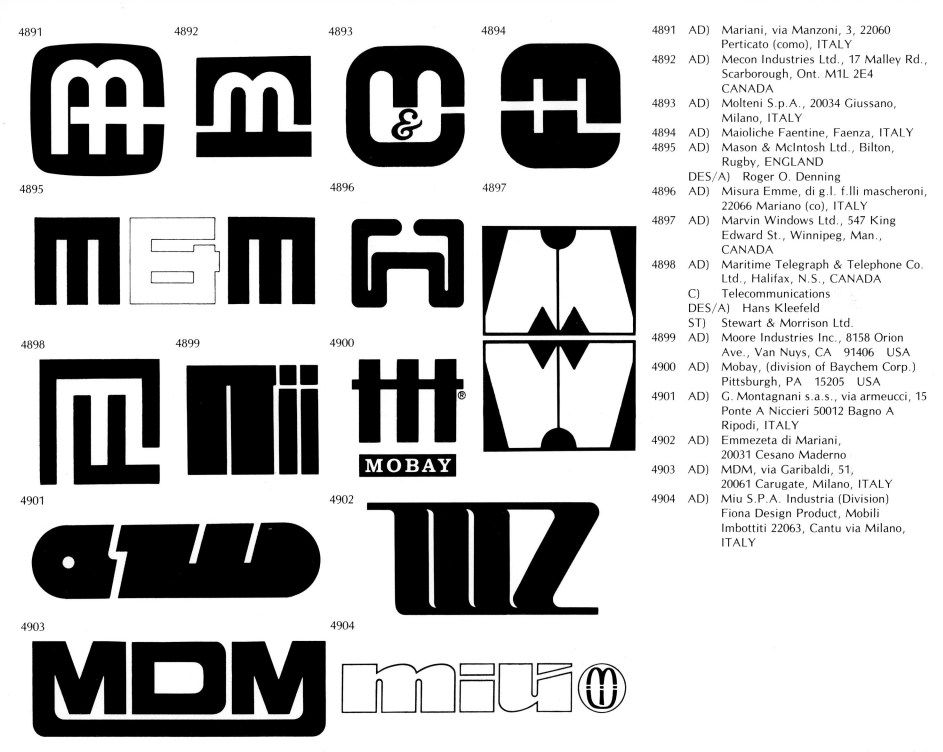

4891 AD) Mariani, via Manzoni, 3, 22060
           Perticato (como), ITALY
4892 AD) Mecon Industries Ltd., 17 Malley Rd.,
           Scarborough, Ont. M1L 2E4
           CANADA
4893 AD) Molteni S.p.A., 20034 Giussano,
           Milano, ITALY
4894 AD) Maioliche Faentine, Faenza, ITALY
4895 AD) Mason & McIntosh Ltd., Bilton,
           Rugby, ENGLAND
      DES/A) Roger O. Denning
4896 AD) Misura Emme, di g.l. f.lli mascheroni,
           22066 Mariano (co), ITALY
4897 AD) Marvin Windows Ltd., 547 King
           Edward St., Winnipeg, Man.,
           CANADA
4898 AD) Maritime Telegraph & Telephone Co.
           Ltd., Halifax, N.S., CANADA
      C)   Telecommunications
      DES/A) Hans Kleefeld
      ST) Stewart & Morrison Ltd.
4899 AD) Moore Industries Inc., 8158 Orion
           Ave., Van Nuys, CA 91406 USA
4900 AD) Mobay, (division of Baychem Corp.)
           Pittsburgh, PA 15205 USA
4901 AD) G. Montagnani s.a.s., via armeucci, 15
           Ponte A Niccieri 50012 Bagno A
           Ripodi, ITALY
4902 AD) Emmezeta di Mariani,
           20031 Cesano Maderno
4903 AD) MDM, via Garibaldi, 51,
           20061 Carugate, Milano, ITALY
4904 AD) Miu S.P.A. Industria (Division)
           Fiona Design Product, Mobili
           Imbottiti 22063, Cantu via Milano,
           ITALY

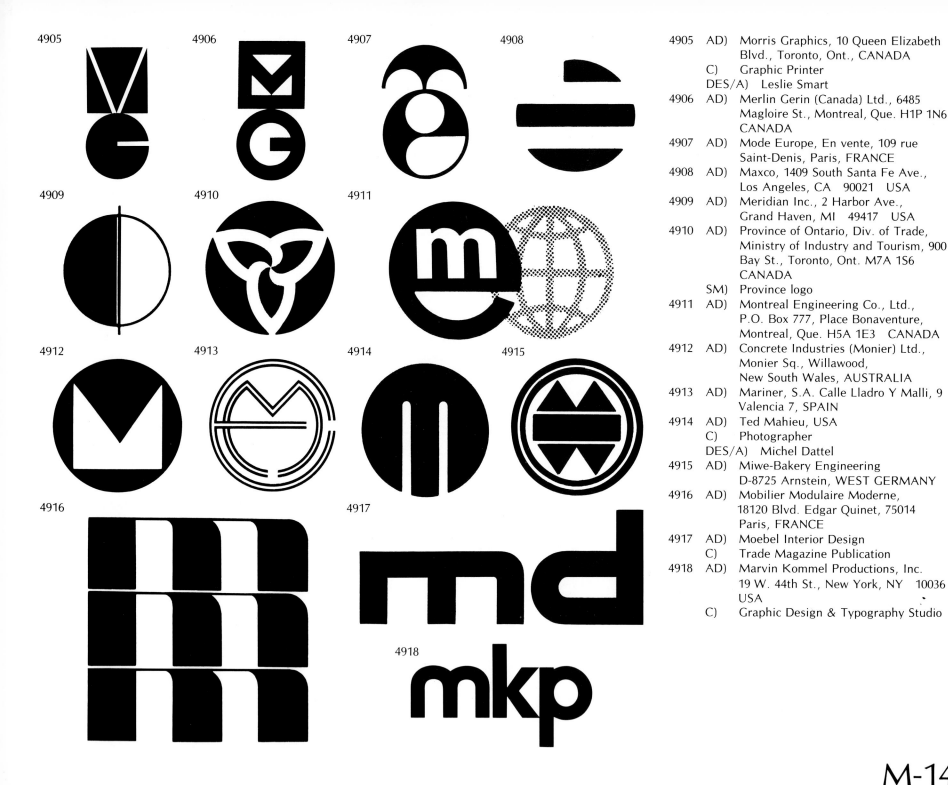

4905
4906
4907
4908
4909
4910
4911
4912
4913
4914
4915
4916
4917
4918

4905 AD) Morris Graphics, 10 Queen Elizabeth
Blvd., Toronto, Ont., CANADA
C) Graphic Printer
DES/A) Leslie Smart

4906 AD) Merlin Gerin (Canada) Ltd., 6485
Magloire St., Montreal, Que. H1P 1N6
CANADA

4907 AD) Mode Europe, En vente, 109 rue
Saint-Denis, Paris, FRANCE

4908 AD) Maxco, 1409 South Santa Fe Ave.,
Los Angeles, CA 90021 USA

4909 AD) Meridian Inc., 2 Harbor Ave.,
Grand Haven, MI 49417 USA

4910 AD) Province of Ontario, Div. of Trade,
Ministry of Industry and Tourism, 900
Bay St., Toronto, Ont. M7A 1S6
CANADA
SM) Province logo

4911 AD) Montreal Engineering Co., Ltd.,
P.O. Box 777, Place Bonaventure,
Montreal, Que. H5A 1E3 CANADA

4912 AD) Concrete Industries (Monier) Ltd.,
Monier Sq., Willawood,
New South Wales, AUSTRALIA

4913 AD) Mariner, S.A. Calle Lladro Y Malli, 9
Valencia 7, SPAIN

4914 AD) Ted Mahieu, USA
C) Photographer
DES/A) Michel Dattel

4915 AD) Miwe-Bakery Engineering
D-8725 Arnstein, WEST GERMANY

4916 AD) Mobilier Modulaire Moderne,
18120 Blvd. Edgar Quinet, 75014
Paris, FRANCE

4917 AD) Moebel Interior Design
C) Trade Magazine Publication

4918 AD) Marvin Kommel Productions, Inc.
19 W. 44th St., New York, NY 10036
USA
C) Graphic Design & Typography Studio

4919   AD)   Mariani Battista S.P.A., 20154 Milano, Via Cenisio, 32, ITALY

4920   AD)   Mathers & Haldenby, 10 St. Mary St., Toronto, Ont., CANADA
      C)   Architects-Planners

4921   AD)   Maple Leaf Press, 2382 Dundas St. W., Toronto, Ont., CANADA

4922   AD)   Marine Construction (UK) Ltd., Willments Shipyard, Hazel Rd., Woolston, Southampton SO2 7GB ENGLAND

4923   AD)   Marine Sciences, Los Angeles, CA, USA

4924   AD)   Mortell Co., Kankakee, IL 60901 USA

4925   AD)   Marr's Marine Ltd., 1470 Willson Pl., Winnipeg, Man. R3T 3N9 CANADA

4926   AD)   Mirage Yachts Ltd., 20 Cartier, Pointe Claire, Que., CANADA

4927   AD)   Maschinenfabrik Wiesbaden GmbH, 62 Wiesbaden, Postfach 409, GERMANY

4928   SM)   Maxalto, product TM

4929   AD)   N.R. Murphy Ltd., 430 Franklin Blvd., Cambridge, Ont. N1R 5T8 CANADA

4930   AD)   Monolithic Systems Corp., 2700 S. Shoshone, Englewood, CO, USA

4931   AD)   Mid-Continent Telephone Corp., USA

4932   AD)   Micro Plastics Co. Ltd., 410 Silvercreek Pky., Guelph, Ont., CANADA
      C)   Custom Profile Extruders

4933   AD)   Metal Koting Continuous Colour Coat Ltd., 1430 Martingrove Rd., Toronto, Ont., CANADA
      DES/A)   Ken Bordon
      ST)   Ken Bordon Ltd.

4934

4935

4936

4937

4938

4939

4940

4941

4942

4943

4944

4945

4934 AD) Meubles Furniture '76, Montreal, Que., CANADA
C) Furniture Trade Show Expositions
4935 AD) Manufacturing Opportunities Show (1976)
4936 AD) Queen Elizabeth Building, Exhibition Park, Toronto, Ont., CANADA
4937 SM) Modulo 3 - Product TM (a subsidiary of Tiffany Industries, Inc.) 100 Progress Parkway, Maryland Heights, MO 63043 USA
4938 AD) The Moorings, Ltd., P.O. Box 50059, New Orleans, LA 70150 USA
4939 AD) Massey Seating Co., Nashville, TN 37208 USA
4940 AD) Montina, Letto/Design Ilmari Tapiovaara, Montina Industria Sedie S. Giovanni Al, Natisone Udine, ITALY
4941 AD) Miami Jai-Alai, Miami, FL, USA A subsidiary of World Jai-Alai Inc.
4942 AD) Milli, 310 Main St. W., Hamilton, Ont., CANADA
4943 AD) Morguard Investment Services Ltd., P.O. Box 110, Toronto Dominion Centre, Toronto, Ont., CANADA
4944 AD) Mazda Motors, JAPAN
4945 AD) Moulds International, Inc.
DES/A) Joseph Addairo

4946 AD) Montgomery Ross & Partners, 365 Bay
St., Toronto, Ont., CANADA
C) Investment Brokers

4947 AD) Mitel Corp., Ltd., P.O. Box 13089,
Kanata, Ont. K2K 1X3   CANADA

4948 AD) Mabuchi Motor Co., Ltd., No. 3-14-11,
Tateishi, Katsushika-ku, Tokyo,
JAPAN

4949 AD) Maritime Computers Ltd.
Halifax, N.S., CANADA

4950 AD) Mariner's Cove, USA
DES/A) Everett Forbes

4951 AD) Montauk Yacht Club & Inn, Star
Island, Montauk, NY   11954   USA
C) Inn, Executive Conference Centre,
Marina and Spa

4952 AD) H.H. Marshall Ltd., 3731 MacKintosh
St., P.O. Box 1590, Halifax,
N.S. B3J 2Y3   CANADA

4953 AD) Gala Cosmetic Group (Smith &
Nephew Group Co.) Surbiton, Surrey
KT6 7LV   ENGLAND
SM) Miners Brand, product TM

4954 AD) Midland Insurance Co., Executive
Offices: One State St. Plaza,
New York, NY   10004   USA

4955 AD) Malcolite Corp., Monteray Park,
CA   91754   USA

4956 AD) The Mountain Shop, Aspen, CO, USA
DES/A) Remo Lavigno

4957 AD) M & T Bank, (Member FDIC)
Head Office: One M&T Plaza,
Buffalo, NY   14240   USA

4958 AD) Michael Hack
C) Dentist
DES/A) Alan Mazetti & Howard York

4959 AD) Management Selection Ltd., 17
Stratton St., London W1X 6DB
ENGLAND
C) Management Consultants

4960 AD) Moss, Lawson & Co., Ltd., 48 Yonge
St., Toronto, Ont. M5E 1G7
CANADA
C) Stock & Investment Broker

4961 AD) Marsh & McLennan, 74 Victoria St.,
Toronto, Ont., CANADA
C) Insurance

4962
4963
4964
4965
4966
4967
4968

MURO

4969
4970
4971

4972

Mappin & Webb

MT_10

4973

maruso

4974

mobilix®

4962 AD) Multiplex Display Fixture Co.,
1555 Larkin Williams Rd., Fenton,
MO 63026 USA

4963 AD) Mauna Kea Beach Hotel, Big Island of
Hawaii, Operated by Rockresorts, Inc.,
Kamuela, HI

4964 AD) Marquette Co., First American Center,
Nashville, TN, USA

4965 AD) The Myrick Co., 618 The Equitable
Building, 100 Peachtree St., N.E.,
Atlanta, GA 30303 USA
C) Realtors

4966 AD) Matheson Gas Products, Safety
Products Group, P.O. Box 85, 932
Paterson Plank Rd., East Rutherford,
NJ 07073 USA

4967 AD) Masson Agencies Ltée, P.O. Box 185,
Longueuil, Que. I4K 3R7 CANADA

4968 AD) Murographics, incorporating
Eurographics, Stafford Rd., Weston-
super-Mare, Avon BS23 3DN
ENGLAND

4969 AD) Meplex AG, St. Gallen,
SWITZERLAND
C) Metal Work
DES/A) Klaus Hofmann

4970 AD) Memphis, Director of Industrial
Development, Memphis, TN, USA

4971 AD) Trak Incorporated, Shawsheen Village
Station, Andover, MA 01810 USA
SM) Product TM

4972 AD) Mappin & Webb, 170 Regent St.,
W1R 6BQ, 25 Old Bond St., W1A 2JH;
65 Brompton Rd., Knightsbridge
SW2 1DB ENGLAND

4973 AD) Maruso, JAPAN
C) Tailor & Men's Shop
DES/A) Sasao Mitsuhiko

4974 SM) Mobilix, product TM
Burkhard Lübke, 483 Gütersloh 12,
Abteilung D Postfach 5070,
GERMANY

4975

4976

4977

4978

4979

4980

4981 4982

4983

4984 4985

4986

4987

4988

4989

4990

4991

4992

4993

4994

4995

4996

meridian
CAPITAL CORPORATION

4997

4998

4999

5000

5001

002

5003

5004

5005

006

5007

5008

009

5010

5011

4998 AD) Museum of Fine Arts, Montreal, Que.,
CANADA
DES/A) Fritz Gottschalk
ST) Gottschalk & Ash Ltd.
4999 AD) Mayatex Carpet Imports, 1201 Story
Ave., Louisville, KY 40206 USA
5000 AD) Italian Marble Industries, 200 Fifth
Ave., New York, NY 10001 USA
5001 AD) Hotel Melia, Puerto la Cruz,
VENEZUELA
5002 AD) Michael's Equipment (Ottawa) Ltd.,
P.O. Box 8232, Ottawa,
Ont. K1G 3H7 CANADA
5003 AD) Monolithic Memories, Inc., Eastern
Area Sales Office, New England
Region, New York Region, Central
Area Sales Office, Western Area Sales
Office; New York City, Long Island,
NY, USA
5004 AD) Magna, Petroleum Treating Div.,
Magnachem Ltd., 626-58th Ave., SE,
Calgary, Alta. T2H OP8 CANADA
5005 AD) Marconi Radar Systems Ltd., Writtle
Rd., Chelmsford CM1 3BN
ENGLAND
A GEC-Marconi Electronics Co.
5006 AD) Majestic Travel Services Ltd.,
Toronto, Ont., CANADA
DES/A) William Tam
ST) Ken Borden Ltd.
5007 AD) Ron Massey Design, Ltd., 4262 .
Belanger St., Montreal, Que.,
CANADA
5008 AD) Musto & Hyde Sails Ltd., Linden Rd.,
Benfleet, Essex SS7 4BQ ENGLAND
C) Sail Boat Builder
5009 AD) Mapleridge Realty Ltd., 101, 7603-104
St., Edmonton, Alta. T6E 4C3
CANADA
5010 AD) Douwe Egberts Koninklijke Tabaks-
fabriek-Koffiebranderijen-
Theehandel B.V., 16-19 Slachtedijk,
Joure, NETHERLANDS
SM) Mullingar's, product TM
5011 AD) Meridien Hotel, operated by
Compagnie Nationale Air France,
1 Square Max Hymans, 75015 Paris,
FRANCE

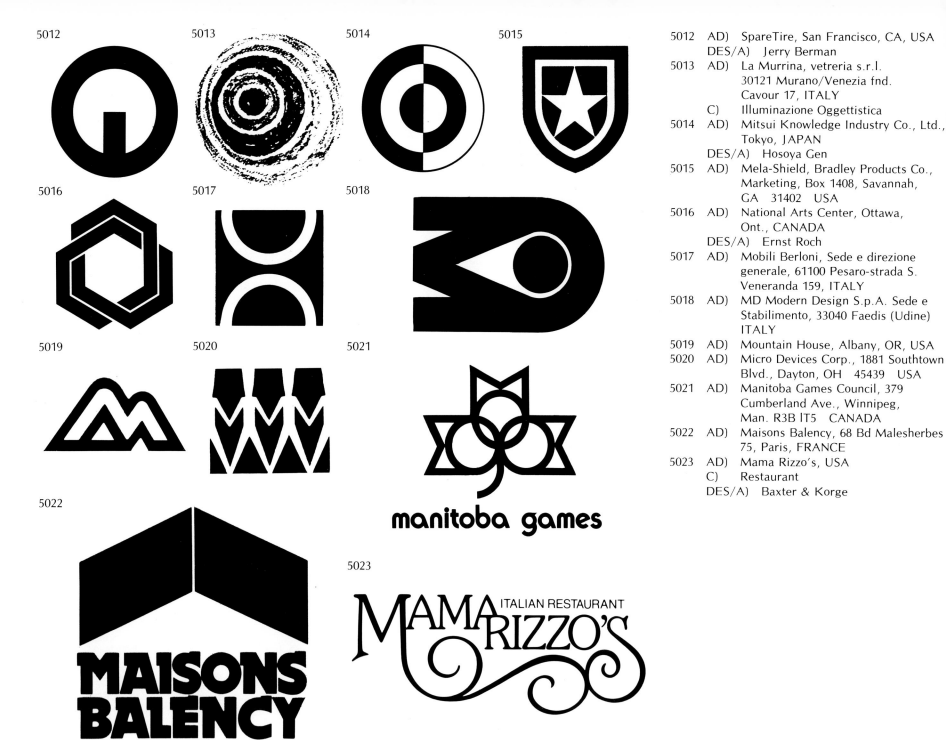

5012   AD)   SpareTire, San Francisco, CA, USA
      DES/A)   Jerry Berman
5013   AD)   La Murrina, vetreria s.r.l.
             30121 Murano/Venezia fnd.
             Cavour 17, ITALY
      C)   Illuminazione Oggettistica
5014   AD)   Mitsui Knowledge Industry Co., Ltd.,
             Tokyo, JAPAN
      DES/A)   Hosoya Gen
5015   AD)   Mela-Shield, Bradley Products Co.,
             Marketing, Box 1408, Savannah,
             GA   31402   USA
5016   AD)   National Arts Center, Ottawa,
             Ont., CANADA
      DES/A)   Ernst Roch
5017   AD)   Mobili Berloni, Sede e direzione
             generale, 61100 Pesaro-strada S.
             Veneranda 159, ITALY
5018   AD)   MD Modern Design S.p.A. Sede e
             Stabilimento, 33040 Faedis (Udine)
             ITALY
5019   AD)   Mountain House, Albany, OR, USA
5020   AD)   Micro Devices Corp., 1881 Southtown
             Blvd., Dayton, OH   45439   USA
5021   AD)   Manitoba Games Council, 379
             Cumberland Ave., Winnipeg,
             Man. R3B lT5   CANADA
5022   AD)   Maisons Balency, 68 Bd Malesherbes
             75, Paris, FRANCE
5023   AD)   Mama Rizzo's, USA
      C)   Restaurant
      DES/A)   Baxter & Korge

manitoba games

MAISONS BALENCY

MAMA RIZZO'S ITALIAN RESTAURANT

5026

5027

5028

5029

5030

5031

Danmark

Designer Artist Profile / Adam Moltke
(Ref. World of Logotypes File No. 120)
Adam Moltke, Graphic Designer
Bøgevej 36, DK-2740 Skovlunde, DENMARK

Training: Danish School of Arts, Crafts and Industrial Design. Professional Association: Industrial Designers Denmark (IDD)
Languages: English
Special Experience: Typography, packaging, total design, free-hand drawing.

5024　AD)　Angli, Herning, DENMARK
　　　　C)　Shirt Fabric
5025　AD)　Sanistaal AS, Vejle, DENMARK
　　　　C)　Steel & sanitary engineering
5026　AD)　Gilcodan AS, Copenhagen,
　　　　　　DENMARK
　　　　C)　Importers
5027　AD)　Laane - og Sparekassen, Copenhagen,
　　　　　　DENMARK
　　　　C)　Loan & Savings Bank
5028　AD)　Forening for Boghaandvoerk,
　　　　　　Copenhagen, DENMARK
　　　　C)　Association for fine book work
5029　AD)　J.P. Schmidt Jun., Copenhagen,
　　　　　　DENMARK
　　　　C)　Tobacco Company
5030　AD)　Danish Giftparcels, Copenhagen,
　　　　　　DENMARK
5031　AD)　J.B.S., Herning, DENMARK
　　　　C)　Men's Underwear

5032

5033

5034

5035

5036

5037

5038

5039

5040

5041

5042

5043

Legend   AD)   Advertiser/Client
          DIR)   Art Director
          DES/A)   Designer, Artist
          ST)   Studio, Agency
          C)   Category
          SM)   Symbol Mark
          TM)   Trademark

5032   AD)   Nymark Drug Stores, Toronto, Ont., CANADA
        C)   Drug Store Chain
5033   AD)   NCA Sinigaglia, Corso di Porta Romana 7, Milano, ITALY
5034   AD)   Nordtek Import-Export GMBH 6946 Weinheim-Lü, Wintergasse 60, GERMANY
5035   AD)   Noresco Manufacturing Co., Ltd., 100 Floral Pkwy., Toronto, Ont., CANADA
5036   AD)   W.H. Nichols Co., USA
        ST)   Ampersano Graphics Communicators
5037   AD)   Newark International Plaza, Newark, NJ, USA
5038   AD)   National Semiconductors Ltd., 331 Cornelia St., Plattsburgh, NY   12901   USA
5039   AD)   Nikko, JAPAN
5040   AD)   Nygren-Dahly Co., 1422 Altgeld St., Chicago, IL   60614   USA
5041   AD)   Nanni s.r.l. via democrito 9, 20127 Milano, ITALY
5042   AD)   National Sea Products Ltd., Duke St. Tower, Scotia Sq., Halifax, N.S., CANADA
5043   AD)   National Home Center, Home Improvement '76, Exposition Offices: 600 Talcott Rd., Park Ridge, IL   60068   USA

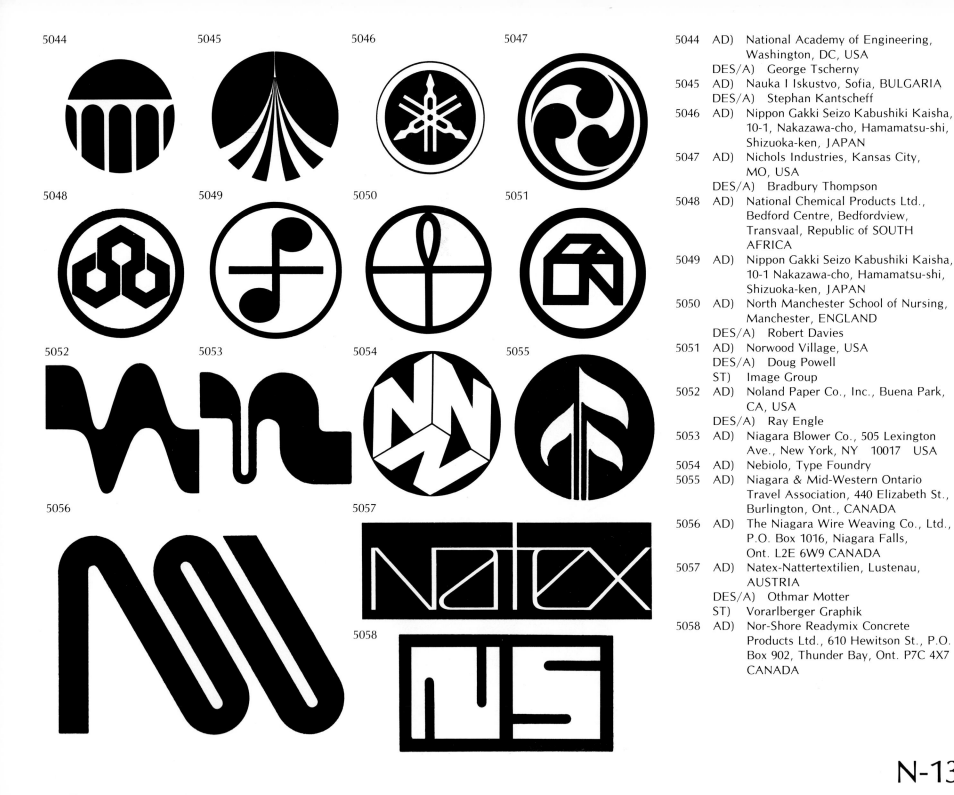

5044
5045
5046
5047
5048
5049
5050
5051
5052
5053
5054
5055
5056
5057
5058

5044 AD) National Academy of Engineering, Washington, DC, USA
      DES/A) George Tscherny
5045 AD) Nauka I Iskustvo, Sofia, BULGARIA
      DES/A) Stephan Kantscheff
5046 AD) Nippon Gakki Seizo Kabushiki Kaisha, 10-1, Nakazawa-cho, Hamamatsu-shi, Shizuoka-ken, JAPAN
5047 AD) Nichols Industries, Kansas City, MO, USA
      DES/A) Bradbury Thompson
5048 AD) National Chemical Products Ltd., Bedford Centre, Bedfordview, Transvaal, Republic of SOUTH AFRICA
5049 AD) Nippon Gakki Seizo Kabushiki Kaisha, 10-1 Nakazawa-cho, Hamamatsu-shi, Shizuoka-ken, JAPAN
5050 AD) North Manchester School of Nursing, Manchester, ENGLAND
      DES/A) Robert Davies
5051 AD) Norwood Village, USA
      DES/A) Doug Powell
      ST) Image Group
5052 AD) Noland Paper Co., Inc., Buena Park, CA, USA
      DES/A) Ray Engle
5053 AD) Niagara Blower Co., 505 Lexington Ave., New York, NY 10017 USA
5054 AD) Nebiolo, Type Foundry
5055 AD) Niagara & Mid-Western Ontario Travel Association, 440 Elizabeth St., Burlington, Ont., CANADA
5056 AD) The Niagara Wire Weaving Co., Ltd., P.O. Box 1016, Niagara Falls, Ont. L2E 6W9 CANADA
5057 AD) Natex-Nattertextilien, Lustenau, AUSTRIA
      DES/A) Othmar Motter
      ST) Vorarlberger Graphik
5058 AD) Nor-Shore Readymix Concrete Products Ltd., 610 Hewitson St., P.O. Box 902, Thunder Bay, Ont. P7C 4X7 CANADA

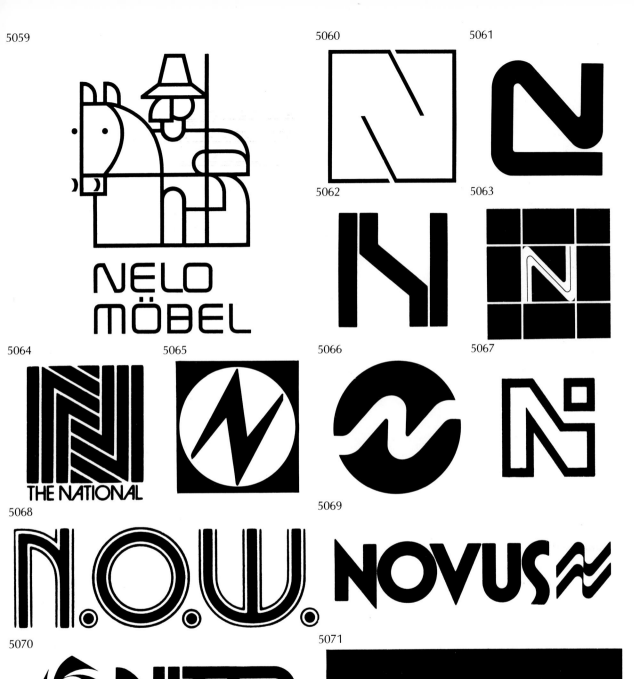

5059

NELO
MÖBEL

5060

5061

5062

5063

5064

THE NATIONAL

5065

5066

5067

5068

N.O.W.

5069

NOVUS≈

5070

NITTO
NITTO KOHKI U.S.A. INC.

5071

nu·west

5059 AD) Nelo Möbel AB, Box 106, 280 61
           Knislinge, GERMANY
5060 AD) Newton Publishing Ltd., Toronto,
           Ont., CANADA
      DES/A) William Newton
5061 AD) Neisler Laboratories, USA
      DES/A) Larry Klein
5062 AD) Neuweiler, SWITZERLAND
      DES/A) Marcel Wyss
5063 AD) Nakamura Architecture Office, Tokyo,
           JAPAN
      DES/A) Ohchi Hiroshi
5064 AD) National Golf Club, Woodbridge,
           Ont., CANADA
      C)   Men Only Golf Club
5065 AD) Northern Canada Power Commission,
           P.O. Box 5700, Station ''L'',
           Edmonton, Alta. T6C 4J8   CANADA
5066 AD) Nihonkai Oil Co., JAPAN
      DES/A) Gan Hosoya & Kohei Miura
5067 AD) Nordisk Insulinlaboratorium,
           Ved Stadion 2, 2820 Gentofte,
           DENMARK
5068 AD) N.O.W. Environments, FL, USA
      DES/A) Michael Segal
5069 AD) Novus Sales Corp., 155 University
           Ave., Suite 704, Toronto,
           Ont. M5H 3B7   CANADA
5070 AD) Nitto Kohki USA Inc., 111 Charlotte
           Pl., Englewood Cliffs,
           NJ 07632 USA
5071 AD) Nu-West Construction & Building,
           301 14th St., N.W., Calgary,
           Alta. T2P 2R6   CANADA

5072

5073

5074 5075

5076 5077 5078 5079

5080 5081

5082 5083

northern
telecom

5072 AD) Nang-Cou Garden, CHINA
DES/A) Isung-Yi Lu
5073 AD) Niemand Custom Packaging Div.,
45-10 94th St., Elmhurst,
NY 11373 USA
5074 AD) Roy Nicholls, Willowdale, Ont.,
CANADA
C) Photographer
DES/A) Carl Brett
5075 AD) National Computer Rental, Ltd.,
Subsidiary of Tiger Leasing Group,
415 Madison Ave., New York,
NY 10017 USA
5076 AD) The Nihon Keizai Shimbun, Tokyo,
JAPAN
DES/A) Hara Hiromu
ST) Nippon Design Centre
5077 AD) Nicor Inc., P.O. Box 529, Aurora,
IL 60507 USA
5078 AD) National Industries for the Blind,
NY, USA
DES/A) Dixon & Parcels Assoc., Inc.
5079 AD) Nippon House, JAPAN
DES/A) Yasaku Kamekura
5080 AD) National Sewer Pipe Ltd., P.O. Box
1800, Oakville, Ont. L6J 5C7
CANADA
5081 AD) Northern Telecom, Inc., International
Plaza, Nashville, TN 37217 USA
5082 AD) Nissenthall Audio Visuals Ltd., 717
Riddle St., Dorval, Que. H9P 1H4
CANADA
5083 AD) International Ltd., Formerly
National Foundry Equipment Co.,
413 W. University, Arlington Heights,
IL 60004 USA

5084

5085

5086 5087

5088 5089 5090

5091 Titanium Pigments

5092 National Can

5093 NEAL

5094 nardi N

5084 AD) Nuratex, Milano, ITALY
     DES/A) Bob Noorda
5085 AD) Niederer-Künzle AG
     DES/A) Eugen & Max Lenz
5086 AD) Norwegian Furniture Manufacturers
     DES/A) Bruno Odani
5087 AD) Arnold Neuweiler AG
     DES/A) Marcel Wyss
5088 AD) Nord-West-Ring, Frankfurt, Federal
     Republic of GERMANY
5089 AD) Government of Newfoundland,
     Department of Industrial Development
     Confederation Bldg., St. John's,
     Nfld., CANADA
5090 AD) Nizzoli Associati, Milano, ITALY
     DES/A) A.G. Fronzoni
5091 AD) NL Industries, Inc., Titanium Pigment
     Div., 100 Chevalier Ave., South Amboy
     NJ 08879 USA
5092 National Can Corp., 8101 W. Higgins
     Rd., Chicago, IL 60631 USA
5093 AD) North East Audio Ltd., 5 Charlotte
     Sq., Newcastle upon Tyne NE1 4XE
     ENGLAND
5094 AD) Nardi Firt, Milano 20010 Bareggio,
     ITALY

5095

5096

5097

5098

5099

5100

5101

5102

5103

5104

5105

5095 AD) National Lock Co., Rockford, IL, USA
DES/A) James Higa

5096 AD) National First Corp., CA, USA
DES/A) Detlef Hallerbach

5097 AD) National Care Services, Inc.,
Los Angeles, CA, USA
DES/A) Carl Seltzer

5098 AD) Nakamichi Research, Carle Pl.,
NY, USA

5099 AD) Nautech Ltd., Portsmouth, Hampshire
PO3 5QF ENGLAND

5100 AD) NV Nederlandse Spoorwegen-
NETHERLANDS
ST) Tel Design Associated

5101 AD) Noble Lowndes Annuities, Surrey,
ENGLAND
DES/A) David Caplan

5102 AD) Napiers Ltd.
ST) Hennion Design Associates

5103 AD) Ninos, Lancashire, ENGLAND
DES/A) Anthony Douglas Forster

5104 AD) Novatec Ltd., 348 Fraser St.,
North Bay, Ont., CANADA

5105 AD) Nobilia-Werke 4830 Guetersloh 11
Dieselstrasse 66 Anbaukuechen
Raumteiler Schrankwaende,
GERMANY
C) International Publication

5106
5107
5108
5109
5110
5111
5112
5113
5114
5115
5116
5117
5118

5106 AD) Nick & Arthur's Under Voisin, 1601
79th St. Causeway, Miami, FL, USA
C) Restaurant
5107 AD) Nova Electronics Industries
C) Calculators
5108 AD) National Citizens' Coalition, 74
Victoria St., Suite 902, Toronto,
Ont. M5C 2A5 CANADA
5109 SM) Norwegian Furniture Control
Organization, NORWAY
5110 AD) Nalco Chemical Co., 2901 Butterfield
Rd., Oak Brook, IL 60521 USA
5111 AD) Neonex Shelter, Industrial Div.,
Vancouver, Edmonton, Calgary,
CANADA
5112 AD) New Atlanta/Tucker Commercial Ind.
Park, Royal Atlanta Dev. Corp., Sub.
of Royal Palm Beach Colony, Inc.,
P.O. Box 747, 4571 Lawrenceville
Hwy., Tucker, GA 30084 USA
5113 AD) The New Brunswick Telephone Co.
Ltd., N.B. CANADA
DES/A) Ernst Roch
5114 AD) New York Aquarium, New York,
NY, USA
ST) Chermayeff & Geismar Associates Inc.
5115 AD) Newell Manufacturing Co., Prescott,
Ont., CANADA
5116 AD) Norwegian Caribbean Lines, Offices:
Major N.A. & European Cities
C) Cruise Shipping
5117 AD) Noodles, 60 Bloor St. W., Toronto,
Ont., CANADA
C) Restaurant
5118 AD) Northern Alberta Institute of
Technology, Melton Building, 10310
Jasper Ave., Edmonton, Alta.,
T5J 2W4 CANADA

5119 AD) Nutrival Inc., Sherbrooke, Que., CANADA
C) Vitamin Protein Food Packaging
DES/A) Ronald Fecteau
5120 AD) North National Properties
DES/A) Wyatt L. Phillips
5121 AD) Nytron, Inc., Palo Alto, CA, USA
DES/A) G. Dean Smith
5122 AD) Nadagokyo Sake, JAPAN
C) Brewing Association
DES/A) Tetsuo Katayama
5123 AD) Norbrasite Comércio e Importação S.A., BRAZIL
DES/A) Alexandre Wollner
5124 AD) National Reality Associates, Inc. Atlanta, GA, USA
5125 AD) Nishimura Shiko, JAPAN
DES/A) Nishiwaki Tomoishi
5126 AD) Nyffeler Bauunternehmung, Bern, SWITZERLAND
DES/A) Kurt Wirth
5127 AD) National Public Affairs Center for TV, USA
DES/A) Ernie Smith
ST) Lubalin, Smith, Carnese, Inc.
5128 AD) Near East Emergency Donations, SWITZERLAND
DES/A) Arnold Saks & Peter Kramer
5129 AD) Nichels Engineering School of Technology, USA
ST) Sharp Assoc.
5130 AD) Northern Gas Co., Omaha, NB, USA

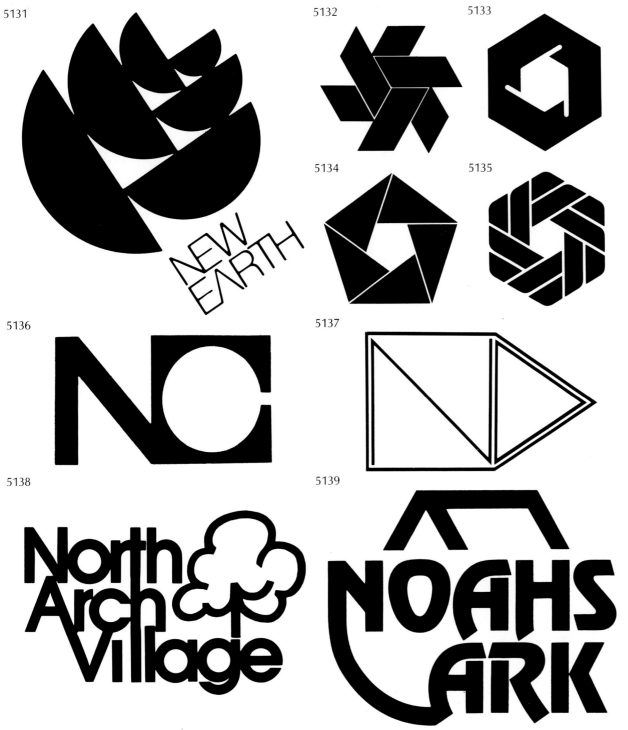

5131

5132

5133

5134

5135

NEW EARTH

5136

5137

5138

5139

North Arch Village

NOAHS ARK

5131 AD) New Earth Continental Can. Co., PORTUGAL
DES/A) Anspach Grossman
5132 AD) Northstar at Tahoe Ski Resort, USA
ST) Robert Peare & Co.
5133 AD) Neumarket Design Associates, USA
ST) Neumarket Design Associates
5134 AD) Nordwestdeutsche Hütten AG., WEST GERMANY
DES/A) Jupp Ernst
5135 AD) National Credit Information Services
DES/A) James Potocki
ST) Huerta Design Associates
5136 AD) Namiki Camera Shop, JAPAN
DES/A) Ohchi Hiroshi
5137 AD) Nippon Design Center, Tokyo, JAPAN
DES/A) Nagai Kazumasa
5138 AD) North Arch Village
5139 AD) Noah's Ark Pet Center, USA
DES/A) Rich Wittosch & Nick Sinadinos
ST) The Shipley Associates

THE CASE of the DUPLICATE LOGO
by William Korbus

condensed from New York

"They've stolen our logo!" said the voice on the telephone. It was New Year's Day and I was still in bed.

"What are you talking about?" I asked my friend from Nebraska's educational network station.

"It's NBC. They're using our logo!"

The "N" logo really began on my 39th birthday when I left Champaign, IL, to join Nebraska ETV Network. I had been hired as the first art director for the network to be in charge of graphics, still photography, scenic design and scenic construction areas. One of my initial responsibilities was to design a network logo.

The Network, the seventh educational television station in the country, founded about 20 years ago, had never had a logo or corporate identity program. My predecessors had made a few valiant attempts to get a logo accepted, but with little success, probably because of a lack of understanding of what a logo is and can do.

Three graphic designers and I worked for about 8 weeks on various designs with a goal of having 3 logos to present to the programming group. Tim Timken, Maria Sun Shih, Michael Buettner and I worked on "N" logos the first week—abstractions of the letter N for Nebraska and Network. The next week we worked on abstract logos—preferably something of a broadcasting nature—such as the iris of a camera, a camera itself, a broadcast tower, something symbolizing the 9 stations in the Network. The third week we dealt with the Nebraska landscape—a distillation of the geography of Nebraska.

At the end of the idea period we asked a small group of people who had been involved in the earlier, abortive logo attempts to give us some impressions of how they felt toward the images we had been creating. After this meeting, we had narrowed our choice to 6 possibilities. My staff and I cut it down to the final 3. These were then made into photostats, all the same size, in black and white so there would be no weighting by presentation. When voting day came those with professional/managerial rank or above who were interested, assembled and cast paper ballots. After the votes were tallied, the "N" logo received 13 votes, the second place abstraction received 13 votes and the third place Nebraska landscape received 9. Since there was a tie vote for first place, the ballots were examined. One ballot for the second place logo was found to have been submitted by a person who belonged to another agency housed in the building. It was declared void, making

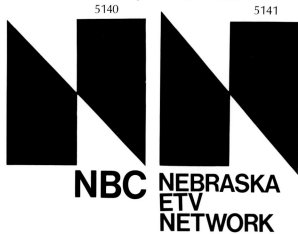

5140   5141

NBC   NEBRASKA ETV NETWORK

the "N" the logo adopted by the Network.

I wanted to implement the new logo immediately so its appearance might begin to pull the people in the organization together under the narrowly-chosen image. By that Friday we had Network logo pads available for those in the building. They were done on a grey stock, and the ink, although reported to be red, is more maroon (PMS 208).

Unlike NBC, our implementation was quite slow. It was very difficult to get anyone to approve new stationery, having the truck repainted, buying stickers for the equipment, ordering business cards, and redesigning production forms used in the building.

The logo that I created probably was done about three-fourths of the way through the development design process. It is very simple in its form. A square with the diagonal going from the upper left corner to the lower right, and then a line 90 degrees to the base half way between the right and left vertical lines. That developed

5142

the form of the "N". I extended the points on the upper left and lower right corners to give it optical balance—something NBC (or Lippincott and Margulies) didn't do with theirs. I also thought it would be wise since the raster lines (horizontal lines that define the video image on the television tube face) have a tendency to clip objects with points, and I didn't want the "N" to appear slanted every time it was used on the air.

The first use I saw of NBC's logo was as a promotion for

a movie that was going to be on that afternoon. It was our logo, except one side is red, the other blue. I was delighted. It looked so good on the screen, and it was being used bigger and better than we had ever used it. I called my wife in to see: she was livid. "Oh my God," she said. "They've ripped you off. You'll never be able to use it again! They've stolen your logo!"

Our FCC attorneys in Washington, lawyers that all broadcasters retain for just such an emergency, began working seriously to solve the problem of the two "N" logos.

Our attorneys decided that the only way to a decision was to go to court with our problem. The suit was filed in the Federal District Court in Lincoln, and finally an offer from NBC was announced.

The settlement consisted of a mobile unit containing videotape machines, 3 color cameras, a color back-pack unit, along with an auxiliary van to carry cables and support equipment. The NETV Network also would receive $25,000 to redo the logo and reimplement what had been done up to that point. $30,000 would be given to our attorneys in Washington as payment for their service.

I think there is a good and valid reason to have a symbol for an organization. This country is becoming more and more overrun with marks that have very little meaning. I call them "bank logos." They're pretty, but without meaning. I believe that a good logo is a simple design. Ideally it will include the image of what the organization represents or manufactures. The CBS logo, the eye, does this. A mark also should be adaptable to many uses and have the ability to be reproduced clearly at any scale, Simplicity, identity, adaptability are the marks of a good logo.

William Korbus is art director, NETV, Lincoln, NB.

Occupational hazard: The more simplicity one seeks in a symbol, the greater the chance for look-alikes. Left: the solution reached by mighty NBC and a tiny Nebraska network.

Joan Kron

ALPHABET SCOOP by Joan Kron

condensed from New York

"...The real rationale for NBC's going to a letter symbol was to differentiate itself from CBS's pictographic eye..."

Unless you're an RCA stockholder, there is something reassuring in catching one of the media wizards looking, not all-powerful and brilliant, but human and fallible. If, with all the brains its money could buy, the National Broadcasting Company, an RCA subsidiary, could come up with merely the same corporate symbol as a little network in Nebraska did with a fraction of the money (and time), there's hope for us all.

Nebraska, as you've heard, placed the design of a new symbol, by which its tiny educational network was to be identified, in the hands of one artist who was on the staff anyway. By one estimate, the whole project ran up about $100 in out-of-pocket expenses.

NBC put its quest for a new symbol to express its "corporate image" in the hand of consultants Lippincott & Margulies. L&M is the design and marketing firm that took mankind's primal need for icons and built it into a super-successful corporate-identity charm-cum-self-consciousness-raising course where graphics is basic to the treatment, and very much a team effort. "I can say with all sincerity," says Walter Margulies, L&M's super-suave French-born president, "that nothing we have ever done was designed by just one person." The firm's New York staff runs about 75, and a "C.I." program, as it's called, can run into years. That costs money.

Whether NBC's program cost the rumored $100,000 to $750,000 is questionable. "It cost so much less than people think," said Margulies, "that I feel like a shnook." But no matter what NBC paid, the network justifies the cost by the money it will save. You understand, NBC is getting more than a super-reductive abstract "N" as its new service mark for that price. It's getting the N plus exhaustive instructions (with layouts) prescribing its use on NBC's own and its affiliates' new letterheads, envelopes, labels, billing forms, checks, etc.

L&M, which has laid hands on the best and biggest—Coca-Cola, Xerox, Amtrak, American Express—did its diagnostic number on NBC. A team of researchers fanned out nationwide to inquire about NBC's image. And the results were that "there was no doubt that NBC was a great company...but it didn't come across as a leader...it's well seated in the public consciousness [I should think so]...but there are too many letters when you put NBC next to local affiliates' call letters..." Obviously, the network needed new graphics.

Even though Margulies is against the "alphabet soup of three-letter titles," at first L&M considered the three-letter route to NBC identity nirvana. By a process of elimination it went through hundreds of design stages. In time, it isolated the "N" as the only letter in NBC that NBC could, in its battle with ABC and CBS, call its own.

Since L&M's London office isn't overworked (corporate identity doesn't generate much anxiety in Britain), the New York office Telexed the London office and asked the staff to put their heads together on a suitable N for NBC—something bold, strong, modern, distinctive, readable, easily recognizable, and lending itself to a large array of treatments and variations in TV animation, card displays at football stadiums, on trucks, cameras, microphones, and, perhaps, needlepoint pillows to cradle the heads of executives with identity crisis.

Now comes the dramatic part. While someone named Jerry in L&M's New York office was coming up with the "N" as we know it, someone in London did the same "N" and sent it over the Telex. Eureka.

So what happens when two companies have the same mark? Who has the right of way? Don't ask. If it's decided that the marks are confusingly similar, and if Nebraska can prove it used the mark before NBC, it could have NBC over a mike boom, at least in Nebraska. But since both marks are normally used in connection with identifying call letters, the marks may not be confusingly similar. Uh-oh, what about the souvenir paper weight NBC gave me? It has no call letters. No distinguishing colors. NBC had better not mail any to its gift list in Nebraska—yet. Legally this kind of case is a morass of conflicting precedents. Since NBC probably registered its mark (for some reason, it isn't saying), it could sue in federal court. The trial of such an issue could pay for fixing the overbites of 1,000 lawyers' children.

PEACOCK V. THE PEA

In the fall of 1974, NBC decided to replace its timeworn symbols, the rainbow-plumed peacock and the cursive cluster of letters known affectionately as "the snake." The network retained Lippincott & Margulies, a Manhattan firm specializing in corporate face-lifts. After 14 months, at a cost estimated to be as high as $750,000, L.&M. produced an abstract N composed of two trapezoids, one red, one blue. NBC is now emblazoning the N on cameras, microphones, stationery, packaging, uniforms and office walls.

Then somebody discovered that the same twin-trapezoid N, only in solid red, has been since last June the official logo of the Lincoln-based Nebraska Educational Television Network. NETV Art Director Bill Korbus, working on salaried time, had developed the design. Total additional cost: less than $100, says Korbus. "Its hysterical," chuckles NBC Newscaster Tom Snyder. "It's one of those things that happen when executives sit down to do something creative."

NBC professes confidence that the carbon-copy symbols will cause no confusion.

Says Program Manager Ron Hull: "If you see that in New York, you're going to say, 'Those Nebraska hicks stole NBC's symbol.' And that's not true." Lawyers for both networks are pondering whether NETV can claim prior use and force NBC to dust off the peacock.

TIME Magazine, January 19, 1976

5143

NEBRASKA ETV NETWORK

In the final chapter of the great logo hassle of the century, the Nebraska Educational TV Network has designed this new ID symbol. Having won a court decision against NBC on the basis of six months' prior usage of the stylized "N" designed by the big network, the Nebraskans agreed to withdraw their claim in return for a color mobile unit and equipment, in addition to a further cash settlement. The new design is by Mike Buettner of the NETV graphic design staff. AD: William Korbus.

1/ Journal of Organizational Communication 1976/2
"The Case of the Duplicate Logo,"
by William Korbus.
2/ New York, January 1976,
Alphabet Scoop" by Joan Kron.
3/ Time, January 19, 1976,
Peacock v. the Pea.

5144

5145

5146

5147

5148

5149

5150

5151

5152

5153

5154

5155

5156

5157

5158

5159

5144 AD) Operation Upgrade/Plant & Power
           Services, Association Symbol
5145 AD) Original Plank, Product TM
5146 AD) Einrichtungshaus OTT GmbH, 6603
           Sulzbach (Saar)   Bonnhofstrasse 9,
           GERMANY
5147 AD) Odec Computer Systems, Inc., A
           sub. of Odec, Inc., 25 Graystone St.,
           Warwick, RI   02886   USA
5148 AD) Omega-Alpha, Inc., P.O. Box 50046,
           Dallas, TX   75250   USA
5149 AD) Oil India
      DES/A) Jock Kinneir
5150 AD) Orowheat, USA
      DES/A) Richard Runyon
5151 AD) Olivetti, ITALY
      DES/A) Giovanni Pintori
5152 AD) Omnitrade Machinery, 78 Torlake
           Crescent, Toronto, Ont., CANADA
5153 AD) Office Overload (A Drake International
           Co.) CANADA, USA, EUROPE,
           AUSTRALIA
5154 AD) Oil Mop Pollution Control Ltd., 80
           Commissioners St., Toronto, Ont.
           M5A 1A8   CANADA
5155 AD) Oakland Chamber of Commerce,
           Oakland, CA, USA
      DES/A) Grabe Smith
      ST)   Chan Miller Smith Design
            Communications
5156 AD) Opermatt & Rosmarie Tissi
      DES/A) Grafisches Atelier Siegfried
5157 AD) Ohio Marine; Harbor Point, Celina,
           OH, USA
      ST)   Company Art Dept.
5158 AD) Opto Ingeniörsfirma AB, S-64031
           Mellösa, SCHWEDEN
5159 AD) Opus, Ceskoslovenske Hudobne
           Vydavatelstvo, Narodny Podnik,
           Dunajska 22, 899 23 Bratislava,
           CZECHOSLOVAKIA

5160 AD) Oktobarski Salon, Beograd,
        JUGOSLAVIA
     DES/A) Draoslav Stojanovie
5161 AD) Ogilvie Hair Preparations, Montvale,
        NJ, USA
     DES/A) Dominik L. Burckhardt
5162 AD) Omega Construction Canada,
        Montreal, Que., CANADA
     DES/A) Jacques Bellemare
5163 AD) Omniscreen Silkscreen Printers,
        Amsterdam, HOLLAND
     DES/A) Wim Croowel
     ST) Total Design
5164 AD) Olympia International,
        Wilhelmshaven, WEST GERMANY
     DES/A) Eberhard Fuchs
5165 AD) Oehler & Co., Aaran, SWITZERLAND
     DES/A) Paul Bühlmann
5166 AD) Ohio Transformer Corp., 1776
        Constitution Ave., Louisville,
        OH 44641   USA
5167 AD) O'Brian Machinery Co., 214 Green St.,
        Downingtown, PA   19335   USA
5168 AD) Office Interiors, Inc., USA
     DES/A) Anita Soos
5169 AD) Office Concepts
     DES/A) William Davis
     ST) George N. Sepetys & Assoc.
5170 AD) Ogeechee Valley Bank, USA
     DES/A) John H. Harland Co.
5171 AD) Ocean Falls Corp., Box 730, Ocean
        Falls, B.C. VOT 1PO   CANADA
5172 AD) Ötex, Dornbirn, AUSTRIA
     DES/A) Othmar Motter
     ST) Vorarlberger Graphik
5173 AD) Overseas Shipholding Group, Inc.
        1114 Ave. of the Americas,
        New York, NY, USA
5174 AD) Oil Equipment Mfg. Corp., P.O. Box
        4186, Hamden, CT   06514   USA

5175 AD) Outer Banks Safari, USA
      DES/A) Everett Forbes
5176 AD) O'Keefe's Fisheries, Montreal,
           Que., CANADA
      DES/A) Ernst Roche
5177 AD) Ontario Credit Union League Ltd.,
           4 Credit Union Dr., Toronto,
           Ont. M4A 2A1   CANADA
5178 AD) Onda Nueva, VENEZUELA
      DES/A) Jesus Emilio Franco
5179 AD) Omnium Technique Hotelier, Paris,
           FRANCE
      DES/A) Gerard Ifert
5180 AD) Oz Restaurant
      ST) The Richards Group
5181 AD) Officine Calabrese, Bari, ITALY
      DES/A) Heinz Waibl
5182 AD) Overseas Marketing Corp., London,
           ENGLAND
      DES/A) Chandrashekhar Kamat
5183 AD) The Open University, P.O. Box 82,
           Walton Hall, Milton Keynes MK7 6AU
           ENGLAND
5184 AD) One Up Restaurant, TX, USA
      ST) The Richards Group
5185 AD) Ocrim S.P.A., Cremona, ITALY
      DES/A) Giulio Confaloneri
5186 AD) Old Colony Envelope Co., Westfield,
           MA, USA

5187 AD) The O'Brien Machinery Co., 214 Green St., Downington, PA 19335 USA

5188 AD) Ontario Science Center, 770 Don Mills Rd., Don Mills, Ont., CANADA

5189 SM) Olympiad for the Physically Disabled, Etobicoke Civic Center, Borough of Etobicoke, Etobicoke, Ont. M9C 2Y2 CANADA

5190 AD) Olympic Yachts S.A. Zea Marina, Piraeus, GREECE

5191 AD) Orion-Yhryma Oy, Nilsiakatu 10, 05100 Helsinki 51, FINLAND

     SM) Normet, Product TM

     C) Skiding winches, skiding grapples, loaders, and rear blades

5192 AD) OCI, Barcelona, SPAIN

DES/A) Perez Sanchez

5193 AD) Ogden Corp., 277 Park Ave., New York, NY 10017 USA

5194 AD) Ogilvie Bloss Ltd., 86 Forsythe St., Oakville, Ont. L6K 3J8 CANADA

5195 AD) Oceanic Products, 814 Castro St., San Leandro, CA 94577 USA

5196 AD) Offshore Mining Co., Ltd., NEW ZEALAND

5197 AD) Olympic Stains, A Div. of Comerco, Inc., 1148 N.W. Learyway, Seattle, WA 98107 USA

5198 AD) Establissements Motte et Cie, société anonyme, 45, Place Alphonse et Antoine Motte, 7700, Mouscron, BELGIUM

     SM) Orckis

     C) Manufacturers of Yarns & Thread

5199 AD) The Chicago Board Options Exchange, LaSalle & Jackson, Chicago, IL 60604 USA

5200 AD) Ceramica, Omega S.P.A., 42013 Casalgrande (R.E.), ITALY

5201 AD) Ocean Inchcape Ltd., No. 5 Bonded Warehouse, Regent Rd., Aberdeen AB1 2NS SCOTLAND

5202

OAKCREST

5203

5204

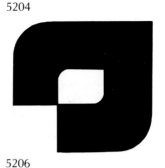

5205

5206

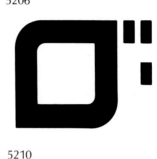

5207

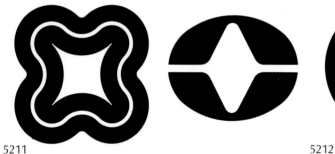

5208

5209

5210

5211

OMNI

5212

OWL

5213

OshkoshBgosh ®

5202 AD) Oakcrest, Santa Barbara, CA, USA
     DES/A) Jess Gruel
     ST) Larson-Bateman, Inc.
5203 AD) Owatonna Tool Co., 655 Eisenhower
     Dr., Owatonna, MN 55060 USA
5204 AD) Olinkraft, Inc., P.O. Box 488,
     West Monroe, LA 71291 USA
5205 AD) Overlock, Howe & Co.
     ST) Overlock, Howe & Co.
5206 AD) William O'Neil & Co., USA
     DES/A) James Cross
5207 AD) Orbon Industries, Inc., USA
     DES/A) Richard Howe
     ST) Overlock, Howe & Co.
5208 AD) Olin Mathieson
     ST) Lippincott & Margulies
5209 AD) Old Mill Towers, Toronto, Ont.,
     CANADA
     DES/A) James Donahue
     ST) Cooper & Beatty Ltd.
5210 AD) Ontario Film Laboratories, North Bay,
     Ont., CANADA
     DES/A) Leslie Smart
5211 AD) Omni, 2401 Virginia Ave., N.W.,
     Washington, D.C. 20037 USA
5212 AD) Owl, CANADA
5213 AD) Oshkosh B'Gosh, Inc., P.O. Box 300,
     Oshkosh, WI 54901 USA

5214

5215

5216

5217

5218

5219

5220

5221

5222

5223

5224

5225

5214 AD) Ontario Automobile Ltd., Toronto, Ont., CANADA
DES/A) Raymond Lee
5215 AD) Ontario Institute for Studies in Education, 252 Bloor St., W., Toronto, Ont., CANADA
DES/A) Leslie Smart
5216 AD) Ontario Dept. of Education, Toronto, Ont., CANADA
C) Student Action for International Dialogue
DES/A) Burton Kramer
5217 AD) Oy Orient-Occident Ltd., Helsinki, FINLAND
DES/A) Jukka Pellinen
5218 AD) Osiguravajuć Zavod, JUGOSLAVIA
DES/A) Vladimir Petrović
5219 AD) Ottagona, Milano, ITALY
DES/A) Pino Tovaglia
5220 AD) Office National Industriel de l'Azote, FRANCE
DES/A) Jacques Douin
5221 AD) Ósrodek Techniki Jadrowej, Warsaw, POLAND
DES/A) Andrzej Zbrozek
5222 AD) Oxidon 2000, USA
C) Whirlpool Corp.
DES/A) Richard Dearforff
5223 AD) Oakland Chamber of Commerce, Oakland, CA, USA
DES/A) Grabe Smith
ST) Chan Miller Smith Design Communications
5224 AD) Opticomp, Washington, D.C., USA
ST) Pat Taylor, Inc.
5225 AD) B. Olivari, Soc. in nome coll. di Ernesto, Ambrogio e Luigi 28021 Borgomanero (Novara) via G. Matteotti, 140, ITALY

5226

5227

5228

5229

5230

5231

5232

5233

5234

5235

5236

5237

5238

5226 AD) Olivetti Canada Ltd., 1390 Don Mills Rd., Don Mills, Ont., CANADA
DES/A) Marcello Nizzoli
5227 AD) Oxford Development Group Ltd., 2400-10025 Jasper Ave., Edmonton, Alta. T5J 1T2   CANADA
5228 AD) Office Away, USA
DES/A) Ron Coates
ST) Unimark International
5229 AD) Old Stone Bank, Providence, RI, USA
5230 AD) Oxford Papers, New York, NY, USA
5231 AD) The Ohio Brass Co., Mansfield, OH, USA
5232 AD) Openbare Bibliotheek, NETHERLANDS
DES/A) Ralph Prins
5233 AD) Omark Industries, Portland, OR, USA
5234 AD) Ohio Trailways, Oxford, OH, USA
5235 AD) Opperman/Harrington, Inc., USA
DES/A) George Opperman
5236 AD) O'Shauguessy's
C) Restaurant
DES/A) Don Weller
ST) Weller & Juett, Inc.
5237 AD) Output Systems Inc., 157 Chambers St., New York, NY   10007   USA
4238 AD) Optibelle Corp., 84 Nassau St., New York, NY   10038   USA

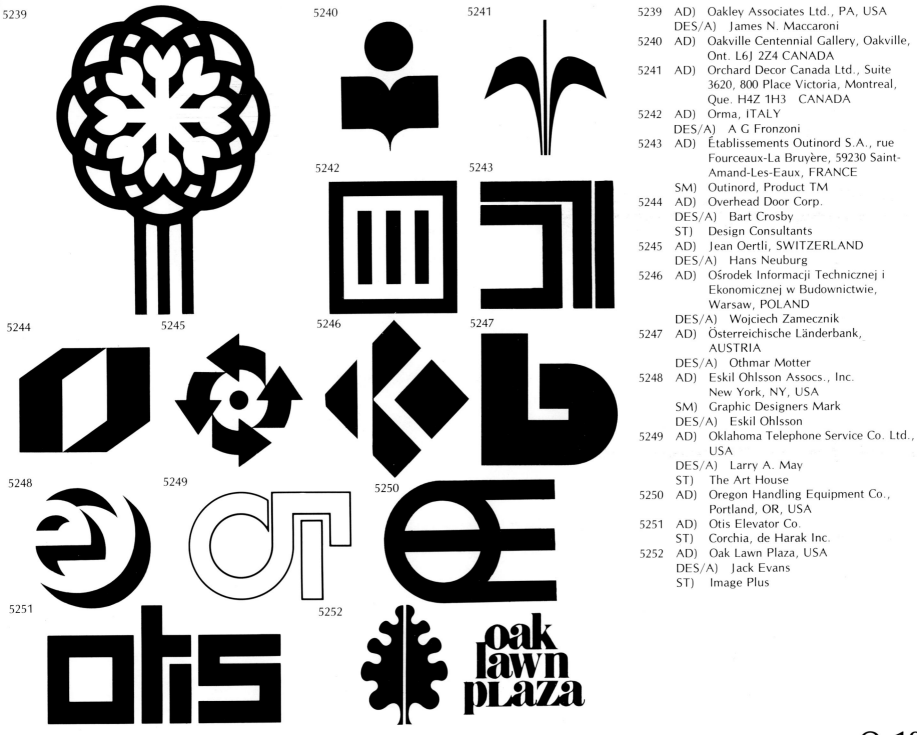

5239 | AD) | Oakley Associates Ltd., PA, USA
| DES/A) | James N. Maccaroni
5240 | AD) | Oakville Centennial Gallery, Oakville, Ont. L6J 2Z4 CANADA
5241 | AD) | Orchard Decor Canada Ltd., Suite 3620, 800 Place Victoria, Montreal, Que. H4Z 1H3 CANADA
5242 | AD) | Orma, iTALY
| DES/A) | A G Fronzoni
5243 | AD) | Établissements Outinord S.A., rue Fourceaux-La Bruyère, 59230 Saint-Amand-Les-Eaux, FRANCE
| SM) | Outinord, Product TM
5244 | AD) | Overhead Door Corp.
| DES/A) | Bart Crosby
| ST) | Design Consultants
5245 | AD) | Jean Oertli, SWITZERLAND
| DES/A) | Hans Neuburg
5246 | AD) | Ośrodek Informacji Technicznej i Ekonomicznej w Budownictwie, Warsaw, POLAND
| DES/A) | Wojciech Zamecznik
5247 | AD) | Österreichische Länderbank, AUSTRIA
| DES/A) | Othmar Motter
5248 | AD) | Eskil Ohlsson Assocs., Inc. New York, NY, USA
| SM) | Graphic Designers Mark
| DES/A) | Eskil Ohlsson
5249 | AD) | Oklahoma Telephone Service Co. Ltd., USA
| DES/A) | Larry A. May
| ST) | The Art House
5250 | AD) | Oregon Handling Equipment Co., Portland, OR, USA
5251 | AD) | Otis Elevator Co.
| ST) | Corchia, de Harak Inc.
5252 | AD) | Oak Lawn Plaza, USA
| DES/A) | Jack Evans
| ST) | Image Plus

O-18

5253

5254

5255

5256

5257

5258

5259

5260

5261

5262

5263

5253 AD) Orindawoods, CA, USA
      ST) Reis & Manwaring
5254 AD) Ogier Boudoul, FRANCE
      DES/A) Gérard Guerre
5255 AD) Országos Villamostávvezeték Vállalat
           Budapest, HUNGARY
      DES/A) Arpád Jzabó
5256 AD) Open Road International, USA
      ST) Overlock, Howe & Co.
           (also see 5205 & 5207)
5257 AD) Organic Nutrients Inc., CA, USA
      DES/A) John Gregg Berryman
      ST) Image Group
5258 AD) Odakyu Department Store,
           Tokyo, JAPAN
      DES/A) Hayashi Yoshio
5259 AD) Order-Mation, Los Angeles, CA, USA
      DES/A) David J. Goodman
      ST) Porter & Goodman
5260 AD) Ole Lynggaard, DENMARK
      DES/A) Morten Peetz-Schou
5261 AD) Ocean State Bank, USA
      DES/A) Don Weller & Dennis Juett
      ST) Weller & Juett Inc.
5262 AD) Objects and Posters,
           WEST GERMANY
      DES/A) Till Neuburg
5263 AD) Orleans Distributing Corp., USA
      DES/A) Joseph Addario

Jeux de la
XXIe Olympiade
Montréal
1976

Games of the
XXI Olympiad
Montréal
1976

O-20

5265 Pictogrammes officiels Montréal 1976

Official Pictograms Montréal 1976

Ref. World of Logotypes
File No. 190

Reproductions from the Graphic Manual, published by The Organizing Committee for the Games of the XXI Olympiad, Montreal 1976
P.O. Box 1976
Montreal, Que., Canada
H3C 3A6

Art Directors
Georges Huel and Pierre-Yves Pelletier

Graphic Designers
Raymond Bellemare and Pierre-Yves Pelletier

The manual is intended for prospective users of the official Symbol of the Games of the XXI Olympiad, which took place in Montreal in 1976. Its purpose is to describe the conditions and standards for the correct and effective use of the Symbol itself and of other graphic representations made available by the Organizing Committee of the 1976 Olympic Games, also known as COJO 76.

In order to exercise some control of the use of the official Symbol and logotypes of the Games, COJO 76 obtained the full protection of national and international laws governing copyright, trade marks and industrial designs. This means notably that the Symbol may not be modified in any way, and that its use must be authorized in writing by COJO 76.

This manual outlines the general licensing programme adopted by COJO 76. It serves primarily as a guide for the correct graphic reproduction of this Symbol and the logotypes but it serves equally as a source of ideas for their possible use under license. It also indicates certain graphic uses which are to be avoided.

The official Symbol of the 1976 Olympic Games was conceived by Georges Huel.

1 Athletisme / Athletics		
2 Aviron / Rowing		
3 Basketball / Basketball		
4 Boxe / Boxing		
5 Canoe / Canoeing	7 Escrime / Fencing	
6 Cyclisme / Cycling	8 Football / Football	
9 Gymnastique / Gymnastics	11 Handball / Handball	13 Judo / Judo
10 Halterophilie / Weightlifting	12 Hockey / Hockey	14 Lutte / Wrestling
15 Natation / Swimming	17 Sports equestres / Equestrian sports	
16 Pentathlon moderne / Modern Pentathlon	18 Tir / Shooting	
	19 Tir a l'arc / Archery	
	20 Volleyball / Volleyball	
	21 Yatching / Yatching	

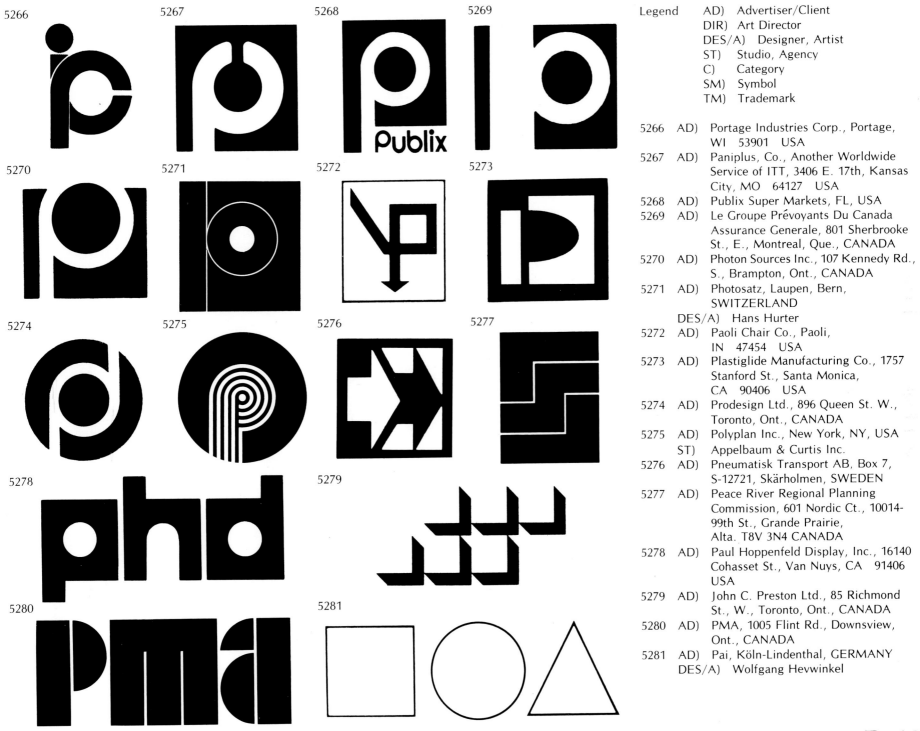

P-13

5282

5283

5284

5285

5286

5287

5288

5289

5290

5291

5292

5293

5294

5295

5296

5282 AD) Photographic Display Laboratories, St. Paul, MN, USA

5283 AD) Plenty & Son Ltd., Hambridge Rd., Newbury, Berkshire, ENGLAND

5284 AD) Power Systems Inc., 1211 E. Tower Rd., Schaumburg, IL 60172 USA

5285 AD) Pavemaster of Canada Ltd., 20 Estate Dr., Scarborough, Ont., CANADA

5286 AD) Per-Pak Corp., Brook, IN 47922 USA

5287 AD) Pharmacia AB, Uppsala, SWEDEN

5288 AD) Pan American Games Society, Winnipeg, Man., CANADA

DES/A) William Mayrs

5289 AD) Polymon Developments Ltd., Bewlay House, 2 Swallow Pl., London W.1. ENGLAND

5290 AD) Property & Casualty Insurance Adjusters, 426 Victoria Ave., St. Lambert, Que., CANADA

5291 AD) Production Tool & Fastener Co., Ltd., P.O. Box 37, 270 Harrop Dr., Milton, Ont. H9T 2Y3 CANADA

C) Golden Triangle Fasteners

5292 AD) Product Development & Mfg. Inc., P.O. Box 727, Mendota, MN 55150 USA

5293 AD) Polster Richter, Polstermöbelfabrik Siegfried Richter 6227 Winkel/ Rheingau, GERMANY

5294 AD) Polargas Project, Toronto, Ont., CANADA

DES/A) A.J. Elliott

5295 AD) Parks Davis Auctioneers, 1211 Citizens Bank Center, 100 N. Central Expwy., Dallas, TX, USA

5296 AD) Positive Electric Co., Ltd., 45 Munham Gate, Unit 5, Scarborough, Ont. M1P 2B3 CANADA

5297   5298   5299

5300   5301

5302   5303   5304   5305

POINT A
LA LIGNE

5306   5307

phillips plastics
INCORPORATED

5308   5309

5297	AD)	The Probe Group, 56 Berkeley St., Toronto, Ont. M5A 2W6 CANADA
5298	AD)	Philips s.p.a., Sezione Illuminazione, piazza IV Novembre 3, 20124 Milano, ITALY
5299	AD)	Palmer-Shile Co., 129 East Dr., Bramalea, Ont., CANADA
5300	AD)	Pierrel, Milano, ITALY
	DES/A)	Albe Steiner
5301	AD)	Plastugil, FRANCE
	DES/A)	Jacques Nathan Garamond
5302	AD)	Point A La Ligne, produzione: 30, avenue Gambetta, 33700 Mérignac (Bourdeaux) FRANCE
5303	AD)	Pittsburgh National, USA
5304	AD)	Wilh. Pahl GMBH, Dortmunder Gummiwarenfabrik, Dortmund-Hombruch, Kieferstr. 35, GERMANY
5305	AD)	Prestolite Battery Div., an Eltra Co., Toronto, Ont., CANADA
5306	AD)	Pacific Far East Line, New York, NY, USA
	C)	Ocean Shipping
5307	AD)	Phillips Plastics Inc., Mississauga, Ont., CANADA
5308	AD)	Pollution Control Products, Inc., Fort Lauderdale, FL, USA
5309	AD)	Pirelli Applicazioni Elettroniche Milano, ITALY
	DES/A)	Aldo Calabresi

5310

5311

5312

5313

5314

5315

5316

5317

5318

PRODUCTEL

5319

palaset

5320

PROVINCIAL CRANE

5310 AD) Patience & Nicholson (Canada) Ltd.,
            39 Voyager Ct., N., Rexdale,
            Ont., CANADA
5311 AD) Piper Aircraft Corp., USA
      DES/A) Bruce L. Bunch
      ST) Designed by Piper Aircraft
            Corp./FF & S
5312 AD) Paint Products Co., Rt. 3, Hwy. 311
            North, Winston-Salem,
            NC 27105 USA
5313 AD) Pennsylvania Crusher Corp., (Sub. of
            Bath Industries) Box 100G, Broomall,
            PA 19008 USA
5314 AD) Plastotype Ltd., 56 Stamford St.,
            London SE1 9LX ENGLAND
5315 AD) Pearson Packaging Systems,
            E. 304 Second Ave., Spokane,
            WA 99202 USA
5316 AD) Plastic Thermoforming Systems,
            (The Shuman Co.) P.O. Box 3347,
            Charlotte, NC 28203 USA
5317 AD) Peripheral Graphics Inc.,
            Andover Industrial Centre, York St.,
            Andover, MA 01810 USA
5318 AD) Productel Inc., 2055 rue Peel, Suite
            325, Montreal, Que. H3A 1V4
            CANADA
5319 AD) Palaset aus Vestyron von Hüls, Treston
            GmbH, 2 Schenefeld, Bez. Hamburg,
            Postfach 1167, GERMANY
5320 AD) Provincial Crane, Equipment Systems
            Div., AMCA International Corp., A
            subsidiary of Dominion Bridge,
            Niagara Falls, Ont. L2E 6W8
            CANADA

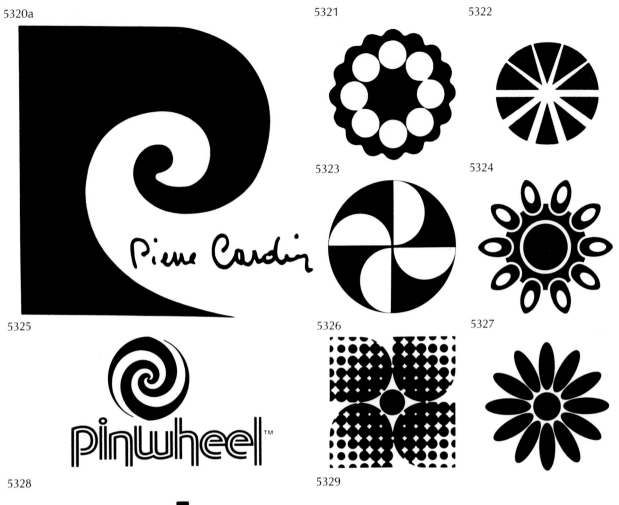

5320a

5321

5322

5323

5324

5325

Pinwheel™

5326

5327

5328

puritan® SPORTSWEAR

5329

PHOTON

5330

5331

PEOPLES⁺ JEWELLERS

5320a AD) Pierre Cardin, Paris, FRANCE
    C) Fashion Designer
5321 AD) Prince Hotel (Toronto) Ltd., 900 York Mills Rd., Don Mills, Ont. M3B 3H2 CANADA
5322 AD) Pacific Lighting Corp., USA
5323 AD) People Plus, Port Credit, Ont., CANADA
    DES/A) Leslie Smart
5324 AD) Pelgrim NV, Gaanderew, NETHERLANDS
    DES/A) A.G. Schillemans
5325 AD) Pinwheel Systems, Inc., 404 Park Ave. S., New York, NY 10016 USA
5326 AD) PF Lugshaupt, Sursee, SWITZERLAND
    DES/A) Atelier Stadelman Bisig
5327 AD) Pharmacraft Ltd., 393 Midwest, Don Mills, Ont., CANADA
    DES/A) Patricia Turnbull
5328 AD) Puritan Sportswear, The Warnaco Group, Altoona, PA 16603 USA
5329 AD) Photon, Inc., 355 Middlesex Ave., Wilmington, MA 01887 USA
5330 AD) Pako Corp., 6300 Olson Memorial Hwy., Minneapolis, MN 55440 USA
5331 AD) Peoples Jewellers, Toronto, Ont., CANADA

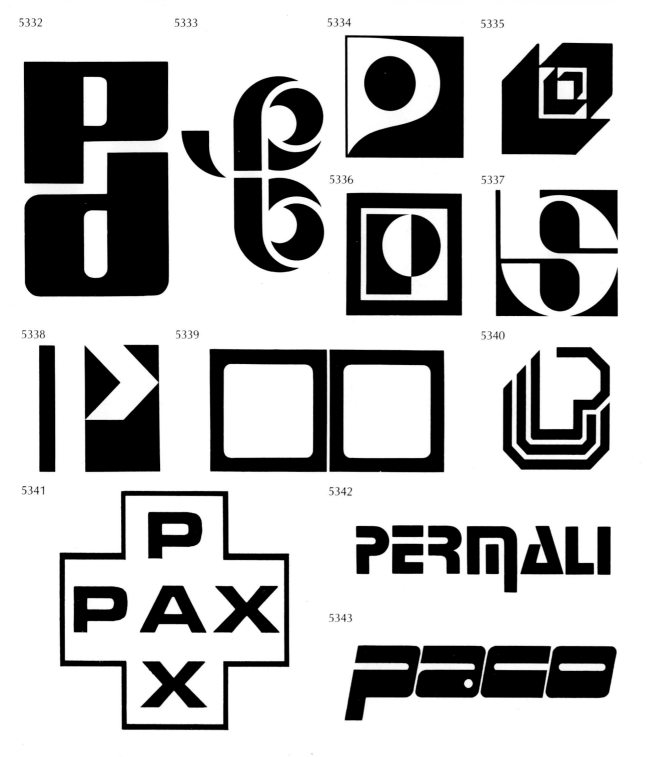

5332   AD)   Parker Drilling Co., OK, USA

5333   AD)   Professional Bank Forms Co., OK, USA

          DES/A)   Jeanie Ruedy

5334   AD)   Progie Paris

          DES/A)   Raymond Loewy

5335   AD)   Panex Exhibits, a div. of CDA Industries Ltd., 1430 Birchmound Rd., Toronto, Ont., CANADA

5336   AD)   Primistères, La Courneuve, FRANCE

          DES/A)   Lonsdale Design Paris

5337   AD)   Pirelli, Milano, ITALY

          DES/A)   Ilio Negri

5338   AD)   Papirfeldolgozók KTSZ, Budapest, HUNGARY

          DES/A)   Istvan Szekers

5339   AD)   Plasticoffre S.A., Lausanne, SWITZERLAND

          DES/A)   Michel Gallay

5340   AD)   Prückl Diamanten, Freilassing, WEST GERMANY

5341   AD)   Pax Save-A-Life Corp., 11186-80th Ave., Delta, B.C. V4C 1W7 CANADA

5342   AD)   Pernali (Canada) Ltd., 2870 Slough St., Malton, Ont., CANADA

5343   AD)   Zev Trading Enterprises Ltd., Suite 1180, Place du Canada, Montreal, Que., CANADA

5343a

5344

5345

5346

5347

5348

5349

5350

5351

5352

5353

5354

5343a AD) Peres Sports, Barcelona, SPAIN
DES/A) José Baques
5344 AD) Public Service Electric and Gas Co.,
USA
5345 AD) Paxton Products Inc., 1664 12th St.,
Santa Monica, CA 90404 USA
5346 AD) Ploudiv International Fair,
Ploudiv, BULGARIA
DES/A) Stephane Kantsheff
5347 AD) Commercial National Bank of Peoria,
USA
5348 AD) Phillipine Airlines, PHILLIPINES
ST) Primo Angeli Graphic
5349 AD) Problematics, Waltham, MA, USA
ST) Gregory Fossella Assocs.
5350 AD) Pennsylvania, New Jersey & Delaware
Committee of Governors,
Philadelphia, PA, USA
5351 AD) Planned Parenthood World Population
DES/A) Rudolph de Harak
5352 AD) The Perfect Mix, 1103A Yonge St.,
Toronto, Ont., CANADA
5353 AD) C. Porter, 522 Plymouth,
Grand Rapids, MI, USA
5354 AD) Peacock Ridge,
Palos Verdes, CA, USA

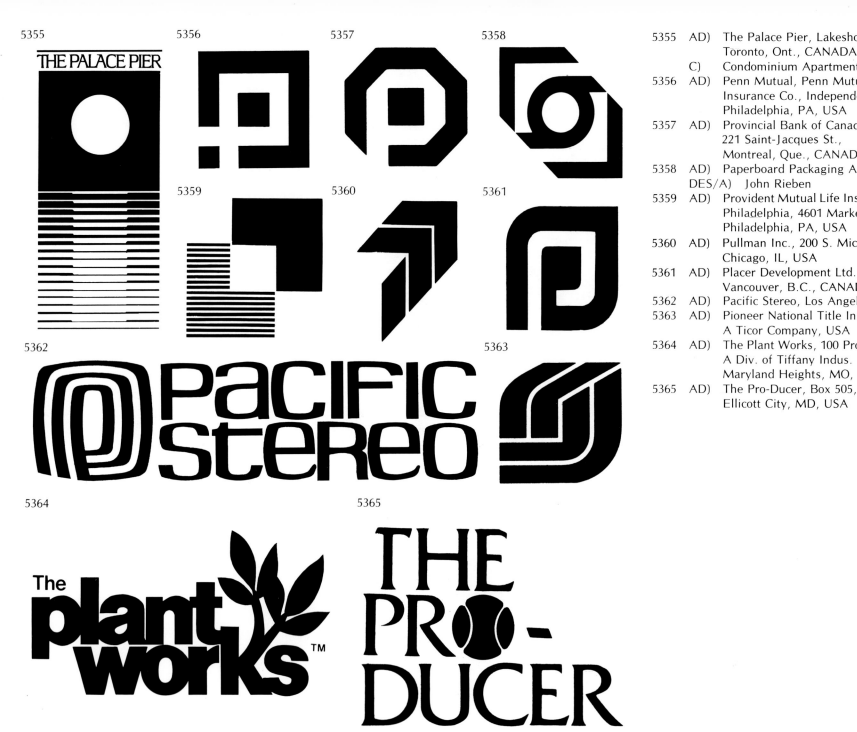

5355

5356

5357

5358

5359

5360

5361

5362

5363

5364

5365

5366

5367

5368

5369

5370

5371

5372

5373

5374

5375

5376

5377

5378

5379

5380

5381

5382

5383

5384

5385

5386

5386a

5387

5388

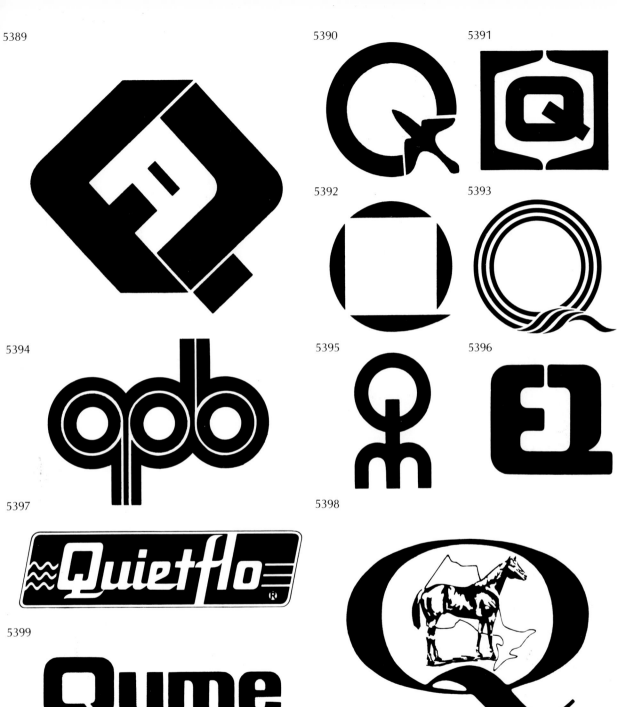

5389

5390

5391

5392

5393

5394

5395

5396

5397

5398

5399

Legend

AD) Advertiser/Client
DIR) Art Director
DES/A) Designer, Artist
ST) Studio, Agency
C) Category
SM) Symbol
TM) Trademark

5389 AD) La Fondation De L'Athlète Québécois, 1415 Est Rue Jarry, Montreal, Que. H2E 2Z7 CANADA

5390 AD) Québecair, Que., CANADA
C) Regional Airline

5391 AD) Questeel (A Division of QSP Ltd.) Longueuil, Que., CANADA

5392 AD) Quad Typographers Inc., New York, NY, USA
DES/A) Mo Lebowitz

5393 AD) Quirra S.p.A., Milano, ITALY
DES/A) Patrizia Pattacini

5394 AD) Quality Paperback Book Service, Inc., PA, USA

5395 AD) Le Quadrimetal Offset, 93300 Aubervilliers, 63, rue de la Haie-Coq, FRANCE
DES/A) Aktuelle Nachrichten

5396 AD) Cunard Shipping Lines, GREAT BRITAIN
SM) Cunard ''Queen Elizabeth''
DES/A) Nick Butteworth

5397 AD) Quietflo Engineering Ltd., West Drayton, Middlesex UB7 7SJ ENGLAND

5398 AD) Ontario Quarter Horse Association Inc. 233 Division St., Welland, Ont., CANADA

5399 AD) Qume, 26203 Production Ave., Hayward, CA 94545 USA

5400

5401

5402

5403

5404

5405

5406

5407

5408

5409

5410

5400 AD) Quatrecolour, Osaka, JAPAN
5401 AD) Quadrant Development Corp., USA
DES/A) Jess Gruel
5402 AD) Quality Photographers, USA
ST) Visual Design Centre
5403 AD) Matsushita Electric Industry Co., Ltd.,
Osaka, JAPAN
5404 AD) Quincy's (23rd Annual Art Show) USA
ST) Don Davis Design
5405 AD) Quebec Telephone, Rimouski,
Que., CANADA
5406 AD) Quik Air, USA
C) Charter Service
ST) Lionhill Studio
5407 AD) Question & Answer, USA
DES/A) Toni Goldmark
5408 AD) Quillayote Camp,
Olympic Peninsula, WA, USA
5409 AD) Los Angeles County Museum of Art,
USA
DES/A) Tom Woodward
5410 AD) Q.R.S. Corp., USA
DES/A) James Potocki

Q-4

AD) Advertiser/Client
DIR) Art Director
DES/A) Designer, Artist
ST) Studio, Agency   SM) Symbol
C) Category   TM) Trademark

5410   AD)   Rodman Industries Inc., Resinwood
              Div., Green Bay, WI 54301   USA
5411   AD)   R & A Plastics, Inc., Higgins Indus.
              Park, Worcester, MA 01606   USA
       SM)   Ramco Plastic Processing Machinery
              Div.
5412   AD)   Roneo Vickers Canada Ltd.,
              129 Carlingview Dr., Rexdale,
              Ont. M9W 5E7   CANADA
5413   AD)   Robicon Corp., 100 Sagamore Hill Rd.,
              Plum Industrial Pk., Pittsburgh,
              PA   15239   USA
5414   AD)   Rodrigo : la linea maschile
5415   AD)   Ridat Engineering Co., Ltd.,
              Fishponds Rd., Wokingham,
              Berkshire, ENGLAND
5416   AD)   Raise Inc., Div. of Heede International
              Ltd., 3070 Lenworth Dr., Mississauga,
              Ont., CANADA, USA, MEXICO, S.A.
5417   AD)   Rappaport Exhibits, Inc., 3608 Payne
              Ave., Cleveland, OH 44114   USA
5418   AD)   Ro-Bar Electronics Systems Ltd.,
              140 Doncaster Ave., Unit 7,
              Thornhill, Ont., CANADA
5419   AD)   Research III
       DES/A)   Gerry Rosentsweig
       ST)   The Graphics Studio
5420   AD)   Roper Whitney, Inc., (Formerly
              Whitney Metal Tool Co.) 2833
              Huffman Blvd., Rockford,
              IL   61101   USA
5421   AD)   Rašica. Ljubljana
       DES/A)   Mojca Vogelnik
5422   AD)   Votre décorateur Ligne Roset
              Chayette, 57 bd Barbés. 606.81.35
              Paris, FRANCE
5423   AD)   Ram Plastics Corp., RR#2,
              Totenham, Ont., CANADA
5424   AD)   Ring-O-Matic Mfg., Co., P.O. Box 305,
              Pella, IA   50219   USA
5425   AD)   Ragsdale Pardoe
       DES/A)   Gary Coo
       ST)   Metzdorf Advertising

5426

5427

5428

5429

5430

5431

5432

5433

5434

5435

5436

5437

5438

5439

5440

5426 AD) Ragno, by Precision Mfg. Co., Montreal, Que., CANADA

5427 AD) Rosemount Partitions, Inc., Airlake Industrial Park, Box D, Lakeville, MN 55044 USA

5428 AD) RUF International, Belgien: S.P.R.L. Claushuis 22-23, Place du Nouveau Marché aux Grains, B-1000 Bruxelles, BELGIUM

5429 AD) Robert's Office Supply Co., 50 Free St., Portland, ME 04111 USA

5430 AD) Otto Rohrbach, SWITZERLAND
DES/A) Marcel Wyss

5431 AD) Rodgers Machinery Mfg. Co., Inc., 2600 S. Santa Fe Ave., Los Angeles, CA 90058 USA

5432 AD) B.M. Root Co., York, PA, USA

5433 AD) Radiomarelli, Programma Habitat

5434 AD) Rotoplas Ltd., Talpiot Industrial Zone, P.O. Box 10285, Jerusalem, ISRAEL

5435 AD) The Ruud Co., Div. of Rheem Manufacturing Co., 7600 S. Kedzie Ave., Chicago, IL 60652 USA

5436 AD) Rexroth

5437 AD) Rostone Corp., 2450 Sagamore Pkwy., S., Lafayette, IN 47901 USA
TM) Rosite Product

5438 AD) Ross Laboratories, Div. of Abbott Laboratories, USA
DES/A) Beman Pound

5439 AD) Room Bar Ltd., Bnei-Brak, ISRAEL

5440 AD) Antonio Ratti, Como, ITALY
DES/A) Giulio Confalonieri

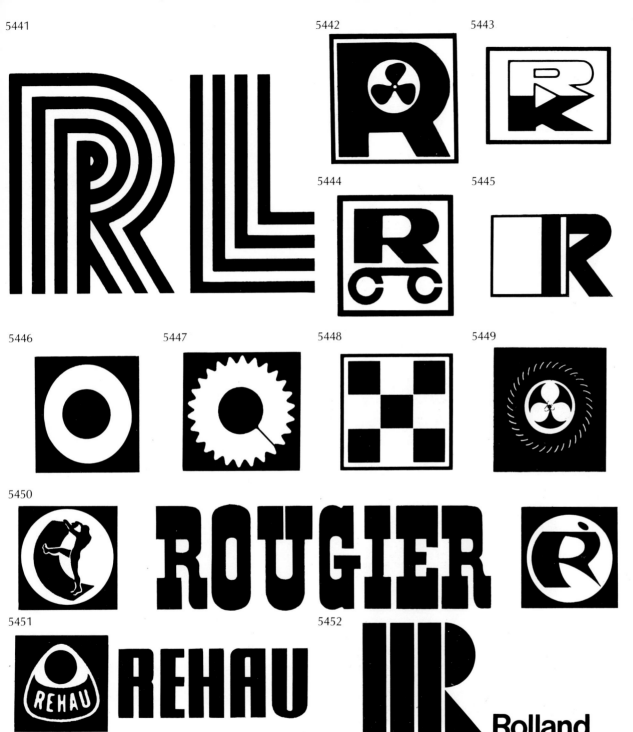

5441

5442

5443

5444

5445

5446

5447

5448

5449

5450

5451

5452

5441 AD) Studio Di Architettura E Arredamento, Mobili Di Design, Oggetti D'Arte-Regali

5442 AD) Eliche Radice, 20052 Bettola di Monza, Milano, ITALY

5443 AD) Ronan & Kunzl, Inc., 1225 S. Kalamazoo Ave., Marshall, MI 49068 USA

5444 AD) Ross Controls Corp. (An Affiliate of American Research & Development Corp.) 257 Crescent St., Waltham, MA 02154 USA

5445 AD) RX/Engineering Thermostats, Rogers Corp., Manchester, CT 06040 USA

5446 AD) Record Club of America, York, PA 17405 USA

5447 AD) Rollem Corp. of America, 41-12 24th St., Long Island City, NY, USA

5448 AD) Ralston Purina Co., Checkerboard Sq., St. Louis, MO 63188 USA
    ST) Overlock Howe & Co.

5449 AD) Revcor Inc., 251 Edwards St., Carpentersville, IL 60110 USA

5450 AD) Rougier, 79040 Niort Cedex, FRANCE

5451 AD) Rehau, Toronto, Ont., CANADA

5452 AD) Rolland Paper Co., Ltd., Suite 3620, 800 Place Victoria, Montreal, Que., CANADA

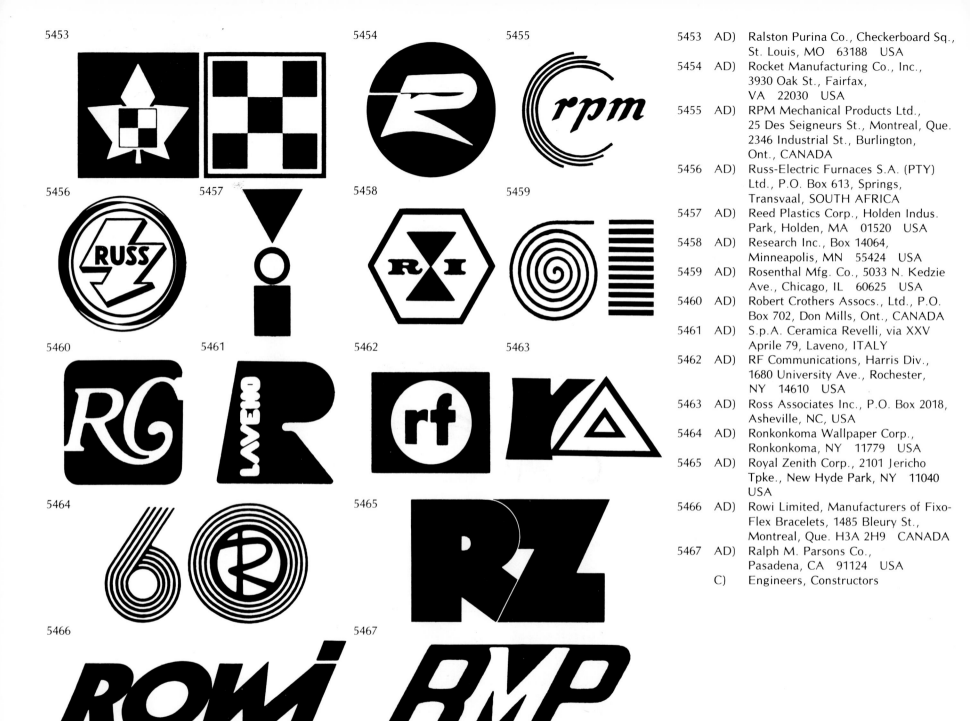

5453	5454	5455
5456	5457	5458	5459
5460	5461	5462	5463
5464	5465		
5466	5467		

5453 AD) Ralston Purina Co., Checkerboard Sq., St. Louis, MO 63188 USA

5454 AD) Rocket Manufacturing Co., Inc., 3930 Oak St., Fairfax, VA 22030 USA

5455 AD) RPM Mechanical Products Ltd., 25 Des Seigneurs St., Montreal, Que. 2346 Industrial St., Burlington, Ont., CANADA

5456 AD) Russ-Electric Furnaces S.A. (PTY) Ltd., P.O. Box 613, Springs, Transvaal, SOUTH AFRICA

5457 AD) Reed Plastics Corp., Holden Indus. Park, Holden, MA 01520 USA

5458 AD) Research Inc., Box 14064, Minneapolis, MN 55424 USA

5459 AD) Rosenthal Mfg. Co., 5033 N. Kedzie Ave., Chicago, IL 60625 USA

5460 AD) Robert Crothers Assocs., Ltd., P.O. Box 702, Don Mills, Ont., CANADA

5461 AD) S.p.A. Ceramica Revelli, via XXV Aprile 79, Laveno, ITALY

5462 AD) RF Communications, Harris Div., 1680 University Ave., Rochester, NY 14610 USA

5463 AD) Ross Associates Inc., P.O. Box 2018, Asheville, NC, USA

5464 AD) Ronkonkoma Wallpaper Corp., Ronkonkoma, NY 11779 USA

5465 AD) Royal Zenith Corp., 2101 Jericho Tpke., New Hyde Park, NY 11040 USA

5466 AD) Rowi Limited, Manufacturers of Fixo-Flex Bracelets, 1485 Bleury St., Montreal, Que. H3A 2H9 CANADA

5467 AD) Ralph M. Parsons Co., Pasadena, CA 91124 USA

C) Engineers, Constructors

5468

5469

5470

5471

5472

5473

5474

5475

5476

5477

5478

5479

5486 AD) RC Galleries, 900 N. Michigan Ave.,
            609 N. Wells St., Chicago, IL, USA
5469 AD) Rick Schreiter, 24 Fifth Ave.,
            New York, NY   10011   USA
5470 AD) Rakennustaiteen Seura, FINLAND
      DES/A) Jukka Pellinen
5471 AD) Rothchild Printing Co. Inc., 52 E.
            19th St., New York, NY, USA
5472 AD) Roy Jacobs Co., 517 Oaklawn Plaza,
            Dallas, TX   75207   USA
5473 AD) Rohde & Schwarz, 8000 München 80,
            Mühldorfstrasse 15, WEST GERMANY
5474 AD) Rockland Colloid Corp., 599 River Rd.,
            Piermont, NY   10968   USA
5475 AD) Rogol Electric Co., Ltd., 408 Ormont
            Dr., Weston, Ont. M9L 1N9
            CANADA
5476 AD) Recticel AB 33200 Gislaved
      SM) Recticel TM
5477 AD) Röder, einrichtungen, 7000 Stuttgart 1,
            Friedrich str. 41, WEST GERMANY
5478 AD) Recorded Publications Laboratories,
            1120 State St., Camden,
            NJ   08105   USA
5479 AD) Research for Better Printing
            Chemical Corp., Milwaukee,
            WI   53214   USA

5480

5481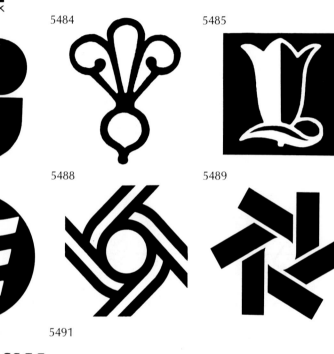

5482 **5483** **5484** **5485**

5486 **5487** **5488** **5489**

5490 **5491**

5492

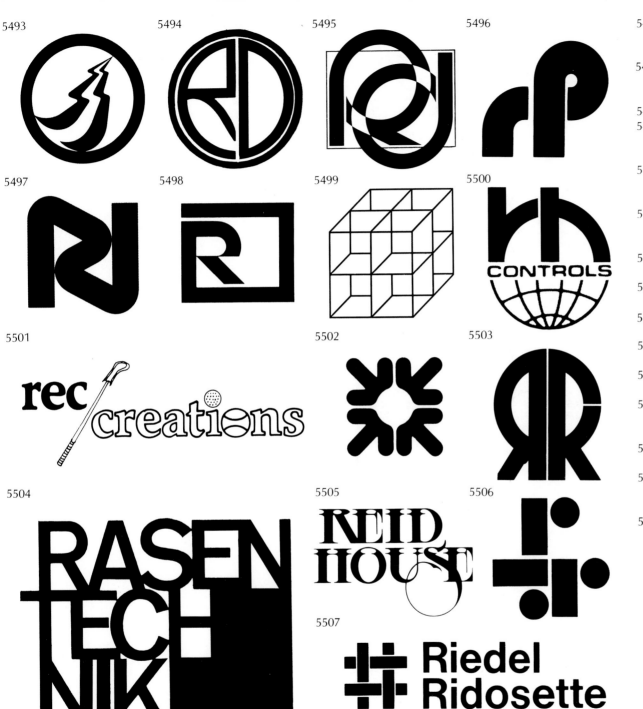

5493

5494

5495

5496

5497

5498

5499

5500

CONTROLS

5501

rec/creations

5502

5503

5504

RASEN TECH NIK

5505

REID HOUSE

5506

5507

‡ Riedel Ridosette

5508

5509

5510

5511

5512

5513

5514

5515

5516

5517

5518

5519

5508 AD) Resilience Ltd., Watford, Hertfordshire, ENGLAND
DES/A) Peter Wilbur

5509 AD) Rees-Hough, Ltd., Dorkin, Surrey, ENGLAND
DES/A) John Gibb & Garth Bell

5510 AD) Ricardo Fayos, Barcelona, SPAIN
DES/A) Ernesto M. Catalá

5511 AD) Rediffusion Television Ltd., London, ENGLAND
DES/A) Arnold Schwartzman

5512 AD) River Steel Co., Ltd., Yokohama, JAPAN
DES/A) Yoshioka Kenichi

5513 AD) Randpax EDP Ltd., London, ENGLAND
DES/A) Roy Walker

5514 AD) Rambler Trailer Co., Burlington, Ont. CANADA

5515 AD) Ramco International, Inc., 3338 Commercial Ave., North Brook, IL 60062 USA

5516 AD) Regency Highland Club, 3912 S. Ocean Blvd., Highland Beach, FL, USA

5517 AD) R.I.F., Box 23444, Washington, D.C. 20024 USA
C) Book Publisher

5518 AD) Rolls Royce (Canada) Ltd., P.O. Box 1000, Montreal AMF, Montreal, Que., CANADA

5519 AD) Regattakomitee Der Ruderwelt Miesterschaften, Luzern, SWITZERLAND
DES/A) Edgar Küng

R-18

5520 AD) Recordati Industria Chimica,
Milano, ITALY
DES/A) Ilio Negri

5521 AD) Rakennuspuusepänteollisus r.y.,
Helsinki, FINLAND
DES/A) Bror B. Zetterborg

5522 AD) Religioni Oggi-Dialogo, Roma, ITALY
DES/A) Michele Spera

5523 AD) RPR Relazioni Pubbliche, Roma,
ITALY
DES/A) Mimmo Castellano

5524 AD) Republic Corp., Los Angeles, CA,
USA
DES/A) Robert Miles Runyan

5525 AD) Raffold Ltd., Guildford, Surrey,
ENGLAND
DES/A) David J. Plumb

5526 AD) Rhodiatoce S.p.A., Milano, ITALY
DES/A) Bob Noorda

5527 AD) Dan River Inc., Webco Knit Div.,
111 W. 40th St., New York,
NY 10018 USA
SM) Dan River TM

5528 AD) Carlo Reggiani, Varese, ITALY
DES/A) Vittorio Antiuori

5529 AD) Franco Ranchetti S.p.A., Milano,
ITALY
DES/A) Heinz Waibl

5530 AD) The New Ruaton Garden Co., Ltd.,
Earls Hall Dr., St. John's Rd.,
Clacton-on-Sea, Essex, ENGLAND
C) Growers and Merchants, Fruits &
Vegetables

5531 AD) Rek-O-Kut Co., Inc., Corona, NY, USA
DES/A) George Nelson & Richard Schiffer

5532 AD) Rhinegold, Toronto, Ont., CANADA
SM) Name of Musical Group
DES/A) Chris Notter

5533 AD) Ritz-Charles of Ritz, USA & FRANCE

5534 AD) Rietz Manufacturing Co., P.O. Box
880, Santa Rosa, CA, USA

5535 SM) Renault TM, Paris, FRANCE
C) Automotive & Military Manufacturer

5536

5537

5538

5539

5540

5541

5542

5543

5544 RIVAL

5545 REALITY T.M.

5546 ROGERS

5547 REAX

5536   AD)   Ridgwood Finance Services,
                  Toronto, Ont., CANADA
      DES/A)   William Tam
      ST)   Ken Borden Ltd.
5537   AD)   Roscoe Brown Sales Co., Inc.,
                  Lenox, IA   50851   USA
5538   AD)   Replacement Lens, Inc., 9025 N.
                  Lindbergh Dr., Peoria,
                  IL   61614   USA
5539   AD)   Rochester Institute of Technology,
                  Rochester, NY, USA
      DES/A)   Roger Remington
5540   AD)   Rockford Screw Supply Co.,
                  Rockford, IL, USA
      DES/A)   Bruce Beck
      ST)   The Design Partnership
5541   AD)   Roco Carpet Co., Inc., A division of
                  Rosecore Carpet Co., Inc., 979 Third
                  Ave., New York, NY   10022   USA
5542   AD)   Rhoades & Jamieson, San Leandro,
                  CA, USA
      C)   Ready-mix Concrete Co.
      DES/A)   Primo Angeli
5543   AD)   Residential Interiors, One Astor
                  Plaza, New York, NY   10036   USA
5544   AD)   Rival, Div. of Southern Boatbuilding
                  Co. Ltd., Willment's Shipyard,
                  Woolston, Southampton SO2 7GB
                  ENGLAND
5545   TM)   Reality, 4776 Yonge St., Toronto,
                  Ont., CANADA
5546   AD)   Rogers Corp., 5259 Minola Dr.,
                  Lithonia, GA   30058   USA
5547   AD)   Westvaco, USA
      TM)   Reax
      DES/A)   Howard York

5548   5549   5550   5551

5552   5553   5554   5555

5556   5557   5558   5559

5560   5661

STAFF LEUCHTEN   **Sheldahl**

5562

cw Stockwell inc.

Legend   AD)   Advertiser/Client
       DIR)   Art Director
       DES/A)   Designer, Artist
       ST)   Studio, Agency
       C)   Category
       SM)   Symbol Mark
       TM)   Trademark

5548   AD)   Slinger, ENGLAND
      ST)   June Fraser & Design Research Unit
5549   AD)   SWF Machinery (formerly General Nailing Machine Corp.) Sanger, CA 93657 USA
5550   AD)   Southwest Forest Industries, Phoenix, AZ, USA
5551   AD)   Swiss Credit Bank, SWITZERLAND
      ST)   Adolf Flückiger & Rosshäusem Be
5552   AD)   Stange Company, USA
      DES/A)   Randall R. Roth
5553   AD)   I.P. Sharp Associates Ltd., P.O. Box 71, Toronto Dominion Centre, Toronto, Ont. M5K 1E7 CANADA
5554   AD)   Superga Industria Scarpe, ITALY
      C)   Shoe Manufacturer
      ST)   Aldo Calabresi & Studio Boggeri
5555   AD)   Scope Furniture, Inc., 407 W. 13th St., New York, NY 10014 USA
      DES/A)   Howard York
5556   AD)   Sullivan Strong Scott, 74 Wildcat Rd., Downsview, Ont. M3J 2V4 CANADA
5557   AD)   Saratoga Performing Arts Centre, Saratoga, CA, USA
      DES/A)   Charles Fuhrman
5558   AD)   Swivelier Nanuet, New York, NY 10954 USA
5559   AD)   Swiss Credit Bank, SWITZERLAND
      DES/A)   Adolf Flückiger & Rosshäusem Be
5560   AD)   Staff Leuchten, Staff KG 4920 Lemgo
5661   AD)   Sheldahl Packaging Machinery Division, 231 Ferris Ave., East Providence, RI 02916 USA
5562   AD)   C.W. Stockwell, Inc., 320 N. Madison Ave., Los Angeles, CA, USA

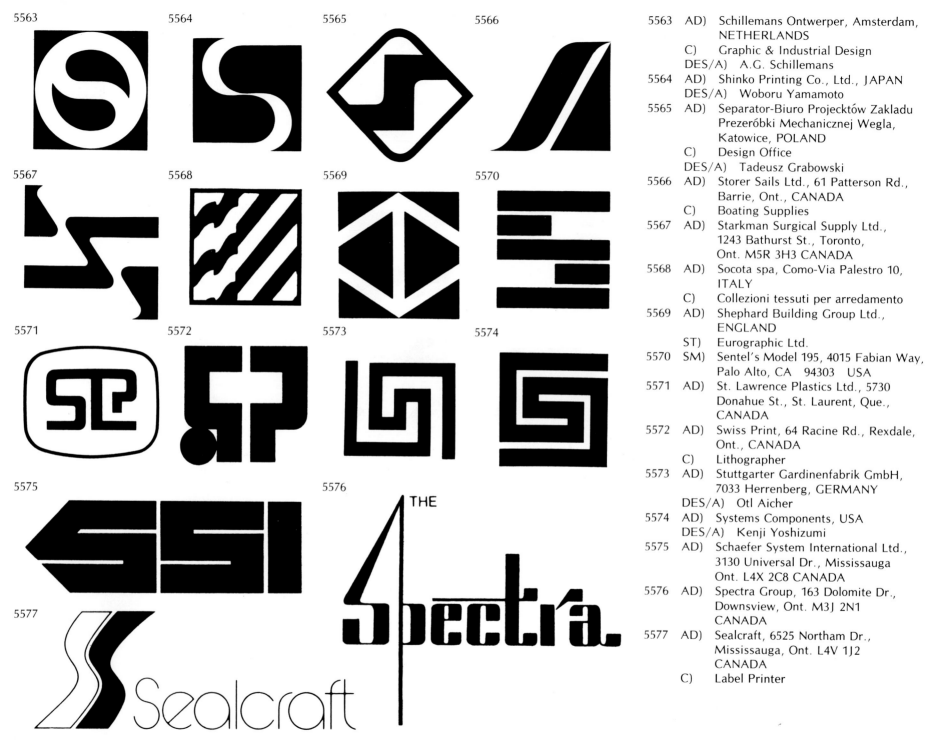

5563

5564

5565

5566

5567

5568

5569

5570

5571

5572

5573

5574

5575

5576

5577

Sealcraft

THE

Spectra

5563 AD) Schillemans Ontwerper, Amsterdam, NETHERLANDS
C) Graphic & Industrial Design
DES/A) A.G. Schillemans

5564 AD) Shinko Printing Co., Ltd., JAPAN
DES/A) Woboru Yamamoto

5565 AD) Separator-Biuro Projektów Zakladu Prezeróbki Mechanicznej Wegla, Katowice, POLAND
C) Design Office
DES/A) Tadeusz Grabowski

5566 AD) Storer Sails Ltd., 61 Patterson Rd., Barrie, Ont., CANADA
C) Boating Supplies

5567 AD) Starkman Surgical Supply Ltd., 1243 Bathurst St., Toronto, Ont. M5R 3H3 CANADA

5568 AD) Socota spa, Como-Via Palestro 10, ITALY
C) Collezioni tessuti per arredamento

5569 AD) Shephard Building Group Ltd., ENGLAND
ST) Eurographic Ltd.

5570 SM) Sentel's Model 195, 4015 Fabian Way, Palo Alto, CA 94303 USA

5571 AD) St. Lawrence Plastics Ltd., 5730 Donahue St., St. Laurent, Que., CANADA

5572 AD) Swiss Print, 64 Racine Rd., Rexdale, Ont., CANADA
C) Lithographer

5573 AD) Stuttgarter Gardinenfabrik GmbH, 7033 Herrenberg, GERMANY
DES/A) Otl Aicher

5574 AD) Systems Components, USA
DES/A) Kenji Yoshizumi

5575 AD) Schaefer System International Ltd., 3130 Universal Dr., Mississauga Ont. L4X 2C8 CANADA

5576 AD) Spectra Group, 163 Dolomite Dr., Downsview, Ont. M3J 2N1 CANADA

5577 AD) Sealcraft, 6525 Northam Dr., Mississauga, Ont. L4V 1J2 CANADA
C) Label Printer

S-14

5578 AD) S.T.A. Air Service Co., BELGIUM
DES/A) Michel Waxmann
5579 AD) South West Fabricating & Welding Co., Inc., Houston, TX 77011 USA
5580 AD) Scotia Factors Ltd., (Assoc. with Bank of Nova Scotia) 630 Sherbrooke St., W., Montreal, Que., CANADA
5581 AD) Superior Car Wash Systems, Inc., 4018 N. 33rd Ave., Phoenix, AZ, USA
5582 AD) Sports Car Unlimited 1974, 1784 Lakeshore Rd. W., Clarkson, Port Credit, Ont., CANADA
DES/A) Diego DiCaro
5583 AD) Simmons Co., Divisions and Affiliates: Living Room, Juvenile Prods., Thonet, Greeff, Bloomcraft, Katzenbach & Warren, Hausted, Raymor/Richards, Morgenthau, Moreddi, Selig, Artisan House, American Acceptance, York-Hoover, Elgin Metal Casket. Intern. Oper: Simmons Ltd. Can.; Simmons De Argentina, S.A.I.C.; Simmons Bedding Co., Pty. Ltd. and V.S. Wright & Sons, Pty. Ltd., AUSTRALIA; Sleepeezee Ltd. and Warner & Sons Ltd., ENGLAND.; Cie, Continentale Simmons, S.A., FRANCE; Cia. Italiana Simmons; Simmons Japan Ltd.; Compania Simmons, S.A. de C.V. MEXICO.; Simmons Inc., PUERTO RICO; Simmons de Venezuela C.A.
5584 AD) Scholven-Chemie AG., 466 Gelsenkirchen-Buer, F.R., GERMANY
5585 AD) Schuylkill Square, 2400 Market St., Philadelphia, PA 19103 USA
5586 AD) Société Française d'Equipements pour la Navigation Aérienne, P.O. Box 59, 78 140-Velizy-Villacoublay, FRANCE
5587 AD) Scott, Syma Italiana Elettronica, via M. Gioia 70-20125 Milano, ITALY
5588 AD) Silverton Marine Corp., Kettle Creek Rd., Toms River, NJ 08753 USA
5589 AD) Selection Tricolore Course, 114 Avenue Charles de Gaulle, Neuilly-sur-Seine, FRANCE
5590 AD) Society of St. Vincent of Paul, 348 Broadview Ave., Toronto, Ont., CAN.
5591 AD) Systems Dimensions Ltd., 770 Brookfield Rd., Ottawa, Ont., CANADA

5592 AD) Standard Elektrik Lorenz AG,
        (a member of the international ITT
        group) Stuttgart 40 (Zuffenhausen)
        Hellmuth-Hirth, Strasse 42, P.O. Box
        40.07.44, WEST GERMANY
     SM) Sel
5593 AD) Styrex Industries Inc., P.O. Box 5706,
        High Point, NC   27262   USA
5594 AD) Starmark of Canada Ltd., Vancouver,
        B.C., CANADA
     C) Office Supply Manufacturer
5595 AD) Sormani/Linea Plus, Ltd., 964 Third
        Ave., New York, NY   10022   USA
5596 AD) Ideal Standard S.p.A., Divisione
        arredamento bagno, 33080 Orcenico
        (PN), ITALY
     TM) Syntex, Div.
5597 AD) F.F. Slaney & Co. Ltd., 402 West
        Pender St., Vancouver, B.C.,
        CANADA
5598 AD) Standard Change-Makers Inc., 422 E.
        New York St., Indianapolis,
        IN 46202   USA
5599 AD) Sutton Place Hotel, 955 Bay St.,
        Toronto, Ont., CANADA
5600 AD) S.A.G.I.M. S.p.A., via Ronzinella,
        95-31021 Mogliano Veneto, ITALY
5601 AD) Sirrah, ITALY
5602 AD) Saverland Trennwandsystem,
        Sauerländer, Spanplattengesellschaft
        mbH & Co. KG, 577 Arnsberg/Westf.
        Postfach 84, WEST GERMANY
5603 AD) Shiawassee Hotel, 17017 West Nine
        Mile, Southfield, MI   48075   USA
5604 AD) Salon Santorian, JAPAN
     DES/A) Hiroshi Konno
5605 AD) Sundance Records
     DES/A) David Bacigalupi

5606

5607 SELECTFORM

5608

5609

5610

5611

5612

5613

5614

5615

5616

5617

5618 **seabrook island**
A Land Logistics Corporation Development

5619

5620 SVETEX

5621

5606 AD) Shaw Festival Theatre, Box 774, Niagara-On-The-Lake, Ont., CANADA
DES/A) Arnold Wicht
ST) Camp Associates Advertising
5607 AD) Select Form, Gesellschaft für modernen, Wohnbedarf mbH & Co. KG., 7 Stuttgart 70, Degerloch, Sigmaringer Strasse 258, WEST GERMANY
5608 AD) Stereo Tape Equipment Ltd., ENGLAND
DES/A) Michael Pacey
5609 AD) Société Générale
5610 AD) Sinclair Valentine Inks, 4590 Dufferin St., Downsview, Ont., CANADA
5611 AD) St. Lawrence Centre for the Arts, Front & Scott Streets, Toronto, Ont., CANADA
5612 AD) Schawkgraphics, 4546 N. Kedzie Ave., Chicago, IL 60625 USA
5613 AD) Shinetso Broadcasting System Inc., JAPAN
DES/A) Kimihito Obashira
5614 AD) Staley (Canada) Ltd., 385 The West Mall, Etobicoke, Ont., CANADA
5615 AD) Steel Service Centre Institute, Cleveland, OH, USA
5616 AD) Santa Barbara Conference & Convention Bureau, P.O. Box 299-E, Santa Barbara, CA 93102 USA
5617 AD) Savogran, Norwood, MA 02062 USA
5618 AD) Seabrook Island Co. (A Land Logistics Corp. Development) P.O. Box 99, Charleston, SC 29402 USA
5619 AD) Sea Grill, 1619 N.E. 4th Ave., Fort Lauderdale, FL, USA
C) Sea Food Restaurant
5620 AD) Svensk Textil Mats Fransson AB, Box 4030, S-511 04 Kinna 4, SWEDEN
SM) Svetex
5621 AD) Standard Manufacturing Co., 220 E. Fourth St., Cedar Falls, IA 50613 USA

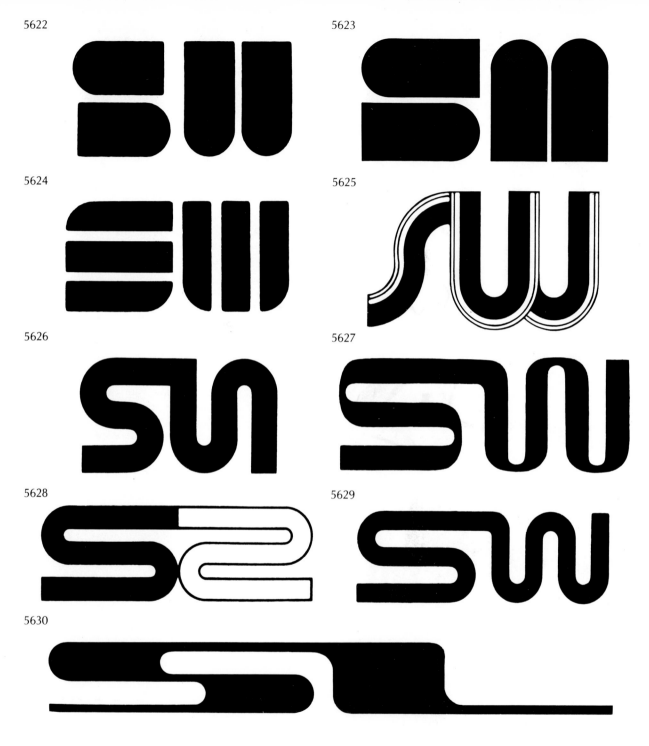

5622

5623

5624

5625

5626

5627

5628

5629

5630

5622   AD)   Shelby Williams Industries Inc.,
               Chicago, IL, USA
5623   AD)   Shand, Morahan & Co., Inc., 801
               Davis St., Evanston, IL   60201   USA
5624   AD)   Shannon & Wilson, Inc., Seattle,
               WA, USA
5625   AD)   Stationers Wholesale Ltd., 1351
               Matheson Blvd., Mississauga,
               Ont., CANADA
5626   AD)   Sun Spice, Inc., JAPAN
        DES/A)   Koji Kato
5627   AD)   Schwartz/Wassyng Inc., USA
        C)   Design Studio
5628   AD)   Solid State Instrument Laboratories,
               USA
        DES/A)   Richard Oborne
5629   AD)   Stowe-Woodward Co., Essex Urethane
               Div., Newton, MA   02164   USA
5630   AD)   Simpson Lee Paper Co., San Francisco,
               CA, USA

5631

5632

5633

5634

5635

5636

5637

5638

5639

5640

5631 AD) South Carolina National Bank, Columbia, SC, USA

5632 AD) Syntex (USA) Inc., 3401 Hillview Ave., Palo Alto, CA, USA

5633 AD) The Robert Simpson Co., Ltd., 176 Yonge St., Toronto, Ont. M5H 3K2 CANADA

C) Simpson's West End Men's Shop

5634 AD) Superior Sanitation Services, 1126 Fewster Dr., Mississauga, Ont., CANADA

5635 AD) Sherwood Selpac, A Hill Acme Co., 120 Church St., Lockport, NY 14094 USA

5636 AD) Simmel, 31033 Castelfranco Veneto (Treviso), Borgo Padova 2, ITALY

C) Military Equipment

5637 AD) Schiffini S.p.A., Casella Postale 321, La Spezia, ITALY

5638 AD) Southeast Ohio Emergency Medical Services, USA

DES/A) Dean R. Lindsay

5639 AD) Sdraio Furniture, ITALY

5640 AD) Summertop, Northpark Shopping Centre, USA

ST) The Richards Group

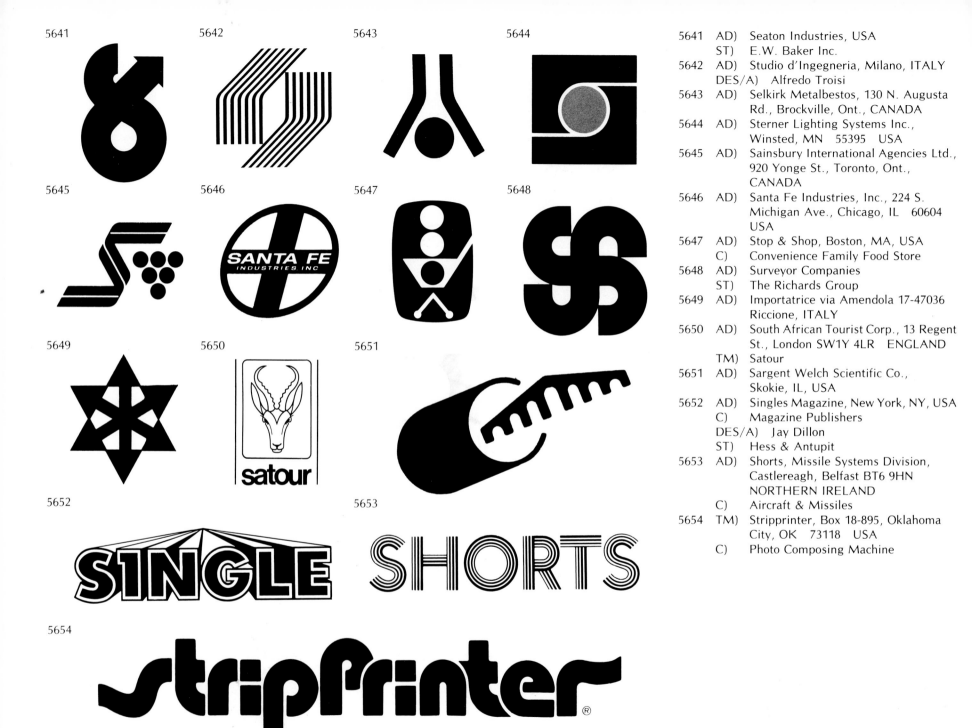

5641

5642

5643

5644

5645

5646

SANTA FE
INDUSTRIES, INC

5647

5648

5649

5650

satour

5651

5652

S1NGLE

5653

SHORTS

5654

stripPrinter®

5641 AD) Seaton Industries, USA
ST) E.W. Baker Inc.
5642 AD) Studio d'Ingegneria, Milano, ITALY
DES/A) Alfredo Troisi
5643 AD) Selkirk Metalbestos, 130 N. Augusta Rd., Brockville, Ont., CANADA
5644 AD) Sterner Lighting Systems Inc., Winsted, MN 55395 USA
5645 AD) Sainsbury International Agencies Ltd., 920 Yonge St., Toronto, Ont., CANADA
5646 AD) Santa Fe Industries, Inc., 224 S. Michigan Ave., Chicago, IL 60604 USA
5647 AD) Stop & Shop, Boston, MA, USA
C) Convenience Family Food Store
5648 AD) Surveyor Companies
ST) The Richards Group
5649 AD) Importatrice via Amendola 17-47036 Riccione, ITALY
5650 AD) South African Tourist Corp., 13 Regent St., London SW1Y 4LR ENGLAND
TM) Satour
5651 AD) Sargent Welch Scientific Co., Skokie, IL, USA
5652 AD) Singles Magazine, New York, NY, USA
C) Magazine Publishers
DES/A) Jay Dillon
ST) Hess & Antupit
5653 AD) Shorts, Missile Systems Division, Castlereagh, Belfast BT6 9HN NORTHERN IRELAND
C) Aircraft & Missiles
5654 TM) Stripprinter, Box 18-895, Oklahoma City, OK 73118 USA
C) Photo Composing Machine

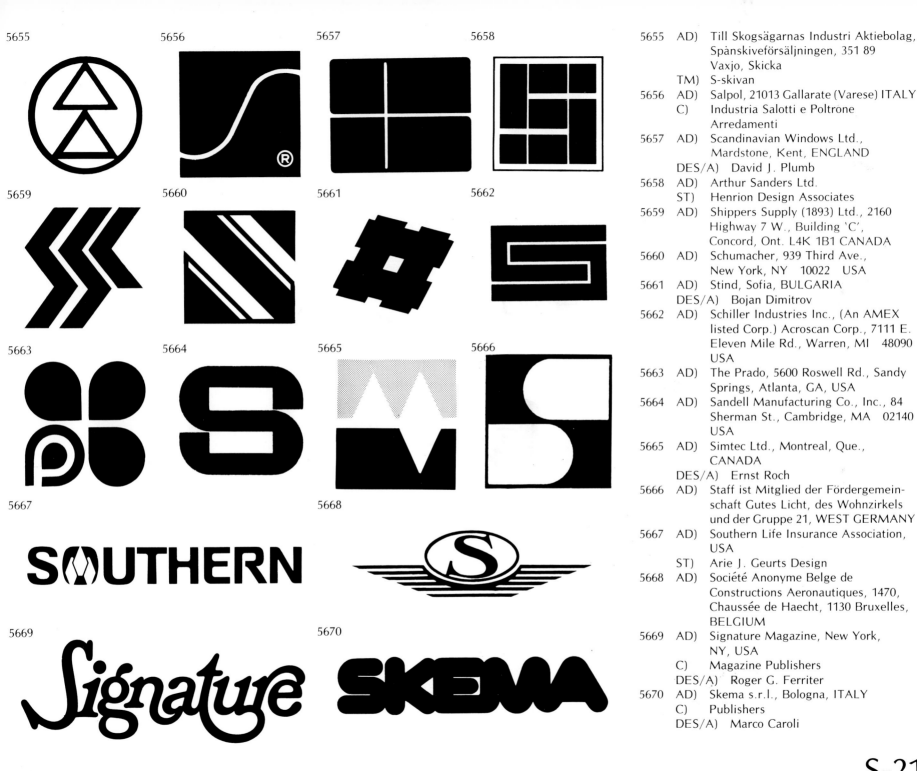

5655 AD) Till Skogsägarnas Industri Aktiebolag, Spånskiveförsäljningen, 351 89 Vaxjo, Skicka
TM) S-skivan
5656 AD) Salpol, 21013 Gallarate (Varese) ITALY
C) Industria Salotti e Poltrone Arredamenti
5657 AD) Scandinavian Windows Ltd., Mardstone, Kent, ENGLAND
DES/A) David J. Plumb
5658 AD) Arthur Sanders Ltd.
ST) Henrion Design Associates
5659 AD) Shippers Supply (1893) Ltd., 2160 Highway 7 W., Building 'C', Concord, Ont. L4K 1B1 CANADA
5660 AD) Schumacher, 939 Third Ave., New York, NY 10022 USA
5661 AD) Stind, Sofia, BULGARIA
DES/A) Bojan Dimitrov
5662 AD) Schiller Industries Inc., (An AMEX listed Corp.) Acroscan Corp., 7111 E. Eleven Mile Rd., Warren, MI 48090 USA
5663 AD) The Prado, 5600 Roswell Rd., Sandy Springs, Atlanta, GA, USA
5664 AD) Sandell Manufacturing Co., Inc., 84 Sherman St., Cambridge, MA 02140 USA
5665 AD) Simtec Ltd., Montreal, Que., CANADA
DES/A) Ernst Roch
5666 AD) Staff ist Mitglied der Fördergemeinschaft Gutes Licht, des Wohnzirkels und der Gruppe 21, WEST GERMANY
5667 AD) Southern Life Insurance Association, USA
ST) Arie J. Geurts Design
5668 AD) Société Anonyme Belge de Constructions Aeronautiques, 1470, Chaussée de Haecht, 1130 Bruxelles, BELGIUM
5669 AD) Signature Magazine, New York, NY, USA
C) Magazine Publishers
DES/A) Roger G. Ferriter
5670 AD) Skema s.r.l., Bologna, ITALY
C) Publishers
DES/A) Marco Caroli

5671 AD) Standards Council of Canada, 350 Sparks St., Ottawa, Ont., CANADA

5672 AD) Symmers Financial Insurance Services, Inc., 1923 S. Andrews Ave., Ft. Lauderdale, FL 33316 USA

5673 AD) Qualitatserzeugwisse Der Schmitz-Werke KG, 4407 Emsdetten, WEST GERMANY

5674 AD) Standard Communications, 639 N. Marine Ave., Wilmington, CA 90744 USA

5675 AD) Sure Paint Ltd., 4525 Chesswood Dr., Downsview, Ont., CANADA

C) Instant Printer

5676 AD) Superior Business Machines Ltd., 34 Progress Ave., Scarborough, Ont. M1P 2Y4 CANADA

5677 AD) Sigma-Kaplan Assoc., 1615 Northern Blvd., Manhasset, NY, USA

5678 SM) Students Union, Hong Kong Polytechnic, HONG KONG

DES/A) Michael Miller Yu

5679 AD) Stant Leisure Products Ltd., Middlemore Lane W., Aldridge, West Midlands WS9 8DY ENGLAND

5680 AD) Standard Management Ltd., HONG KONG

DES/A) Michael Miller Yu

5681 SM) 163rd. Street Shopping Center, Miami Beach, FL, USA

5682 AD) Spider Ltd., 23 Salme, ISRAEL

5683 AD) Sherwin-Williams Paints, USA

ST) F. Eugene Smith Assoc.

5684 AD) Segal Assoc., 5800 W. Jefferson Blvd., CA, USA

5685 SM) Small World Children's Day School

ST) Jess Gruel, Larson-Gateman Inc.

5686 AD) The Sterling Trusts Corp., 372 Bay St., Toronto, Ont., CANADA

5687

5688

5689

5690

SIGNALTONE
CORPORATION

5691

5692

5693

5694

5695

5696

5697

San
Vicente
RACQUET CLUB

See & Sea

5698

5699

SCOTTSDALE
EXECUTIVE OFFICE
PARK

Sonic
A UNIT OF GENERAL SIGNAL

5700

5701

SULZER®

Scheherazade

5687 AD) Signaltone Corp., 34039 Schoolcraft
            Rd., Livonia, MI   USA
5688 AD) Sitcap; Torino, ITALY
      DES/A)   Emanuele Centazzo
5689 AD) Safeguard International Ltd.,
            HONG KONG
      DES/A)   Michael Miller YU
5690 AD) Sagdos Printing, Brugherio, Milano,
            ITALY
      DES/A)   Piero Sansoni
5691 AD) Shimano Industrial Co., Ltd., 77,
            3-Cho Oimatsu-Cho, Sakai-Shi,
            Osaka, JAPAN
5692 AD) Société des Produits Nestlé S.A.,
            Vevey, Vaud, SWITZERLAND
5693 AD) Spartan Controls Ltd., Calgary,
            Alta., CANADA
5694 AD) San Vicente Raquet Club, 4000 San
            Vicente Rd., Sandiego Country
            Estates, Ramona, CA   92065   USA
5695 AD) Steury Corp., 310 Steury Ave.,
            Goshen, IN   46526   USA
5696 AD) Splendix Musical Instruments,
            HONG KONG
      DES/A)   Michael Miller YU
5697 AD) See & Sea Travel Service, Inc., 680
            Beach St., San Francisco, CA   94109
            USA
5698 AD) Scottsdale Executive Office Park, 8009
            Via De Ventura, Scottsdale,
            AZ   85258   USA
5699 AD) Sonic Corp., a General Signal Div., 350
            Fairfield Ave., Stamford, CT   06902
            USA
5700 AD) Sulzer Brothers Ltd., CH-8401
            Winterhoe, SWITZERLAND
5701 AD) Ahmad Saidi, Sharonsaidi & Mahoud
            Saidi, USA
      SM) Scheherazade
      DES/A)   Jagdish J. Chavda

5702

5703

5704

5705

5706

5707

5708

5709

5710

5711

5712

5713

GTE SYLVANIA

5714

5715

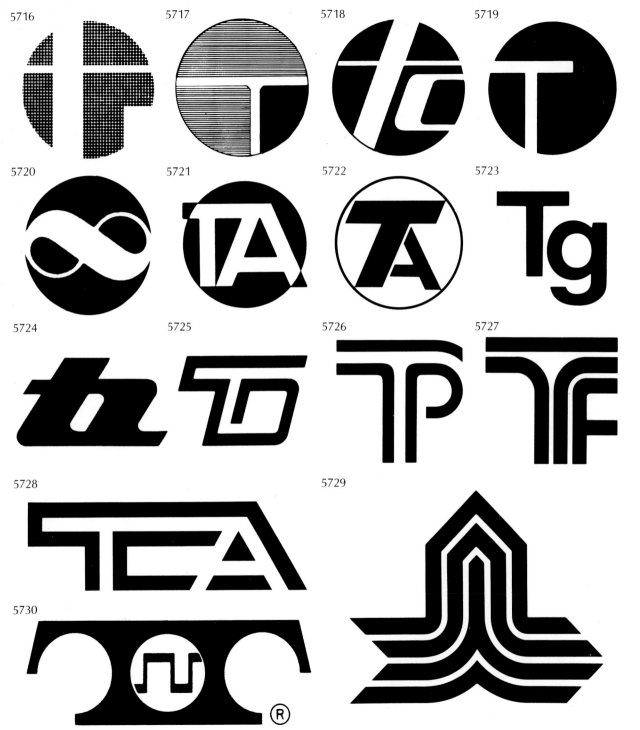

Legend   AD)   Advertiser/Client
            DIR) Art Director
            DES/A) Designer, Artist
            ST)   Studio, Agency
            C)   Category
            SM) Symbol Mark
            TM) Trademark

5716 AD) Trabeco S.A., 96, Rue Montmartre 75002, Paris, FRANCE

5717 AD) Texas Office Supply Co., 6628 Gulf Freeway, Houston, TX 77017 USA

5718 AD) Twin-Cee Ltd., 20 Armstrong Ave., Georgetown, Ont., CANADA

5719 AD) Toilet Laundries Ltd., CANADA
        DES/A) Ernst Roch

5720 AD) Taiyo Kobe Bank, Subsidiary: Taiyo Kobe Finance Hong Kong Ltd., Tokyo, Kobe, JAPAN

5721 AD) Tobias Associates, Inc., 50 Industrial Dr., Ivyland, PA 18974 USA

5722 SM) Toyota Astre, JAPAN
        DES/A) Yasaburo Kuwayama

5723 AD) Texas Gulf, Inc., 200 Park Ave., New York, NY 10017 USA
        DES/A) George Tscherny

5724 AD) Tulli Zuccari, Borgo Trevi, (Perugia), ITALY

5725 AD) Tri-Data, 800 Maude Ave., Mountain View, CA 94043 USA

5726 AD) Tioga Pipe Supply Co., Inc., Philadelphia, PA, USA

5727 AD) Trend Financial, Inc.
        ST) RKP Associates
        DES/A) Joseph Addario

5728 AD) Textcomp Associates Ltd., 2104 Yonge St., Toronto, Ont. M4S 2A5 CANADA

5729 AD) Teleglobe Canada, 625 Belmont St., Montreal, Que. H3B 2M2 CANADA

5730 AD) Teletype Corp., Dept. 71F, 5555 Touhy Ave., Skokie, IL 60076 USA

5731   AD)   Toho Shigyo Co., Ltd., JAPAN
          DES/A)   Yusaku Kamekura

5732   AD)   Tscharnergut Immobilien AG, Bern, WEST GERMANY
          DES/A)   Peter Kräuchi

5733   AD)   Trelement-Dau, Frankfurt, GERMANY
          DES/A)   Eberhardt G. Rensch

5734   AD)   Tamminen & Havaste, Helsinki, FINLAND
          DES/A)   Seppo Polameri

5735   AD)   Tyndale Hall, Bristol, ENGLAND
          ST)   Alan Wagstaff & Partners Ltd.

5736   AD)   Massachusetts Bay Transportation Authority
          ST)   Chermayeff & Geisman Associates

5737   AD)   Tero Corvette, IL, USA
          DES/A)   Jim Lienhart

5738   AD)   Takahashi Shoji Co., Ltd., Tokyo, JAPAN
          DES/A)   Nakayo Masayoshi

5739   AD)   Toyo Printing Co., Los Angeles, CA, USA
          DES/A)   J. Cullimore and F. Cheatham

5740   AD)   Tartan Marine Co., Grand River, OH, USA

5741   AD)   Termia, ITALY

5742   AD)   Tulip Inc., Philadelphia, PA, USA

5743   AD)   Tennis Magazine, Published by Tennis Features Inc., 495 Westport Ave., Norwalk, CT   06856   USA

5744

5745

5746

5747 **telak**

5748 tacon

5749

5750 ®

5751

5752

5753 TILT

5753a rubinetterie **teorema**

5754 **TOURNUS**

5755 **tipco»**

5756

5757

5758

5759

5760

5761

5762

5763

5764

5765

5766

5767

5756 AD) Type-Graphics & Lettering, Div. of
Artissimo, Inc., 223 E. 31st St.,
New York, NY 10016 USA
C) Design/Logotypes, Trademarks &
Symbols/Headlines
DES/A) Tony Dispigna
5757 AD) Telemecanique Canada Ltd., 303
Lesmill Rd., Don Mills, Ont.
M3B 2V1 CANADA
5758 AD) Charles Tennant & Co. (Canada) Ltd.,
34 Clayson Rd., Weston, Ont.
M9M 2G8 CANADA
TM) Tennant Chemicals
5759 AD) É Maillée Au Titane
5760 AD) Tanaka of Tokyo, 5 Sultan at Bay,
Toronto, Ont., CANADA
C) Restaurant
5761 AD) Canadian Motor Industries, 1291
Bellamy N., Scarborough, Ont.,
CANADA
SM) Toyota Emblem
5762 AD) Tretorn Aktiebolag, Fack, S-25100,
Helsingborg, SWEDEN
5763 AD) Oy Tilgmann Ab, Helsinki, FINLAND
C) Printing
DES/A) Alfons Eder
5764 AD) Trident Pool and Recreation Service,
4400 Bathurst St., Downsview,
Ont., CANADA
5765 AD) Toronto Office, 42 Mercer St., Toronto,
Ont. M5V 1H3 CANADA
C) Office Supplies Consumer Magazine
5766 AD) TCC, Inc., 3807 Wilshire Blvd., Los
Angeles, CA 90010 USA
5767 AD) Transair, Palermo, ITALY
DES/A) Silvio Coppola

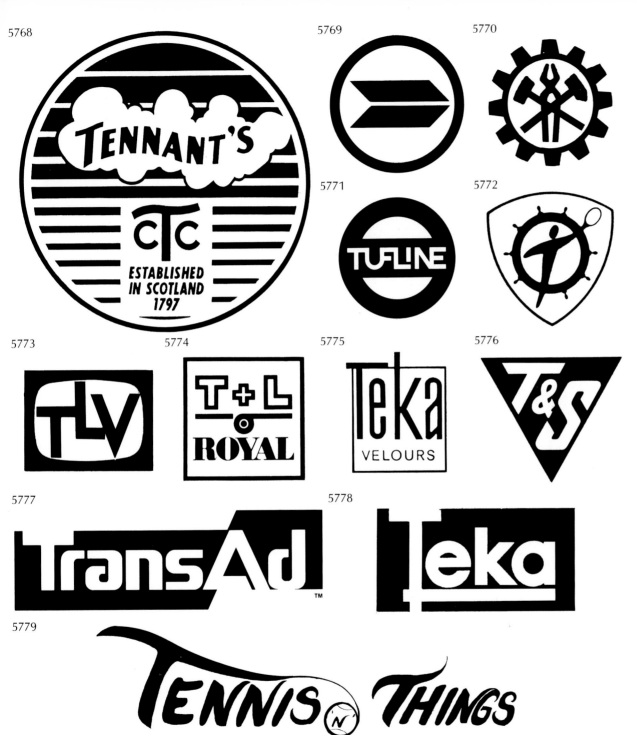

5768 AD) Charles Tennant & Co. (Canada) Ltd.,
         34 Clayson Rd., Weston, Ont.,
         CANADA (Ref. also see #5758)
     SM) Tennant's Product TM
5769 AD) Travel Dynamics, New York, NY, USA
     DES/A) George Mileos
     ST) Mileos Industrial Design
5770 AD) Transocean Machine Co. Inc.,
         5500 Royalmount Ave., Montreal,
         Que. H4P 1H9 CANADA
5771 AD) Tufline Ltd., 222 Norfinch Dr.,
         Downsview, Ont., CANADA
5772 AD) Treasure Island Tennis & Yacht Club,
         400 Treasure Island Causeway,
         Treasure Island, FL 33706 USA
5773 AD) Time-Life Video, Time & Life
         Building, Rockefeller Center, New
         York, NY 10020 USA
5774 AD) Twick & Lehrke KG., 483 Gütersloh,
         Postfach 3140 ABT. MD.,
         WEST GERMANY
5775 AD) Theodor Kreimer, Textilwerke, 4412
         Freckenhorst 02581 4015 Ruf
     SM) Teka Velours
5776 AD) T & S Brass & Bronze Works, Inc.,
         128 Magnolia Ave., Westbury,
         NY 11590 USA
5777 AD) Trans-Ad, Ltd.
     DES/A) Don Primi
5778 AD) Teka-Apparatebau, Sieber & Schiele,
         6 Frankfurt am Main-Süd, Postfach
         700942 FR GERMANY
5779 AD) Tennis N' Things, 3025 Las Vegas
         Blvd. S., Las Vegas, NV 89109 USA

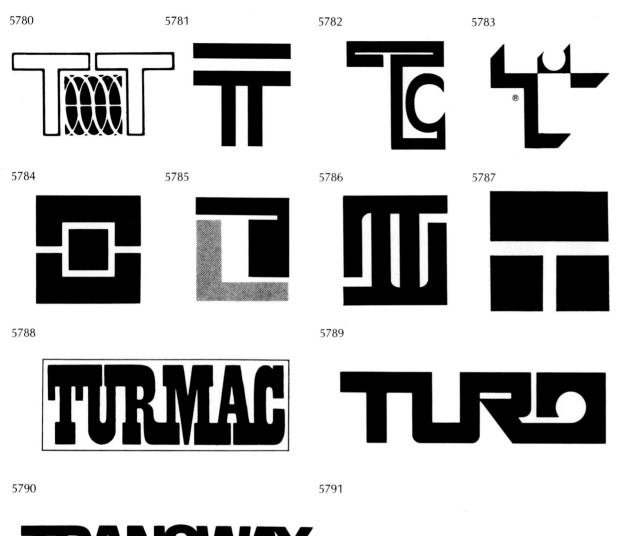

5780

5781

5782

5783

5784

5785

5786

5787

5788

5789

TURMAC

TURO

5790

TRANSWAY

5791

5792

TOPIOKA™

5780 AD) Tech-Tran Corp., 50 Indel Ave., Rancocas, NJ 08073 USA

5781 AD) Terminus Media, 1720 Peachtree Rd. N.W., Atlanta, GA 30309 USA

5782 AD) Toronto Learning Centre, 272 Lawrence Ave. W., Toronto, Ont. M5M 4M1 CANADA

5783 AD) Tol-O-Matic, 246 Tenth Ave. S., Minneapolis, MN 55415 USA

5784 AD) Transformatoren Union AG, A company founded by AEG-Group and Siemens, Deckerstrasse 1, D-7000 Stuttgart 50, WEST GERMANY

5785 AD) Thunderline Corp., Wayne, MI, USA

5786 AD) Textil Lassen, Vallensbaekvej 22A, DK-2600 Glostrup, DENMARK

5787 AD) Telle-Büromöbel AG, Windisch, WEST GERMANY
C) Office Furniture Manufacturers
DES/A) Hans R. Woodtli

5788 AD) Turmac Industries Ltd., Montreal, Que., CANADA

5789 AD) Turo Construction Corp.
DES/A) Don Primi

5790 AD) Transway International Corp., 747 Third Ave., New York, NY, 10017

5791 AD) Type/Graphics
DES/A) Michael Fountain
ST) George Monagle/Graphic Production Ltd.

5792 AD) Cosaco Sales Corp. Ltd., 9600 Meilleur St., Suite 850, Montreal, Que., CANADA
TM) Topioka

5793

Type Trends Inc.

5794

5795

5796

5797

5798

TEMPE RACQUET & SWIM CLUB

5799

TÉLÉ-CAPITALE LTÉE

5800

5801

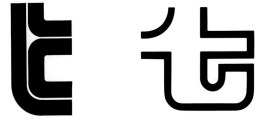

5802

5803

Toscana

5804

tred 2 T.M.

5805

5806

5793 AD) Type Trends Inc., 222 E. 46th St., New York, NY 10017 USA
DES/A) Ray Cruz
ST) Type Trends, Inc.
5794 AD) Test Drilling Service Co., Maryland Heights, MO, USA
DES/A) Tim McLandsborough
ST) PR&D Advertising
5795 AD) Tjernlund Manufacturing Co., 2140 Kasota Ave., St. Paul, MN 55108 USA
5796 AD) Team Concept, 1925 Century Blvd., N.E., Atlanta, GA 30345 USA
5797 AD) Taller 《Ensamblaje》 Caracus, VENEZUALA
C) Assembly Workshop
DES/A) Gerd Leufert
5798 AD) Tempe Racquet & Swim Club, 2140 E. Broadway Rd., Tempe, AZ, USA
5799 AD) Télé-Capitale Ltée, 2136 Chemin Ste-Foy, Ste-Foy, Que., CANADA
5800 AD) Tonelli & C, Mobili, Via Ciro Menotti 9, 61100 Pesare, ITALY
5801 AD) Typography Shop, 2161 Monroe Dr., N.E., Atlanta, GA 30324 USA
5802 AD) TelAlpha, Inc., 358 Mathew St., Santa Clara, CA 94050 USA
C) Audio & Video Systems
5803 AD) Rubinetterie Toscane, Ponsi-Viareggio, ITALY
5804 AD) Tred 2, Inc., Dept. 101, 2510 Channing Ave., San Jose, CA 95131 USA
5805 AD) Techman Ltd., 320-9th Ave., S.W., Calgary, Alta. T2P 1K6 CANADA
C) Engineers and Environmental Scientists
5806 AD) Texco Construction, Div. of Mayan, 4111 Directors Row, Houston, TX 77018 USA

5807

5808

5809

5810

5811

5812

5813

5814

5815

5816

TUMBLER

5817

5818

THORENS

Timex

5819

5820

Tyler

TYLER

TEXAS AMERICAN BANCSHARES INC.

5807 AD) Telefonos de Mexico, S.A., MEXICO
5808 AD) Typographie Métro Inc., Montreal, Que., CANADA
      C)   Typographic Studio
      DES/A) Pierre-Yves Pelletier
5809 AD) Tunnel Refineries Ltd., London, ENGLAND
      C)   Edible Oil Refining
      DES/A) Anthony Hobbs
      ST)   Hiller Rinaldo Associates
5810 AD) Terra Furniture Inc., Los Angeles, CA, USA
      DES/A) Frank R. Cheatham & David J. Goodman
      ST)   Porter & Goodman Design
5811 AD) Tecnicas de Comunicación, Barcelona, SPAIN
      C)   Advertising Agency
      DES/A) Francesc Guitart
5812 AD) Toyota Motor Co., Ltd., Toyota, JAPAN
      C)   Automobile Manufacturers
      DES/A) Tanaka Ikko
5813 AD) The J.A. Tumbler Laboratories Ltd., 2135 Lawrence Ave. E., Scarborough, Ont., CANADA
5814 AD) Teleflex Inc., North Wales, PA, USA
      C)   Cable System
      DES/A) David L. Burke
5815 AD) Tyrolean Village Resorts, Collingwood, Ont., CANADA
5816 AD) Trans-Africa Marketing Services Ltd., Tel-Aviv, ISRAEL
      C)   Dispensing Machines
5817 AD) Thorens Electronic Transcription Turntable, USA
5818 AD) Tow. Handlu Zagraniczn, Warsaw, POLAND
      TM)   Timex
      DES/A) Ryszard Sidorowski
5819 AD) Tyler Boat Co., Ltd., Sovereign Close, Tonbridge, Kent TN9 1RP ENGLAND
5820 AD) Texas American Bancshares Inc., P.O. Box 2050, Fort Worth, TX 76101 USA

5821 AD) Thumbody, Princeton Partners Inc., 245 Nassau St., Princeton, NJ, USA
C) Advertising Agency/Promotional & Public Relations Services
5822 AD) Tri-Canada, Cherry-Burrell Ltd., 6500 Northwest Dr., Malton, Ont., CANADA
5823 AD) Ernest Treganowan, Inc., Interior Design Bldg., 306 E. 61st St., New York, NY 10021 USA
5824 AD) Tikkaustuote, Loimaa, FINLAND
C) Textile Factory
DES/A) Rolf Christianson
5825 AD) Treco Inc., Champlain Division, Centre Industriel, St. Romuald Co., Lévis, Que., CANADA
5826 AD) Tee-Pak, Inc., 915 N. Michigan Ave., Danville, IL 61832 USA
5827 SM) Toy Maker, JAPAN
DES/A) Hiroshi Ohchi
5828 AD) Products Pluperfect, 48 Massapequa Ave., Massapequa, NY 11758 USA
SM) Tennis Doctor
5829 AD) Tammsco, Inc., N. Front St., Tamms, IL 62988 USA
5830 AD) Telegraph Press, P.O. Box 1831, Harrisburg, PA 17105 USA
5831 AD) Tollycraft Corp., Kelso, WA, USA
5832 AD) Torrid Oven Ltd., 7500 Bath Rd., Malton, Ont., CANADA
C) Manufactured Industrial Equipment

5832a

5833

5834

5835

5836

5837

5838

5839

TAYLOR
SYBRON CORPORATION

5840

5841

Transcontinental Gas Pipe Line Corporation

5832a AD) Trans-Canada Liquidations Ltd.,
111 Richmond St., W., Toronto,
Ont., CANADA
DES/A) Steve Gill
5833 AD) Tubertini-Hillhouse Insurance
Agency, Inc.
DES/A) Anita Soos
5834 AD) Trend Associates Inc., USA
ST) Addario Design Associates
5835 AD) Tele-Communications Consultants
Inc., USA
DES/A) Don Primi
5836 AD) Teledyne Inc., Los Angeles, CA, USA
ST) Robert Miles Runyan & Assoc.
5837 AD) Triplett Corp., Bluffton, OH, USA
5838 AD) Trust Company Bank, Atlanta,
GA, USA
5839 AD) Taylor Instruments of Canada Ltd.,
A Sybron Corp., 75 Tycos Dr.,
Toronto, Ont., CANADA
5840 AD) Sas-Scandinavian Airlines,
Bromma Airport, Stockholm,
SWEDEN
SM) Thai
5841 AD) Transcontinental Gas Pipe Line Corp.,
USA

5842

5843

5844

5845

5846

5847

5848

5849

5850

5851

5852

5853

5854

5855

5856

5857

Legend   AD;   Advertiser/Client
          DIR)   Art Director
          DES/A) Designer, Artist
          ST)   Studio, Agency
          C)   Category
          SM)   Symbol Mark
          TM)   Trademark

5842   AD)   Ultraflex, via Sturdia, 36-16131
               Genova, ITALY
5843   AD)   Universal Geneve of Canada Ltd.,
               123 Bartley Dr., Toronto, Ont.,
               CANADA
5844   AD)   Unarco Industries, Inc., 332 S.
               Michigan Ave., Chicago, IL 60604
               USA
5845   AD)   Unternehmensberatung Der
               Industriepraktiker Hans-Georg Schu
               München-Grünwald, GERMANY
5846   AD)   U.I.P. Corp., 1970 Estes Ave., Elk
               Grove Village, Chicago, IL 60007
               USA
5847   AD)   Unifair Inc., New York, NY, USA
        ST)   Appelbaum & Curtis Inc.
5848   AD)   Usemco, Inc., Chicago, IL, USA
        DES/A) William Cagney
        ST)   RVI Corp.
5849   AD)   Utet Sansoni Edizioni Scientifiche,
               ITALY
        ST)   Studio Genovesi
5850   AD)   Universal Data Systems, 2611 Leeman
               Ferry Rd., Huntsville, AL 35805
               USA
5851   AD)   Universal Match Corp., 404 Paul Ave.,
               St. Louis, MO 63135   USA
5852   AD)   United Business Products Corp.,
               P.O. Box 1315, Southfield, MI 48075
               USA
5853   AD)   United Fruit Co., USA
5854   AD)   University of Alberta, Alta., CANADA
        DES/A) Walter Jungkind
5855   AD)   United Yacht Brokers, 2260 S.E. 17th
               St., Fort Lauderdale, FL 33316   USA
5856   AD)   Underwater Mechanics International,
               P.O. Box 654, Spring, TX 77373
               USA
5857   AD)   Universal Water Systems, Inc.,
               1425 Hawthorne Lane, West Chicago,
               IL 60185   USA

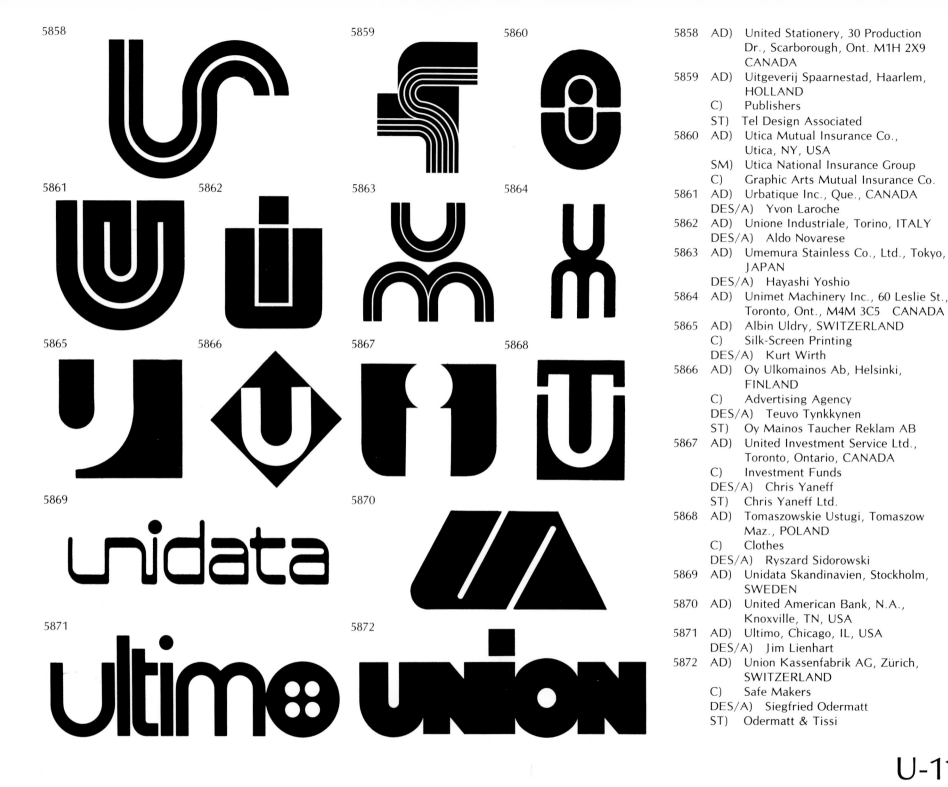

5858

5859

5860

5861

5862

5863

5864

5865

5866

5867

5868

5869

unidata

5870

5871

ultimo

5872

UNION

5858   AD)   United Stationery, 30 Production
                Dr., Scarborough, Ont. M1H 2X9
                CANADA
5859   AD)   Uitgeverij Spaarnestad, Haarlem,
                HOLLAND
        C)   Publishers
        ST)   Tel Design Associated
5860   AD)   Utica Mutual Insurance Co.,
                Utica, NY, USA
        SM)   Utica National Insurance Group
        C)   Graphic Arts Mutual Insurance Co.
5861   AD)   Urbatique Inc., Que., CANADA
        DES/A) Yvon Laroche
5862   AD)   Unione Industriale, Torino, ITALY
        DES/A) Aldo Novarese
5863   AD)   Umemura Stainless Co., Ltd., Tokyo,
                JAPAN
        DES/A) Hayashi Yoshio
5864   AD)   Unimet Machinery Inc., 60 Leslie St.,
                Toronto, Ont., M4M 3C5   CANADA
5865   AD)   Albin Uldry, SWITZERLAND
        C)   Silk-Screen Printing
        DES/A) Kurt Wirth
5866   AD)   Oy Ulkomainos Ab, Helsinki,
                FINLAND
        C)   Advertising Agency
        DES/A) Teuvo Tynkkynen
        ST)   Oy Mainos Taucher Reklam AB
5867   AD)   United Investment Service Ltd.,
                Toronto, Ontario, CANADA
        C)   Investment Funds
        DES/A) Chris Yaneff
        ST)   Chris Yaneff Ltd.
5868   AD)   Tomaszowskie Ustugi, Tomaszow
                Maz., POLAND
        C)   Clothes
        DES/A) Ryszard Sidorowski
5869   AD)   Unidata Skandinavien, Stockholm,
                SWEDEN
5870   AD)   United American Bank, N.A.,
                Knoxville, TN, USA
5871   AD)   Ultimo, Chicago, IL, USA
        DES/A) Jim Lienhart
5872   AD)   Union Kassenfabrik AG, Zürich,
                SWITZERLAND
        C)   Safe Makers
        DES/A) Siegfried Odermatt
        ST)   Odermatt & Tissi

U-11

5873   AD)   U.S. National Park Service, Washington, D.C., USA
       C)   Government Agency
       DES/A)   Tom Geismar

5874   AD)   United Tape, 57 Glencameron Rd., Thornhill, Ont., CANADA
       C)   Packaging Products Dist.

5875   AD)   United Oilseed Products Ltd., P.O. Box 68, Lloydminster, Alta., CANADA

5876   AD)   Unione Produttori Di Sintetico Per Calzature, Milano, ITALY
       C)   Union of Footwear Synthentics Producers
       ST)   G & R Associati

5877   AD)   United Technologies Corp., Hartford, CT 06101 USA
           Div. Group: Pratt & Whitney Aircraft Group, Otis, Essex Group, Sikorsky Aircraft, Hamilton Standard, Norden, Chemical Systems Division, Power Systems Division, Turbo Power & Marine Systems, United Technologies International, United Technologies Research Center.

5878   AD)   United States Polo Association, Chicago, IL, USA
       C)   National Polo Association
       DES/A)   Jim Lienhart

5879   AD)   U.S. Photo Exhibition, NY, USA
       DES/A)   Kissiloff & Wimmershoff

5880   AD)   Unitech Inc., 1005 East St. Elmo Rd., Austin, TX, USA

5881   AD)   United Hospital Fund and Greater New York Hospital Association, New York, NY, USA
       C)   Hospital fund raising and consultants
       DES/A)   Beau Gardner

5882   AD)   Union Trust, USA
       ST)   The Richards Group

5883   SM)   United Israel Appeal of Canada, H.O. Montreal, Que., CANADA

5884   AD)   Cimco Ltd., 65 Villiers St., Toronto, Ont., CANADA
       TM)   Unipak Product

5885
5886
5887
5888

5889
5890
5891
5892

5893
5894
5895
5896

5897
5898

5885 AD) S.C. Johnson & Son, Inc., 1525 Howe St., Racine, WI, USA
      SM) Product TM
5886 AD) Union Bank of Switzerland
5887 AD) Upton Bradeen & James, Inc., 7200 E. 15 Mile Rd., Sterling Heights, MI, USA
5888 AD) U.S. Air Force Systems Command, Washington, D.C., USA
      C) Electronics div. of Air Force
      DES/A) Ben Dennis
5889 AD) Universal Greetings Ltd., 24 St. Mary Axe, London EC3 ENGLAND
5890 AD) Union Bank of Finland, Formerly ''Pohjoismaiden Yhdyspankki-Nordiska Föreningsbanken,'' Head Office: Helsinki, FINLAND
5891 AD) Union Des Foires Internationales
5892 AD) U.S. Department of Health, Washington, D.C., USA
      C) Government Department
      DES/A) Edmond P. Sullivan
5893 AD) United Jersey Banks, 210 Main St., Hackensack, NJ 07602 USA
5894 AD) United Cansco Oil & Gas Ltd., USA
5895 AD) Charles Ulmer, Inc., 175 City Island Ave., City Island, NY 10464 USA
      C) Sailmakers
5896 AD) Universal Aviation Supply Co., Ltd., 232 Tolworth Rise S., Tolworth, Surrey, ENGLAND
5897 AD) United Federal Savings & Loan Association, 3600 North Federal Hwy., Fort Lauderdale, FL, USA
5898 AD) Twelve Stone Flagons Ltd., 4001 Greenridge Rd., Castle Shannon, PA 15234 USA

5899

5900

5901

5902

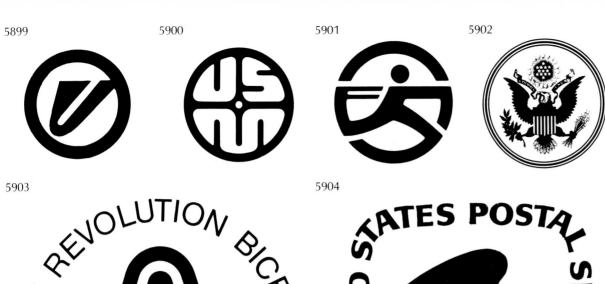

5903

5904

AMERICAN REVOLUTION BICENTENNIAL 1776-1976

UNITED STATES POSTAL SERVICE

U.S. MAIL

5905

5906

Uniflite INC

underwood *Yachting Centers*

5907

5908

Ungermann

THE UNSTUCKER™

5899 AD) Unimax Switch, Wallingford, CT, USA
5900 AD) U.S. Microfilm Sales Corp., 235 Montgomery, San Francisco, CA, USA
DES/A) Paul Hagen
5901 AD) UAP, 7025 est, Rue Ontario St., E., Montreal, Que., CANADA
5902 AD) The Great Seal of The United States, USA
5903 SM) Bicentennial Symbol, American Revolution (1776-1976) Bicentennial Celebration, USA
5904 SM) United States Postal Service, USA
5905 AD) Uniflite Inc., USA
5906 AD) Underwood Yachting Centers, USA
5907 AD) Erwin Ungermann, Kälte & Klimatechnik, 5600 Wuppertal 2, Mollenkotten 155, GERMANY
5908 AD) Noremco Marketing Systems Ltd., 151 Birge St., Hamilton, Ont., CANADA
        TM) Product Name, The Unstucker

5909 AD) Union of Oil and Soap Industries, Bulgaria
      DES/A) Kantscho Kanev
5910 AD) Union Tiefban GmbH, München, GERMANY
      DES/A) Pham Phu Oanh
5911 AD) University of Toronto, Toronto, Ont., CANADA
      SM) Sesquicentennial
      DES/A) Allan Fleming
5912 AD) Universal, Paris, FRANCE
      C) Paris Travel Agency
      DES/A) Jean Delunay
5913 AD) Unilever Ltd., London, ENGLAND
      C) Manufacturers of Consumer Products
      DES/A) Collis Clements
5914 AD) Unican Security Systems Ltd., 5795 de Gaspe Ave., Montreal, Que., CANADA
5915 AD) Unión de Centros de la Edificación, SPAIN
      DES/A) Jose Baqués
5916 AD) Unione Costruttori, Serramenti Alluminio Acciaio, Leghe, ITALY
      ST) Studio GSZ
      SM) Uncsaal
5917 AD) Union Internationale De La Presse
      C) Professionelle De L'Ameublement
      SM) UIPPA
5918 AD) U.S. Department of Commerce, Washington, D.C., USA
      ST) Appelbaum & Curtis Inc.
5919 AD) Urban Systems Development Corp., USA
      DES/A) Shirley Olsen Jones

5920

5921 5922

5923 5924

5925 5926 5927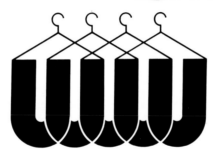

5928 unit1

5929 THE UNITED NATIONS TWENTY FIFTH 1945 1970

5930 U&lc.

5920 AD) United American Realty, USA
ST) Miller/Hernandez Design
5921 AD) University Plaza, USA
ST) Miller/Hernandez Design
5922 AD) United Graphics Corp., USA
DES/A) Nash Hernandez
5923 AD) Trend Industries, Atlanta, GA, USA
SM) Uptrend
5924 AD) Universal Industries Ltd., Box 766,
Lloydminster, Alta. S9V 1C1
CANADA
5925 AD) U.S. Plywood, New York, NY, USA
5926 AD) U.S. Ski Association, USA
DES/A) James Adler
ST) Genesis Inc.
5927 AD) Uniforms Unlimited, Inc.,
Los Angeles, CA, USA
DES/A) Thomas A. Rigsby
ST) TriArts Inc.
5928 AD) Unit 1, Denver, CO, USA
5929 AD) United Nations, USA
DES/A) Herb Lubalin
ST) Lubalin, Smith, Carnase, Inc.
5930 AD) International Typeface Corp.
(Publisher) 216 E. 45th St., New York,
NY 10017 USA
SM) "Upper & Lower Case" masthead for
Trade Paper
DES/A) Herb Lubalin
ST) Lubalin, Smith, Carnase, Inc.

What a way to run a "monopoly!"

You're looking at some of the brands and names of companies that sell gasoline. Some people say oil companies are a monopoly. If so, it's the world's most inept "monopoly."

The "monopoly" is so inept that it offers the world's richest country some of the world's most inexpensive gasoline.

This "monopoly" is so inept that it lets everybody and his brother horn in on the action. Did you know that of the thousands of American oil companies, none has larger than an 8.5% share of the national gasoline?

In fact, this "monopoly" is so inept that you probably wouldn't recognize that it is a monopoly because it looks so much like a competitive marketing system.

People who call us a monopoly obviously don't know what they're talking about.

5931
5932 KM KERR McGEE
5933
5934 Gulf
5935 THRIFTY
5936 TESORO

5937 TIME
5938 CLARK
5939  MOHAWK
5940 TEXACO
5941 LERNER
5942 CONOCO

5943 CROWN
5944 CRYSTAL
5945 QUAKER STATE
5946 MFA OIL
5947 MALCO
5948 MARTIN

5949 WESTERN
5950 FINA
5951 ARCO
5952 SUNOCO
5953 Colonial
5954 EXXON

5955 CHEKER
5956 Vickers
5957 TERRIBLE HERBST
5958 POWERINE
5959 DERBY
5960 BEACON

5961 SPUR
5962 STAR GAS
5963 MIDWEST
5964 CENEX
5965 HESS
5966 USA GASOLINE

5967  PENNZOIL

5968 Ashland

5969 BILLUPS

5970  POWER TEST

5971 SOHIO

5972 COLÓNIAL MINUTEMAN

5973 TOTAL

5974 FS

5975 CERTIFIED

5976  AMOCO

5977 Getty

5978  C TRESLER COMET

5979 Chevron

5980 Texgas

5981  WOOD RIVER

5982 76

5983 CO OP

5984  TENNECO

5985 SHELL

5986 APCO

5987 SOUTHLAND

5988  SHAMROCK

5989 Mobil

5990 M MIDLAND

5991 Zephyr

5992 DIXIE

5993  FCX

5994 ETNA

5995 PHILLIPS 66

5996  UCO

Union "Monopoly" Logotype Ad
Prepared for Union Oil Company of California.
Agency: Leo Burnett U.S.A. Advertising

5997 CITGO

5998 HUSKY

5999 champlin

6000 KEYSTONE

6001 SUNLAND

6002 SOC

6003  UNION 76
Union Oil Company of California
Los Angeles, California 90017

U-18

6005

6006

6007

6008

6009

6010

6011

6012

6013

6014

6015

6016

6017

6018

6019

6020

Legend AD) Advertiser/Client
DIR) Art Director
DES/A) Designer, Artist
ST) Studio, Agency   SM) Symbol Mark
C) Category   TM) Trademark

6005 AD) Varielectric Industries Ltd.,
2800 Pitfield Blvd., Montreal,
Que. H4S 1G9   CANADA

6006 AD) Versatec, Inc., 10100 Bubb Rd.,
Cupertino, CA 95014   USA

6007 AD) Varco-Pruden Metal Building Systems,
Inc., A Division of Dombrico, Inc.
DES/A) Tom Henton

6008 AD) Victor Business Personnel, Div. of
Victor Canada Ltd., 390 Bay St.,
Toronto, Ont. M5H 2G2 CANADA

6009 AD) Vibra Screw Inc., 755 Union Blvd.,
Totowa, NJ 07512   USA

6010 AD) Vinyl-Weld, Inc., 1900 South Western
Ave., Chicago, IL 60608   USA

6011 AD) VBM Corporation, 1402 W. Main St.,
Louisville, KY 40201   USA

6012 SM) Voko, Büromöbelfabriken,
Pohlheim Ortsteil, Garbenteich
Postanschrift: 63 GieBen
Postfach 6540, GERMANY

6013 AD) Victor Graphic Systems Inc.,
Sub. of Victor Comptometer Corp.,
3900 N. Rockwell St.,
Chicago, IL 60618   USA
C) Scanatron Facsimile/Electrowriter
Systems
ST) Dimensional Concepts

6014 AD) Vetter Fairing Co., Dept. CW, Box
927, Rantoul, IL 61866   USA

6015 AD) Viking Products, 929 Broadway,
Riviera Beach, FL 33404   USA

6016 AD) Viceroy Mfg. Co., Ltd., 1655 Dupont
St., Toronto, Ont. M6P 3T1   CANADA

6017 AD) Veart sas, via Moglianese
30037 Scorzè/Venezia, ITALY

6018 AD) Victor Duncan, Inc., 676 St. Clair,
Chicago, IL 60611   USA

6019 SM) Vamply, FL, USA, Vancouver, B.C.
CANADA
DES/A) Ted Baker

6020 AD) Vancouver Community College,
250 West Pender St., Vancouver,
B.C. V6B 1S9   CANADA

6021

6022

6023

6024

6025

6026

6027

6028

Vanda

6029

VIEᔓMANN

6030

VIKING CLOCK COMPANY

6031

VCR

6021 AD) Vac Offset & Printing Co., 338 Est Rue Craig, Montreal, Que., CANADA

6022 AD) Vail Resort Association, Box NY5N, Vail, CO 81657 USA

6023 AD) Michael Vijuk Bindery Consultants Co., Ltd., 630 Rivermede Rd., Concord, Ont. L4K 1C7 CANADA

6024 SM) Volkswagen Automobile Co., GERMANY

6025 AD) Vision Craft Ltd., Fayetteville, NY, USA

6026 AD) VT Industries Inc., 1000 Industrial Park, Holstein, IA 51024 USA

6027 AD) Visual Graphics Corp., Posteriter Div., 1398 N.E. 125th St., N. Miami, FL 33161 USA

6028 AD) Vanda Beauty Counselor, Orlando, FL, USA
DES/A) Rudolf Meyer

6029 AD) Viessmann Werke KG, GERMANY
DES/A) Anton Stankowski

6030 AD) Viking Clock Co., The Viking Building, Foley, AL 36535 USA

6031 AD) Philips Electronics Industries Ltd., (Professional E.L.A. Division) 116 Vanderhoof Ave., Toronto, Ont., CANADA
SM) Video Cassette Recording

6032

6033

6034

6035

6036

6037

6038

6039

6040

6041

6042

6043

6044

6045

6032 AD) Les Productions Videodio Inc.,
1572 Rue De Parc, Ste-Foy, Que.,
CANADA

6033 AD) Visual Dynamics
DES/A) Brian Schuiling

6034 AD) Vorarl Berger, Landesverband För
Fremdenverkehr, Bregenz,
AUSTRIA
DES/A) Othmar Motter

6035 AD) Vendorafa, Valenza PO, Alessandria,
ITALY
DES/A) Alfredo Troisi

6036 AD) Varefakta-Komiteen, Oslo, NORWAY
DES/A) Paul Brand

6037 AD) Vallourec, Société Anonyme,
7 Place Chancelier Adenaver,
75016 Paris, FRANCE

6038 AD) Video 9, Paris, FRANCE
DES/A) Anne-Marie Latremolière

6039 AD) Verband Schweiz . Reform-und Diätf
Achgeschäfte, Zurich,
SWITZERLAND
DES/A) Walters Diethelm

6040 AD) Van Gelder Papier, Amsterdam,
HOLLAND
DES/A) Karen Munck

6041 AD) Tervcon Ltd., 7520 Bath Rd., Malton,
Ont., CANADA
TM) Verifire

6042 AD) Hercules, Inc., 910 Market St.,
Wilmington, DE 19899 USA
TM) Vantage, from the makers of Herculon

6043 AD) Vasold & Schmidt, Neunkirchen,
WEST GERMANY
DES/A) Am Brand

6044 AD) Vacumite, 549 Bosler Ave.,
Lemoyne, PA 17043 USA

6045 AD) Vickers & Benson Advertising Ltd.,
22 St. Clair Ave. E., Toronto,
Ont. M4T 2T3 CANADA
DES/A) Hans Kleefeld

6046   6047   6048   6049

6050   6051

6052   6053

6054   6055

6056

6046	AD)	Victoria Joanne Wynnychuk, 9836-78 Ave., Edmonton, Alta., CANADA
6047	AD)	Valtur, Roma, ITALY
	C)	Tourist Organization
	DES/A)	Hazy Osterwalder
6048	AD)	Vorarlberger Treuhandgesellsell- Schaft, Dornbirn, AUSTRIA
	DES/A)	Othman Motter
6049	AD)	Vierlinger-Käse, Bizau, AUSTRIA
	C)	Cheese Wholesalers
	DES/A)	Othmar Motter
6050	AD)	Van Wijk & Visser, NV, Geldermalsen, NETHERLANDS
	DES/A)	Jan Jaring
6051	AD)	Valextra Design, Milano, ITALY
	DES/A)	Giulio Confalonieri
6052	AD)	Viganò Olympio Muggiò, Industria Mobili Imbottiti, ITALY
	SM)	Vom
6053	AD)	Varispace Items, Inc., 1259 University Ave., Rochester, NY 14607 USA
6054	AD)	Viva Zapata, 1234 Yonge St., Toronto, Ont., CANADA
	C)	Restaurant
	DES/A)	Chris Notter
6055	AD)	Village Palos Verdes, USA
	DES/A)	Wayne Hunt, Connie Beck
	ST)	John Follis & Associates
6056	AD)	Vision Center, USA
	DES/A)	Crawford Dunn
	ST)	RYA Graphics, Inc.

V-10

6057

6058

6059

6060

6061

6062

6063

6064

6065

6066

Vodax Limited

6067

Vanleigh

6068

VLIER BARRY MOUNTS

6069

velosef®

6057 AD) Vail Institute, USA
      ST) Unit 1 Inc.
6058 AD) Vance Industries, USA
      DES/A) Randall R. Roth
      C) Sinks & Faucets
6059 AD) Vargas Zippers, Los Angeles, CA, USA
      ST) Adrian Loos Design Studio
6060 AD) Verolme United Shipyards, Rotterdam,
            Botlek, NETHERLANDS
      DES/A) Michael Russell
6061 AD) Virax, FRANCE
      DES/A) Rémy Peignot
6062 AD) Ville De Montreal, Montreal,
            Que., CANADA
      DES/A) Jacques Roy
6063 AD) Velsicol Chemical Corp.,
            Chicago, IL, USA
6064 AD) Vozila Gorica, JUGOSLAVIA
      DES/A) Oskar Kogoj
6065 AD) Vinylgrain, USA
      ST) Clayton-Davis & Assoc. Inc.
6066 AD) Vodax Limited, 6 Lilliput Rd.,
            Poole Dorset, ENGLAND
6067 AD) Vanleigh, Washington, D.C., USA
6068 AD) Vlier Barry Mounts, Div. of Barry-
            Wright Corp., 2333 Valley St.,
            Burbank, CA, USA
6069 AD) E.R. Squibb & Sons Ltd., 2365 Côte
            De Liesse, Montreal, Que., CANADA
      C) Product, Cephradine, Squibb
      TM) Velosef

Legend AD) Advertiser/Client
        DIR) Art Director
        DES/A) Designer, Artist
        ST) Studio, Agency   SM) Symbol Mark
        C) Category   TM) Trademark

6070 AD) Weyerhaeuser Co., Crocker Hamilton
           Papers, Inc., Subsidiary, 230 Park
           Ave., New York, NY 10017 USA
6071 AD) Wheelabrator Corp. of Canada Ltd.,
           235 Speers Rd., Oakville,
           Ont. L6K 2E8 CANADA
6072 AD) Western Research & Development
           Ltd., Sub. of Bow Valley Ind. Ltd.,
           932 Pacific 66 Plz., Calgary,
           Alta. T2P OT8 CANADA
6073 AD) Wyldewood Golf & Country Club,
           6198 Trafalgar Rd., Oakville, Ont.,
           CANADA
6074 AD) Wesdrill, 280 Viking Way, Richmond
           B.C. V6V 1N5 CANADA
6075 AD) Wix Corporation Ltd., 25 Curity Ave.,
           Toronto, Ont., CANADA
6076 AD) Weston Publishing Co., Ltd.,
           109 Railside Rd., Don Mills,
           Ont., CANADA
6077 AD) Werbeagentur, Dr. Marion & Walter
           Diethelm, Zurich, SWITZERLAND
      DES/A) Walter J. Diethelm
6078 AD) Al Wright, 651 McCowan Rd.,
           Toronto, Ont., CANADA
6079 AD) H. Wennberg GMBH, Musterkarten-
           fabrik, 7250 Leonberg-Ramtel,
           Böblinger Str. 27, WEST GERMANY
6080 AD) Warnock Hersey International Ltd.,
           250 Madison Ave., Toronto,
           Ont. M4V 2W6 CANADA
6081 AD) Windmöller & Hölscher, D454
           Lengerich/Westf.
6082 AD) West Mersea Yacht Charters, Pyefleet
           House, The Strood, Peldon,
           Essex, ENGLAND
6083 AD) Wilkenson Mfg. Co., Inc., Div. Alleg-
           heny Steel & Brass, 4950 S. Kilbourn
           Ave., Chicago, IL 60632 USA
6084 AD) Wirefil Inc., 8585 Langelier,
           Montreal, Que. H1P 2C7 CANADA
6085 AD) Western Farmers Mutual Insurance
           Co., Woodstock, Ont., CANADA

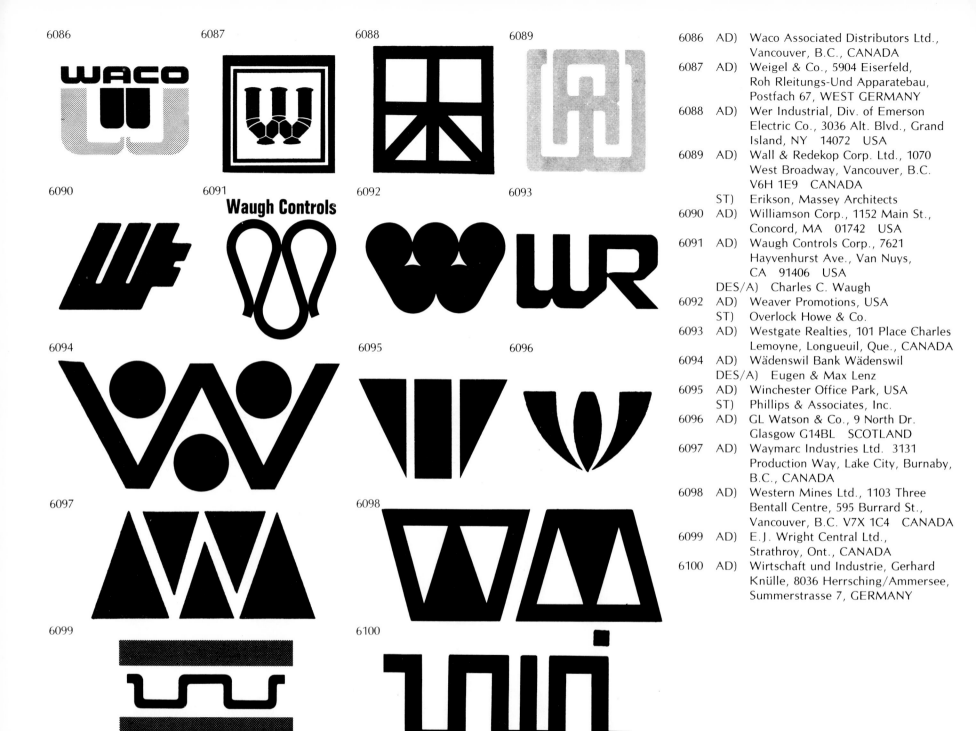

6086
6087
6088
6089

6090
6091 **Waugh Controls**
6092
6093

6094
6095
6096

6097
6098

6099
6100

6086 AD) Waco Associated Distributors Ltd., Vancouver, B.C., CANADA

6087 AD) Weigel & Co., 5904 Eiserfeld, Roh Rleitungs-Und Apparatebau, Postfach 67, WEST GERMANY

6088 AD) Wer Industrial, Div. of Emerson Electric Co., 3036 Alt. Blvd., Grand Island, NY 14072 USA

6089 AD) Wall & Redekop Corp. Ltd., 1070 West Broadway, Vancouver, B.C. V6H 1E9 CANADA
      ST) Erikson, Massey Architects

6090 AD) Williamson Corp., 1152 Main St., Concord, MA 01742 USA

6091 AD) Waugh Controls Corp., 7621 Hayvenhurst Ave., Van Nuys, CA 91406 USA
      DES/A) Charles C. Waugh

6092 AD) Weaver Promotions, USA
      ST) Overlock Howe & Co.

6093 AD) Westgate Realties, 101 Place Charles Lemoyne, Longueuil, Que., CANADA

6094 AD) Wädenswil Bank Wädenswil
      DES/A) Eugen & Max Lenz

6095 AD) Winchester Office Park, USA
      ST) Phillips & Associates, Inc.

6096 AD) GL Watson & Co., 9 North Dr. Glasgow G14BL SCOTLAND

6097 AD) Waymarc Industries Ltd. 3131 Production Way, Lake City, Burnaby, B.C., CANADA

6098 AD) Western Mines Ltd., 1103 Three Bentall Centre, 595 Burrard St., Vancouver, B.C. V7X 1C4 CANADA

6099 AD) E.J. Wright Central Ltd., Strathroy, Ont., CANADA

6100 AD) Wirtschaft und Industrie, Gerhard Knülle, 8036 Herrsching/Ammersee, Summerstrasse 7, GERMANY

6101   AD)   Wildfire Records Inc., 118 Balliol St., Toronto, Ont., CANADA

6102   AD)   Westburne Division, Westburne Alberta Electric Supply Ltd., 3604 8th St., S.E., Calgary, Alta., CANADA

6103   AD)   J.A. Wilson Display Ltd., 1645 Aimco Blvd., Mississauga, Ont. L4W 1H8 CANADA

6104   AD)   Washington Mutual Savings Bank, Seattle, WA, USA

          DES/A)   Ken Parkhurst

6105   AD)   Wards Ateliéer AB, Box 96-S-54301 Tibro 1, SWEDEN

6106   AD)   Dr. A. Wander AG, Bern, SWITZERLAND

          DES/A)   Peter Megert

6107   AD)   WBAP, Fort Worth, TX, USA

          DES/A)   Crawford Dunn

6108   AD)   Württembergische Bibelanstalt, Stuttgart, WEST GERMANY

          DES/A)   Anton Stankowski

6109   AD)   Wako Shoken Co., Ltd., Osaka, JAPAN

          DES/A)   Ohtaka Takeshi

6110   AD)   T.F. Wilks MRPA & Son Ltd., Sanderstead, Surrey, ENGLAND

          DES/A)   Herman Hecht

6111   AD)   Warsaw Agency, USA

          DES/A)   Anita Soos

6112   AD)   Oy Wulff AB, Helsinki, FINLAND

          ST)   Oy Mainos, Taucher Reklam AB

6113 AD) Westransco, USA
C) Freight Lines
DES/A) James Cross

6114 AD) Warrington Presbyterian Church, USA
DES/A) Everett Forbes

6115 AD) White Cross Surgical Medical Ottawa Ltd., 504 Kent St., Ottawa, Ont., CANADA

6116 AD) Wisconsin Power and Light Co., WI, USA

6117 AD) Ward Hydraulics, Fluid Power Group, Alden, NY, USA

6118 AD) Willows North, Niagara Falls, Ont., CANADA

6119 AD) Western Canada Steel Ltd., CANADA

6120 AD) George Walter, USA
C) Landscape Designers
DES/A) Clemente Lagundiamo

6121 AD) Wigwam Mills, Inc., Sheboygan, WI, USA

6122 AD) Urs Walther AG, Zollikofen, Bern, SWITZERLAND
DES/A) Hans Knöpfli

6123 AD) The William Byrd Press, Inc., Richmond, VA, USA
DES/A) W.B. Propert

6124 AD) Wel-tex, Wroclaw, POLAND
DES/A) Franciszek Winiarski

6125 AD) The Wigmore Hall, London, ENGLAND
DES/A) Nicholas Jenkins

6126 AD) WESC, Greenville, SC, USA
DES/A) Arnold Roston

6127 AD) Waldmann, USA

6128

6129

6130

6131

6132

6133

6134

6135

6136

6137

6138

6139

6140

6141

6128 SM) WAIF, Box 2004,
New York, NY 10017 USA

6129 AD) Young & Rubicam, London,
ENGLAND

DES/A) Marcello Minale & Brian
Tattersfield

6130 AD) Walker Croswell and Co., Ltd.,
Whaddon Works, Clyde Crescent,
Cheltenham, Gloucestershire
GL52 5EP ENGLAND

6131 SM) Walt Disney World, Lake Buena Vista,
FL, USA

6132 AD) Fr. Lürssen Werft, GERMANY

6133 AD) Thomas Walker & Sons Ltd.,
Birmingham, ENGLAND

C) Ship Instruments

DES/A) James White

6134 AD) World Wildlife Fund

ST) Lans Bouthillier Corporate Designs
Systems

6135 AD) Wallis Laboratory, London, ENGLAND

C) Table Manufacturing

DES/A) David Lock & Tor A. Petterson

6136 AD) WRNG Radio Station, Atlanta, GA,
USA

6137 AD) Washington Industries Inc., 224
Second Ave. N., Nashville, TN, USA

6138 AD) Woolsey Marine Industries, Inc.,
P.O. Box 1328, 100 Saw Mill Rd.,
Danbury, CT 06810 USA

6139 AD) Water Peds, USA

DES/A) Marie Martel

6140 AD) Williams Companies, Tulsa, OK, USA

6141 AD) WKSU-TV, Kent State University,
Kent, OH, USA

DES/A) Paul S. Weiser

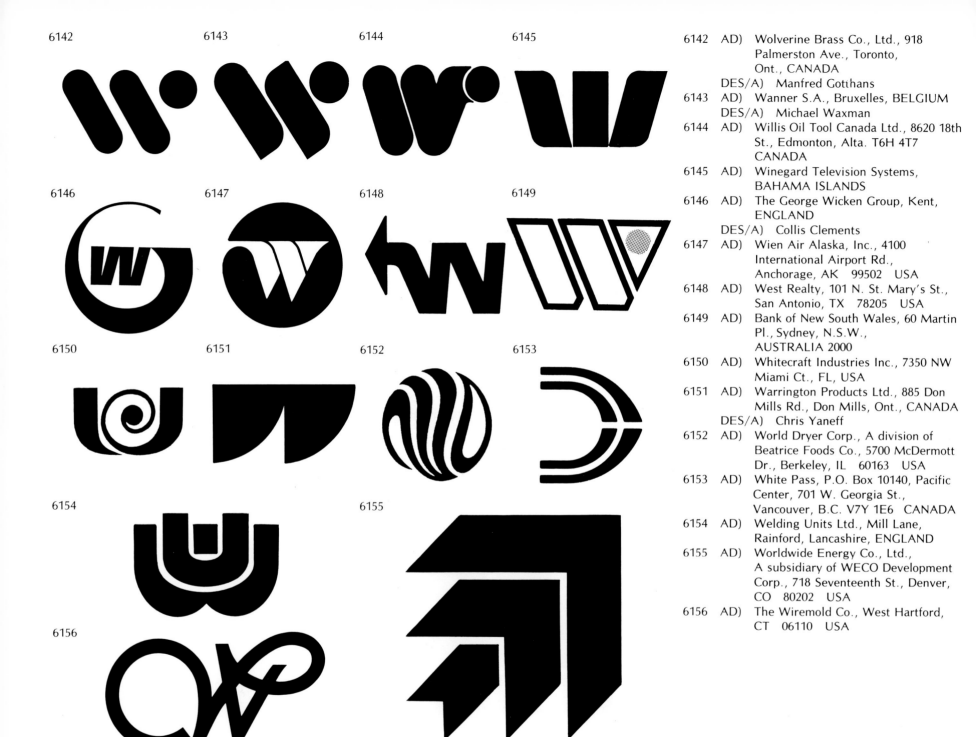

6142 AD) Wolverine Brass Co., Ltd., 918 Palmerston Ave., Toronto, Ont., CANADA
  DES/A) Manfred Gotthans
6143 AD) Wanner S.A., Bruxelles, BELGIUM
  DES/A) Michael Waxman
6144 AD) Willis Oil Tool Canada Ltd., 8620 18th St., Edmonton, Alta. T6H 4T7 CANADA
6145 AD) Winegard Television Systems, BAHAMA ISLANDS
6146 AD) The George Wicken Group, Kent, ENGLAND
  DES/A) Collis Clements
6147 AD) Wien Air Alaska, Inc., 4100 International Airport Rd., Anchorage, AK 99502 USA
6148 AD) West Realty, 101 N. St. Mary's St., San Antonio, TX 78205 USA
6149 AD) Bank of New South Wales, 60 Martin Pl., Sydney, N.S.W., AUSTRALIA 2000
6150 AD) Whitecraft Industries Inc., 7350 NW Miami Ct., FL, USA
6151 AD) Warrington Products Ltd., 885 Don Mills Rd., Don Mills, Ont., CANADA
  DES/A) Chris Yaneff
6152 AD) World Dryer Corp., A division of Beatrice Foods Co., 5700 McDermott Dr., Berkeley, IL 60163 USA
6153 AD) White Pass, P.O. Box 10140, Pacific Center, 701 W. Georgia St., Vancouver, B.C. V7Y 1E6 CANADA
6154 AD) Welding Units Ltd., Mill Lane, Rainford, Lancashire, ENGLAND
6155 AD) Worldwide Energy Co., Ltd., A subsidiary of WECO Development Corp., 718 Seventeenth St., Denver, CO 80202 USA
6156 AD) The Wiremold Co., West Hartford, CT 06110 USA

6157   6158

6159   6160   6161

6162   6163

6164   6165

6166   6167

6157	AD)	Widom & Abronson, Architects, USA
	ST)	Ray Engle & Associates
6158	AD)	World Associates Inc., USA
	DES/A)	W. Wayne Webb
	ST)	RVI Corporation
6159	AD)	Worthen Bank & Trust Co., Little Rock, AR, USA
6160	AD)	Wright State University, USA
	DES/A)	David Battle
	ST)	Vie Design Studio
6161	AD)	Westinghouse Learning Corp., USA
	ST)	Tom Woodward Design
6162	AD)	Wates Ltd., Forest Dale, London, ENGLAND
	ST)	Henriou Design Associates
6163	AD)	Water Refining Co., Inc., USA
	DES/A)	David Battle
	ST)	Vie Design Studios
6164	AD)	Wilson Co., SCANDANAVIA
6165	AD)	Woodstream Corp., Niagra Falls, Ont., CANADA
6166	AD)	Weber Bros. Realty Ltd., 620-9th Avenue S.W., Calgary, Alta., CANADA
6167	AD)	Walker Manufacturing Co., Los Angeles, CA, USA

6168 AD) Watts Pool Co., USA
DES/A) Baxter & Korge
6169 AD) Westinghouse Electric Corp., Pittsburgh, PA, USA
DES/A) Peter Megert
6170 AD) The Wickes Corp., Saginaw, MI, USA
DES/A) John Greiner
6171 AD) Weltifurrer, Zurich, SWITZERLAND
DES/A) Hansruedi Scheller
6172 AD) Western Art, Amsterdam, NETHERLANDS
DES/A) Jan Jaring
6173 AD) Donald C. Williamson Ltd., St. Catherines, Ont., CANADA
6174 AD) West End Bally, Antwerpen, BELGIUM
DES/A) Paul Ibou
6175 AD) Wevery de Ploeg, Bergeyck, NETHERLANDS
DES/A) Teunissen Van Manen
6176 AD) Woningbouwvereniging de goede woning, Voorburg, NETHERLANDS
DES/A) Ralph Prins
6177 AD) Wolters . Noordhoff nv, Groningen, NETHERLANDS
DES/A) Otto Truemann
6178 AD) Wandlyn Motor Inns, Winnipeg, Man., CANADA
6179 AD) Waring, Dorval, Que., CANADA
6180 AD) Wynn's Canada Ltd., 23 Racine Rd., Rexdale, Ont., CANADA

6181

6182

CITIZENS SAVINGS®

6183

6184

6185

AUTOMOTIVE MAINTENANCE PLAN

6186

Designer Artist Profile/Benedict Norbert Wong
(Ref. World of Logotype File No. 80)
Illustration & Design
1719 Monticello Rd.,
San Mateo, CA 94402 USA

6181 AD) Wadsworth Publishing Co., Inc.,
10 Daris Dr., Belmont, CA 94002
USA
DES/A) Ben Wong

6182 AD) Citizens Savings and Loan
Association, 700 Market St.,
San Francisco, CA 94102 USA
DES/A) Ben Wong & Madeleine Weidner

6183 AD) Whitecliff Homes, 895 North San
Mateo Dr., San Mateo, CA 94401
USA
DES/A) Ben Wong & Bill Gin

6184 AD) Citizens Savings and Loan Association,
700 Market St., San Francisco,
CA 94102 USA
DES/A) Ben Wong & Madeleine Weidner

6185 AD) Car Care of California, 405 24th St.,
Richmond, CA 94804 USA
DES/A) Ben Wong

6186 AD) Arizona's Juniperwood Ranch,
8671 Wilshire Blvd., Beverly Hills,
CA 90211 USA
DES/A) Ben Wong

W-19

6187

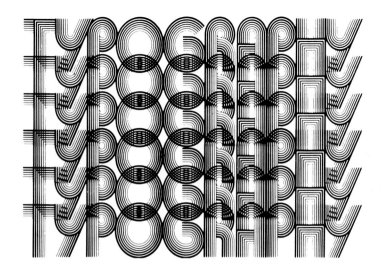

6188

6189

6190   6191   6192

6193

6194   6195

6196

6197

6198   6199

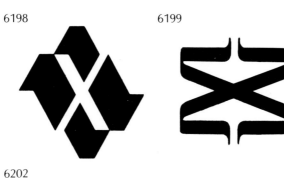

6200   6201   6202

6203   6204

6196 AD) Art Gallery X
        DES/A) Paul Orvath
6197 AD) X-Tex, Herning, DENMARK
        DES/A) Morten Peetz-Schov
6198 AD) Xerox Do Brasil, S.A.,
             Rio De Janeiro, BRASIL
        DES/A) Aloisio Magalhàes
6199 AD) Xonics, 6849 Hayvenhurst Ave.,
             Van Nuys, CA 91406 USA
6200 AD) York Regional School of Nursing,
             1255 Sheppard Avenue, East,
             Toronto, Ont., CANADA
        DES/A) William Newton
6201 AD) Yasuda Trust & Banking,
             Head Office: Yaesu 1-Chome,
             Chuo-Ku, Tokyo, JAPAN
6202 AD) Xerca S.A., Paris, FRANCE
        DES/A) Rémy Peignot
6203 AD) Zyma, Nyon, SWITZERLAND
        DES/A) Hansruedi Widmer
6204 AD) Albert Ziegler Agency, Grellingen,
             SWITZERLAND
        DES/A) Paul Bühlmann

XYZ-5

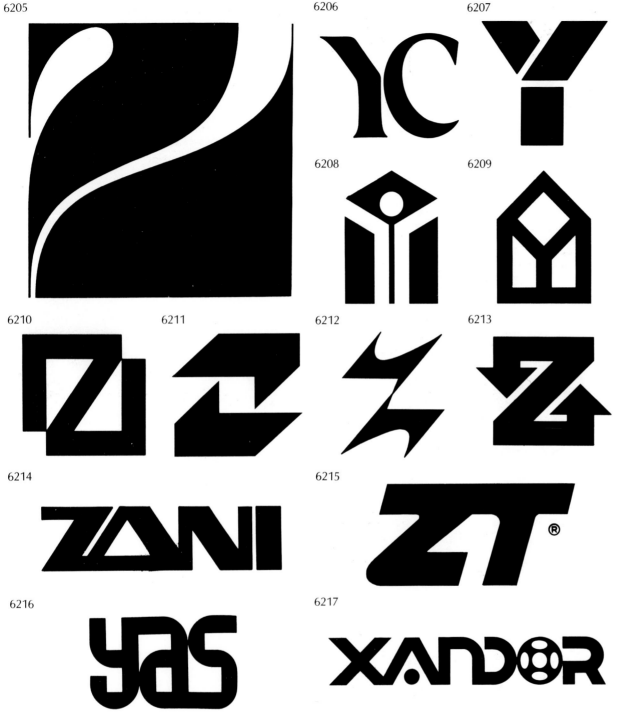

6205

6206

6207

6208

6209

6210

6211

6212

6213

6214

6215

6216

6217

6205 AD) Bernard Zins, FRANCE
C) Men's Ready-Made Suits
DES/A) Daniel Maurel
6206 AD) Yankee Communications, Inc., Providence, RI, USA
DES/A) Dick Cady
6207 AD) Kenneth Yost, Chicago, IL, USA
DES/A) David L. Burke
6208 AD) Young Home Builders of Northern California, Berkeley, CA, USA
DES/A) Robert Pease
6209 AD) Ytong Schweden, SWITZERLAND
DES/A) Joseph P. Grabner
6210 AD) Zingg Möbelwerkstätten, Bern, SWITZERLAND
DES/A) Werner Mühlemann
6211 AD) Zurcher Zeigeleien, Zurich, SWITZERLAND
DES/A) Jörg Hamburger
6212 AD) Zosit, Kōdž, POLAND
DES/A) Zbiginiew Marjanowski
6213 AD) Zahner Elektrotechnische Artikel, Rüshlikon, SWITZERLAND
DES/A) Hansruedi Scheller
6214 AD) Zani Industria Dell' Acciaio
6215 AD) The Zippertubing Co., 13000 S. Broadway, Los Angeles, CA 90061 USA
6216 AD) Yuasa, JAPAN
C) Watch Bank Maker
DES/A) Akira Inada & Yuichi Nishiwaki
6217 AD) Xandor Recording Studios, USA
DES/A) Charles R. Thomas

WYZ-6

6218

6219 6220

6221

6222 6223 6224

6225 6226

yanKee **Zuntz**

6227 6228

ZAND **YKK**

6218 AD) The Yachtsmans Exchange, USA
DES/A) Michael Vanderbyl
6219 AD) Yancey Bros. Co., Atlanta, GA, USA
USA
DES/A) Robert C. Manning
6220 AD) The Yorkviller, 75 Yorkville Ave.,
Toronto, Ont., CANADA
6221 AD) Zambeletti S.p.A., Divisione
Pediatrica, ITALY
ST) Studio GSZ
6222 AD) Youngs Drug Products Corp., USA
ST) Dixon & Parcels Assoc.
6223 AD) Yokohama Japanese Restaurant, USA
ST) Supergraphics Design
6224 AD) Zeefdrekkerij B. Wijtmans,
NETHERLANDS
DES/A) Baer Cornet
6225 AD) Yankee, 11295 W. Washington Blvd.,
Culver City, CA, USA
6226 AD) A Zuntz sel Wwe, WEST GERMANY
DES/A) Ulrich Maass
6227 AD) David M. Zand Advertising Ltd.,
1000 Yonge St., Suite 303, Toronto,
Ont., CANADA
6228 AD) YKK, 1251 Valley Brook Ave.,
Lyndhurst, NJ, USA
C) Zipper Manufacturer

6229

6230

6231

6232

6233

6234

6235

6236

6237

6238

6239

6240

6241

PANSONIC 全音
SING TAO PANSONIC LTD.

6242

6243

6244

Designer Artist Profile / Michael Miller Yu
(Ref. World of Logotypes File No. 78)
48-78 High St., Hang Sing Mansion 6/F Flate 8,
Sai Ying Poon, HONG KONG
ST)   Creation House

6229   AD)   Standard Management Ltd.,
                HONG KONG
6230   AD)   Students Union Hong Kong
                Polytechnic, HONG KONG
6231   AD)   Hong Kong Photographic Club,
                HONG KONG
6232   AD)   Acumen Electronic Products,
                HONG KONG
6233   AD)   Hutchison House Ltd., HONG KONG
6234   AD)   Design Exhibition of Hong Kong
                Polytechnic, HONG KONG
6235   AD)   Utility Clothing Ltd., HONG KONG
6236   AD)   Teletron Electronics, HONG KONG
6237   AD)   International Vinyl Transfer Ltd.,
                HONG KONG
6238   AD)   Philippine Marine Food Group,
                Manila, PHILIPPINES
6239   AD)   Lantern Festival '75 Hong Kong,
                HONG KONG
6240   AD)   Marcelo Flooring Tiles, Manila,
                PHILIPPINES
6241   AD)   Sing Tao Panasonic Ltd., HONG
                KONG
        C)   Recording Studio
6242   AD)   Splendix Musical Instruments,
                HONG KONG
6243   AD)   Creation House Design Studio,
                HONG KONG
6244   AD)   Interprint Co., Ltd., HONG KONG

INDEX
to Art Directors, Design Artists & Studios